CHARLES JAMES FOX
MAN OF THE PEOPLE

David Powell

Foreword by Tony Benn

HUTCHINSON
London Sydney Auckland Johannesburg

Hutchinson
An imprint of Century Hutchinson Ltd
62–65 Chandos Place, London WC2N 4NW

Century Hutchinson Australia (Pty) Ltd
89–91 Albion Street, Surry Hills,
NSW 2010, Australia

Century Hutchinson New Zealand Limited,
PO Box 40–086, Glenfield, Auckland 10,
New Zealand

Century Hutchinson South Africa (Pty) Ltd,
PO Box 337, Bergvlei, 2012 South Africa

First published by Hutchinson 1989

British Library Cataloguing in Publication Data
Powell, David, *1930–*
  Charles James Fox : Man of the People.
  1. Great Britain. Politics. Fox, Charles, James.
  1749-1806
  I. Title
  941,07'3'0924

ISBN 0 09 174188 2

Typeset in Times 11/12pt
Printed and bound in Great Britain by
Mackays of Chatham PLC, Chatham, Kent

Contents

'History is neither written nor made
without love or hate.'

Theodore Mommsen

Foreword

Although, on the face of it, British politics could hardly have been more different in the last quarter of the eighteenth century than they are today, it is impossible, reading this life of Charles James Fox, to escape noticing the parallels with the present.

Of course the electorate then was tiny – all rich and all men
– and many of the constituencies were owned by patrons and represented in the Commons by their placemen. At the start of the period when Fox was first elected to the House of Commons the American colonies still owed allegiance to the king, and France had not yet had its revolution. King George
exercized enormous power and influence, and Prime Ministers were made and unmade at his command. Corruption was
widespread. Women were disfranchized, trade unions were unknown or illegal, and the ideas of socialism had not been formulated.

All this is well described in the pages which follow, and it is hard to avoid a strong distaste for most of the figures who march across the stage, including Burke and Pitt, Lord North and occasionally Charles James Fox himself – none of whom were actually representing the day-to-day concerns of the vast majority of the citizens, who looked, in vain, to the House of Commons of protect their interests and secure their rights.

We are taken through the history of the American Revolutionary war, and how it was debated at Westminster, the French Revolution and the conflicts with France, and given some insight into the events in Ireland. But these appear as incidents in the lives of the leading parliamentarians with whom Fox worked, or whom he opposed at various stages in his glittering career as a Commons orator.

But having said all that, the way that Parliament worked and the fluctuating alliances that grouped and re-grouped around a handful of colourful personalities looks, in retrospect, to have many similarities to the situation we have two hundred years later.

The extreme flexibility of political principle, and the play of personal ambition; the concentration of attention on the top people at the expense of the common people; and the financial dealings which are the backcloth against which the political system worked, will sound familiar to anyone who now follows late twentieth-century British politics, each suggesting that an ancient regime is struggling to survive at a time when new and disturbing political and economic forces are coming into play.

Then, it was the American and French revolutionaries whose ideas were challenging the rotten feudalism that hung like a pall over the Court and the Palace of Westminster. In our period it has been the Russian and anti-colonial revolutionaries who have destroyed the British Empire and changed the rules of politics.

The vulnerability of the British establishment at the time when Fox was at the height of his powers, emerges quite clearly from the way in which his own ideas developed against the executive power of the king when his prerogatives and patronage seemed unassailable. It was, indeed, his opposition to these abuses that earned Fox his reputation as a man of the people; though he was by modern standards, in his life-style and habits, a somewhat improbable champion of the masses.

Yet, allowing for the very different circumstances of his time, it is possible to detect the influence of the enlightenment on his own thinking, encouraging his espousal of parliamentary reform and his toast to the sovereignty of the people, which cost him his membership of the Privy Council.

It is also possible to detect, from the harshness of the repressive measures introduced by Pitt and the treason trials which followed, something of the strength of the popular resistance which was growing up, and the panic this caused among those who held power. For the threat of democratic reform would have undermined the whole framework of privilege in government, as established in 1688, and which still characterized the then British system of government.

Just as the English Revolution of 1649 profoundly influenced the thinking of the American colonists and the French revolutionaries, so now their ideas were filtering back to undermine the unreconstructed politics of the British monarchy and its control of parliament. Charles James Fox – the precocious and gifted orator, the young aristocrat who entered the Commons almost as of right, the gambler who was almost always in debt, the man who fought a duel to settle an argument – sensed these movements and began to articulate some of the demands that were coming from below.

The strength of those demands may be gauged from the enormous amount of radical activity that was beginning at that time, with the corresponding societies and street demonstrations that, on one occasion, attracted two hundred thousand people in London alone – a city that was then tiny as compared to its later size.

The idea of annual parliaments and equal representation was a very real threat to the status quo. They were seen as such and put down with ferocity, and those who advocated these politics were also terrorized by the 'King and Country' mobs who could be mobilized whenever they were needed to assist the forces of reaction.

The pressure of all these events broke the Whigs, and the fluctuating coalition, in and out of office. They sometimes made Fox sound like a voice in the wilderness, though a century or more later his little minority had certainly won the day – and therein lies the importance of Fox as a major figure in the period through which he lived.

This book offers us a useful insight into the political life of the time, concentrating, as Fox's contemporaries would have done, on the arguments, alliances and deals that were taking place in the corridors of power.

It thus re-creates most vividly the atmosphere that must have prevailed behind the scenes, while these debates were taking place across the floor of the House; leaving others to describe the social changes that were taking place under the surface, and which transformed the nature of British politics in the nineteenth and twentieth centuries.

Tony Benn
March 1989

Introduction

Pitt the Younger and Charles James Fox died within eight months of one another in 1806, and if George III wept for the former, he was to say of the latter: 'I never thought I would have regretted his death as much as I do.' Thus ended a feud that wracked British politics during the Age of Revolution. The phrase comes easily now, and in the imagination Robespierre still rages against the blasphemy of kingship – while some Scarlet Pimpernel or other makes a sport of the night, before riding a tumbril to the Place de la Revolution where the *tricoteurs* gather, interrupting their knitting only to follow the fall of the blade. 'La Guillotine ne va pas mal'!

Two centuries on, the Age of Revolution is in danger of becoming a peepshow for voyeurs, careless of the principles involved. Ultimately, however, principles are immutable, and the issues addressed in the last quarter of the eighteenth century have as much relevance today as when Burke railed against the rights of man, and Paine called up his vision of building the world anew. And if it was Pitt who came to represent reaction during those turbulent years, then it was Fox who led the war against what he regarded as the despotism of prerogative.

As such, the intention of *Charles James Fox: Man of the People* is to explore the character of a man who was adored and vilified in equal parts not only during his own times, but also the times through which he lived – for the former is incomprehensible without the latter. Indeed, Fox was at the political forefront of virtually every issue of his day. Above all the rest, however, towered his unremitting defence of the rights of the individual against an increasingly coercive state which led to his being struck off the Privy Council for proposing a toast to 'Our Sovereign Lord, the People'.

Even today, the words have a certain shock value. In the late eighteenth century, they were tantamount to sedition – the more so when voiced by a scion of the aristocracy who, it seemed, was turning on his own kind to elevate what the Quality were pleased to call 'the mere people'. The defection was widely regarded as the final proof of Fox's political instability – though it had been long in the making. For a decade and more, Fox had been becoming as critical of eighteenth-century political practices as he was disenchanted with the rakehell life he had formerly lived.

Not that the transition was seamless. Fox was too complex a character for that. Indeed, it is this very complexity that has continued to tease biographers down to the present day. What was it that transformed 'one of the most egregious coxcombs in Europe' who thought little of losing 12,000 guineas at the tables in a night, into the man who enjoyed 'a little gardening' at St Anne's hill? How was it that the young favourite of the Court party who had endeared himself to George III for asserting that he would 'pay no regard whatever to the voice of the people', became 'The Man of the People' to be excoriated by George for being 'as contemptible as he is odious'? And, above all else, why should the child of privilege become, if not the father, then the godfather of what many feared would be an English revolution?

The answers are as diverse, and the speculation as intriguing, as the character of Fox and the times through which he lived continue to be compelling. For Britain in the second half of the eighteenth century was in a restless mood. It seemed that the old prescriptions (as old, that is, as the Glorious Revolution of 1688) no longer served, and if the author of Tom Jones could rue the fact that 'the very Dregs of the People . . . aspire still to a degree beyond that which belongs to them', then their ambitions were to take more concrete form as the century progressed – inspired, in part, by the suspicion that George III had designs on absolutism; in part, by resurgent memories of the times when free-born Englishmen had sent Charles I to the block, and James II on his travels; in part, by the revolutions in America and France.

The connection between each may have been tenuous, none the less, they were there. Possibly George's aspirations on sovereignty were no more than a figment of the Whig's imaginings, but there can be no doubt that an obduracy whose regal proportion was matched only by its petty mindedness led to the break with America which, in its turn, was a part cause of that July day in 1789 when Louis XVI wondered whether a rebellion had occurred in Paris, to be told by the Grand Master of his Wardobe: 'No, sire, this is a revolution.'

Individually, each development was significant enough. Collectively they raised profound questions, as much among ordinary people as among their representatives in Westminster. If the colonists could demand improved representation, then why not the disenfranchised mass 'out of doors' in Britain? If the French could elevate the Rights of Man above the Rights of Kings, then why not join Fox in his toast to the majesty of the people? Within thirty years of George III's accession in 1760, the issues were to divide England more radically than at any time since the Civil War – and it was Pitt and Fox who led the opposing factions: the one, armed with the king's unfailing support; the other, with a band of followers that diminished to the point where it was quipped that the entire Opposition could travel to the Commons in a single coach.

Gillray's malign cartoons, whether or not paid for out of the Secret Fund, were warmly admired by Pitt's ministry, and capture the full extent of the government's antipathy towards Fox – of Fox being hounded out of Brooks's Club; of Fox praying at the altar of revolution at St Anne's Hill; of Fox's dismembered head, wearing the bonnet rouge of the revolution, mounted on a pike planted among the skulls of his friends. But Gillray's venom reveals fear as much as animosity – the fear that Fox might, indeed, be right; that the future might, indeed, be on the side of the sovereign people.

For a class whose sole occupation was to safeguard its own privileges, it was a monstrous prospect – and the establishment reacted monstrously. Incapable of adapting to changed, and changing circumstances, executive power was reinforced to drive through a series of measures which, by the mid 1790s, had made a deformity of the free-born Englishman's traditional liberties. In short, the secret state was as much a feature of the late eighteenth century as it is a concern of the late twentieth, while its agents continue to share much in common.

In *The British Cabinet*, published twenty years ago, John Mackintosh wondered whether the Cabinet system was becoming a Prime Ministerial one. The tendency has accelerated over the past decade. In March 1988, Lord Jenkins of Hillhead charged the government with presiding over a centralization of power which was snuffing out long established democratic practices: 'I have the impression that a greater number of issues and appointments, which I should have regarded as wholly within the prerogative of a senior Secretary of States, are now settled in Downing Street.' The culture of liberty, he implied, was at risk – books banned, placemen imposed, dissent prosecuted.

Such a concentration of executive power with diminished accountability to the Westminster legislature is exactly the issue that Fox addressed two centuries ago, holding that Parliament was the ultimate source of constitutional authority. For George III, for Pitt the Younger, and for their placemen on the benches in the Commons during the 1790s, the notion was an unpalatable one – the more so when articulated by one of their own kind. As an anonymous correspondent of the *Anti-Jacobin Magazine* noted:

> It must be a matter of infinite regret, not only to his relatives and friends, but to all who are properly jealous of our national character, to see a man who, from his birth and talents, might fairly have aspired to proud pre-eminence . . . sink to become

the repeater of clumsy and foolish, but seditious, toasts to the Whig Club, the hero only of mobs, and the constant champion of every man who pants for patriot fame by dabbling in sedition.

Thus the enigma remains? Why should Fox have exposed himself to such abuse? What was it that led him to prefer twenty years of political exile to the place that both his birth-right and his talents would certainly have secured for him? How was it that in little more than two decades the Court favourite should have come to invite the opprobrium of the establishment in the name of the people he had formerly denied?

These are among the questions that *Charles James Fox: Man of the People* attempts to answer and if, at the conclusion, the enigma is unresolved one thing remains certain: that it was Fox's championship of the rights of the free-born Englishman that kept the ideal alive during the early years of the Age of Reaction. It may have been that Pitt won the present, but as A. J. P. Taylor wrote on the 150th anniversary of Fox's death, it was Fox who won the future. It is a legacy that demands renewed vigilance in a world that bears so many similarities to the period through which Fox lived.

David Powell
Lewes

1

'A Very Sensible Little Fellow'

Charles James Fox, the second son of Henry and Lady Caroline Fox, was born in Conduit Street in the fashionable quarter of London on 24 January 1749, an ugly child of whom his father wrote: 'it's incredible how like a monkey he looked before he was dressed'. The remark, soon to be retracted, disguised Henry Fox's pleasure. It was sons the needed, if only to prove himself. A vain man, the memory of the uproar caused by his runaway marriage to the eldest daughter of the Duke of Richmond in 1744 still rankled; of society's outrage that he, a parvenu, should aspire so high. The Quality had been shocked, the Court appalled, and the Prime Minister, Pelham, had made so much of the matter that Lord Carteret 'thought our fleet was beaten, or Mons had been betrayed' – and now, five years later, the Richmonds had still to forgive their daughter, though she had borne the family two sons.

The proscription was intolerable, a reflection as much on Fox's standing as a member of the Privy Council as on the family name. If life was a bagatelle, then who was to distinguish a Richmond from a Fox? Indeed, both families claimed links with the Crown that reached back for a century and more, and if his wife was the great grandaughter of Charles II by his mistress, Louise de Keroualle, then he, Henry Fox, was the son of the man who had stood with Charles I on the scaffold, who had managed the financial affairs of Charles II when in exile, and who had been appointed Paymaster General to the Forces at the Restoration.

They were proud enough bearings for any man, yet the

interdict remained, a slur as much on Henry as on his father, Sir Stephen. In the hope of having an heir to inherit a fortune 'honestly got and unenvied' according to the diarist John Evelyn, the old man had married for a second time at the age of 77, and had written 'God's grace had blessed the union with seasonable tokens' – among them four children, of whom Henry was the second, born in 1705.

It had been a troubled year in troubled times. Memories of a Commonwealth which had demonstrated that even kings have a bone in their neck still haunted the gentry, while only seventeen years had passed since the Glorious Revolution had sent James II on his travels. A high Tory and lifelong Royalist, Sir Stephen had chafed as much at the new restrictions imposed on sovereign power by the Bill of Rights, as at the rampant ambitions of the new Whig oligarchs – though he had kept his counsel to himself to serve the House of Orange as well as he had the Stuarts.

As for the Richmonds, they had made no pretence at dissembling. Like Louise de Keroualle before them, they'd bedded down where their fortunes would prosper best – good Tories one day, good Whigs the next. Following the times of troubles, it had proved a sound policy (by the 1740s their rent rolls alone totalled more than £20,000 a year)* though in this they were by no means alone. The Whigs may have turned out James in the name of life and liberty, but they were no more democrats than republicans as their mentor, John Locke, had made clear. The whole of Locke's *Second Treatise on Government* had echoed and re-echoed with the sentiment that 'the great and *chief end* of Mens uniting into Commonwealths . . . is the *Preservation of their Property*' – and first the Whigs, then the Tories had assiduously practised what Locke had preached to the point where by the mid eighteenth century there was little to choose between them.

Six years before Charles James's birth, in fact, the young

---

*To obtain a current approximation of mid eighteenth-century money values, multiply by 50.

Scottish philosopher David Hume had noted that 'to determine the nature of these [political] parties is, perhaps, the most difficult problem to be met with'. He had every right to be confused. The names remained – Tory and Whig – and on high days and holy days their disciples paid deference to the old principles (Church and Crown, Commons and Commonweal), but for the rest they made their godhead of property and power.

And what power, what property. The Crown remained, though often as little more than a figurehead. The oligarchs had not broken James to reconsecrate absolutism, but rather to secure their own authority – the authority of a constitution they had written, of a law that they regulated, and of a church that they governed. Only recently, Voltaire had considered that England had established a system of government in which the king, all-powerful for doing good, had his hands tied for doing evil; in which the aristocrats were great without arrogance, and in which the people shared in government without confusion. The theory was all very well as far as it went, as long as it conformed to the grandee's prescriptions.

By the 1740s neither Whigs nor Tories looked for a return to the chaos that had been a feature of the seventeenth century when radicals could proclaim that 'the poorest he in England had a life to lead as the greatest he'. In the years between, they had come to appreciate the value of strong government, and while the one might still toast 'the Glorious Revolution' and the other 'The Prince across the water', the Young Pretender was to learn at Culloden in 1745 that England had lost its taste for political adventuring. The country, and its political masters, had better things to do. Sir Robert Walpole had taught them that.

The apotheosis of the new power-brokers, Walpole's governing principle was straightforward: 'All men have their price'. It was a policy that appealed to the oligarchs, something which they knew and understood, and which Walpole had pursued in practice as first Minister for almost twenty years–the measure of his administration being determined by the depth of its pocket. As Hans Stanley MP had once remarked:

If I had a son, I would say to him 'Get into Parliament, make some tiresome speeches. Do not accept the first offer, but wait until you can make provision for yourself and your family and then call yourself an independent country gentleman.

The advice was unnecessary. By the mid eighteenth century, and in the absence of clear party distinctions, venality had become the staple of government, for Stanhope Spencer to opine: 'A man who could obtain a seat by corruption could be managed by bribery'. Unquestionably, there were occasional policy differences, but in one thing Tories and Whigs shared common cause, their own self-interest, and if it served to vote with one faction one day, then it served equally well to vote with another the next. As for principle, it counted for little when set against patronage, the whole machinery of government being determined by its capacity to secure votes with the promise of place.

As Horace Walpole noted, jobbery was subject to growing refinement, and he was uniquely qualified to comment. The son of Sir Robert, he once listed the sinecures his father's family had reaped during his years in office – the Clerkship of the Pells for one brother, an £8000 a year income as Auditor of the Exchequer for another, and the Clerkship to the Estreats before Horace left Eton. As for Sir Robert, he put £150,000 through only one of his four bankers in as many years – a high proportion of which was spent on building and furnishing his great new house at Houghton, demolishing a whole village in the process.

Landed property, political property, domestic property, there was little to choose between them. A vote was as marketable as a dowry, a political place as an estate – though it was the latter that provided the most visible, the most prodigal expression of these new men of power, Dr Johnson marvelling at the extravagance of Lord Scarsdale's new country seat: 'Why sir, all this excludes but one evil, poverty.'

And as at Scarsdale, so at Woburn and Goodwood, Wentworth and Castle Howard – the country houses that formed the nuclei of the grandee's world. Dominated by a handful of great families it was a small world, and a jealous one,

13

its exclusivity being vigilantly preserved by intermarriage. Indeed, half the novels of the eighteenth century turned on the problems of love and marriage in a society dominated by issues of landholding, and for the Quality the flight of an heiress with an adventurer for marriage by a Fleet parson was more a matter for nightmares than novelettes.

This was the essence of Henry Fox's crime, that he had reached above himself in a society where class was the measure of all men. Only a handful of years before Fox's elopement, Defoe had identified a sevenfold division in society, based on status and wealth –

1 The Great, who lived profusely;

2 The Rich, who lived plentifully;

3 The Middle Sort, who lived well;

4 The Working Trades, who laboured hard but felt no want;

5 The Country People, Farmers etc., who fared indifferently;

6 The Poor, who fared hard;

7 The Miserable, who really pinched and suffered want.

Henry Fox may have been among The Rich, but his sin was to have aspired to The Great. Such presumption was unforgivable, the more so when the Quality again felt threatened as a result of growing economic prosperity which encouraged 'the lower sorts' to imitate their masters. Little more than half a century had passed since the oligarchs had imposed their own order on society, yet in 1745 Henry Fielding, author of Tom Jones, was writing: 'while the Nobleman will emulate the Grandeur of a Prince and the Gentleman will aspire to the proper state of a Nobleman; the Tradesman steps out from behind his Counter into the vacant place of a Gentleman. Nor doth the confusion end there: It reaches the very Dregs of the People, who aspire still to a degree beyond that which belongs to them'.

To the grandees it was a formula for anarchy, of a restless ambition that threatened the social order they had so carefully constructed since 1688 – and Henry Fox's marriage to Lady Caroline was a realization of all their worst fears. No question the man had talents, but, for all that, he aspired above his station. Shortly before her death, Lady Fox had warned her second son: 'You, Harry, having less of a fortune, won't be subject to so many temptations, but withstand those you have when you grow up.'

He was to prove as cavalier with her advice as he was of his fortune. By the age of 30, Fox had raked about to such effect that with what little remained of his inheritance he became a student of jobbery. Returned as Member of Parliament for Hindon, in Wiltshire, in 1735, he immediately attached himself to Sir Robert Walpole, and proved an apt pupil. Two years after his marriage, he was appointed Secretary of State for War, and became a Privy Councillor the following year. For all this, however, Henry Fox still needed sons to prove that a Fox was a match for a Richmond, and on the night of 24 January 1749, he held his second son, Charles James, in his arms.

Since Charles II had conferred his own names on his illegitimate son by de Keroualle they had been the property of the Richmond's – but now they were his. The child might look like a monkey, wrinkled and dark, but he was to be the agent of all his father's hopes. True, there was an elder brother, Stephen, but he had been sickly from birth with what Henry Fox termed 'Sanvitoss dance', while Charles James . . . .

A man whose corruption was to become a byword, Henry Fox was to spend the last quarter century of his life indulging his children as if trying to exorcise his public guilt. Shortly after his marriage to Lady Caroline he had secured a lease on Holland Hose, a rundown property in its own grounds on what was then the western outskirts of London, and it was there that he built a retreat for himself from a world that came to execrate his name.

In 1841, Macaulay wrote of the Foxs, father and son: 'The first Lord Holland [Henry Fox] was educated by Sir Robert Walpole. Mr [Charles] Fox was educated by his Father . . . .The pernicious maxims early imbibed by the first Lord

Holland, made his great talent useless, and worse that useless, to the state. The pernicious maxims early imbibed by Mr Fox led him, at the commencement of his public life, into great faults which, though afterwards nobly expiated, were never forgotten.'

It is as close as any of the Whig apologists of the nineteenth century came to admitting that there was something rotten at the centre of the idyll they made of Holland House. The Whigs had no monopoly of doting on their heirs, but from the outset there was something unhealthy, wanton even in Henry Fox's relationship with his second son – 'dear Thumb' as he used to call him.

In the first years of his life virtually nothing was denied the boy, his father continually reiterating his belief that 'young people are always in the right, and old people in the wrong' – an opinion that may have been influenced by the work of Rousseau. In 1749, the self-tortured genius wrote his Dijon prize essay, arguing that the progress of art and science had led to the corruption of morals. It presaged much that was to come, a philosophy that helped fuse a revolution with its fervent advocacy of the social contract, its championship of the noble savage, and its impassioned belief in the innocence of childhood whose joy and unthinking wisdom irradiate a lost world.

Henry Fox knew enough of lost innocence, but was it something that his son could redeem? True to his father's precept 'Do nothing to break his spirit. The world will do that business soon enough', Charles James's early childhood was an orgy of self indulgence. He only had to rage that a wall had been dynamited when he was absent for it to be rebuilt and dynamited once again. He could destroy a gold watch, wash his hands in cream at the dinner table, or burn a state document all without admonition, so that the 'sensible' 3-year-old with whom Henry Fox dined tête à tête had, by his fifth year, become a 'very pert, very argumentative child' whose passionate temper threatened to dominate more than the nursery at Holland House.

And as Charles's precocity continued to delight his father, so his father's career began to impinge on Charles's life.

Having squandered his inheritance, Henry Fox had little money to spare for the restoration of his London retreat. A £10,000 lottery prize and three legacies following the deaths of the Duke and Duchess of Richmond had temporarily eased his problems, but there was always a concern to secure the longer-term future – yet in 1754 his political career, and the prospects of a lucrative place, looked particularly bleak.

Fox's chief, Henry Pelham, who had succeeded Walpole, had died in March, to be succeeded in his turn as Prime Minister by his brother, the Duke of Newcastle. Although a weak man, more than thirty years in high office ensured that Newscastle had guile enough to compensate for any lack of character, the more so when he controlled seven parliamentary seats in his own right, had decisive influence in at least four more, and spent the lion's share of the £30,000 a year that came from his rent rolls on buttressing the Whig interest.

For Fox the signs were not propitious. He had made powerful enemies in the new faction, Horace Walpole writing: 'The Lord Chancellor hates Fox and the Duke of Newcastle does not pretend to love him.' However, while fashionable London abounded with rumours that Fox 'must very soon be first Minister, or ruined', he was not without resources. If he needed Newcastle, then Newcastle needed him to reinforce his ministry, as he needed one other candidate well qualified for power – William Pitt.

The great grandson of a country parson, the grandson of 'Diamond' Pitt who had sailed for India at the age of 20, and returned home a merchant prince, Pitt the Elder had followed Henry Fox first to Eton, then to Oxford, and finally into the Commons in 1736. Ten years later, Fox was to hold the more prestigious post of Secretary of State for War, Pitt the more lucrative one of Paymaster General to the Forces, and in 1754 both men accepted places in Newcastle's new administration though each harboured a grievance against their chief for having offered neither of them the leadership of the Commons.

Although nominally both members of the same ministry, Pitt and Fox had little else in common, and the alliance between them was to be as short-lived as it was expedient. Each had only one objective, to break Sir Thomas Robinson who had accepted Newcastle's offer of the post that both men coveted, Walpole writing to Sir Horace Mann that:

> Mr Pitt has broke with the Duke of Newscastle, on the want of power . . . and Mr Fox is not at all more in humour. If I should tell you in my next, that either of the Gorgons has kissed hands for Secretary of State, only smile, snakes are as easily tamed as lap dogs.

Walpole's waspish humour was matched by his political intelligence, and within the month he was reporting on Fox's appointment to Newcastle's Cabinet, to conclude: 'The more I see, the more I am confirmed in my idea of this being the age of abortions!'

If Fox appreciated the observation, he scorned it. Once again opportunism had served, though he can hardly have imagined that his desertion of Pitt marked the beginning of a feud which, with only brief respites, was to wrack the two families for more than half a century. As it was, while Fox's reputation suffered, that was incidental to his ambitions, and he could even amuse himself by reporting a remark by his 5-year-old son: 'He [Charles] says I look like a villain, and is sure that everybody in the House of Commons that don't know me, must take me for such.'

Villain or not, Fox could always escape his critics at Holland House which, in itself, justified all the rest – the corruption, the intrigue, the vilification. By the mid 1750s, with restoration work virtually complete, the house had become one of the most fashionable rendezvous in London, a vantage point from which Charles could study society and its mores between schooling and playgoing ('Stage mad' wrote his father 'but it makes him read a good deal') and developing what his mother feared was becoming 'a dreadfully passionate' character.

Henry Fox was unconcerned. 'Never mind' he is said to have replied 'he is a very sensible little fellow, and will learn to curb himself.' Lady Caroline did not share his optimism. Six years of paternal indulgence may have done much for

Charles James's confidence, but had made him none the easier to live with, and there may well have been some truth in the taunt later levelled against him of how:

> born a disputant, a sophist bred.
> His nurse he silenced, and his tutor led.

It is not an attractive portrait, of a braggart 6-year-old whose precocity his father actively encouraged as if to reassure himself that the sacrifices he made for his 'sensible boy' compensated for the loss of his public reputation; as if to pleasure himself with the surety that his son was already word perfect in his favourite axiom: 'Aspire to the first employments, but never *trust* as I did.'

The miracle, as Macaulay noted, was that Fox survived his father's influence, though it was to take him half a lifetime to recover from its worst effects. As it was, Fox had already decided that he had enough of home schooling and determined to enter M. Pampellone's academy for young gentlemen in Wandsworth. His parents were undecided. Charles James Fox had no doubts – first Wandsworth, and then Eton, and on 22 June 1758, aged 9 years, he paid his 5 guinea entrance fee and enrolled at the latter.

2

'You Need Not Interrupt Your Amusements'

A Reynolds's portrait of Fox in his last year at Eton, commissioned by Fox himself, shows an unsmiling and earnest 15-year-old whose neat cravat and modest brown coat belie the playboy of whose profligate influence Lord Shelburne was later to write: 'the great change that has taken place amongst our youth dated from the time of his [Henry Fox's] sons going to Eton'. Shelburne exaggerated, Eton had an unsavoury reputation well before Fox arrived for the autumn term of 1758, Pitt the Elder noting that he had never observed a boy 'not cowed for life at Eton'.

No milksop, Pitt had witnessed for himself the barbarity that passed for a gentleman's education in the greatest of English public schools. Once, possibly, Eton had upheld its founder's exhortation to 'excel all other grammar schools' in the kingdom, but those days were long gone. By the mid eighteenth century, the college had degenerated to a point where the savagery of the staff was only exceeded by the savagery of the pupils, the practice of 'fagging' providing older boys with a menial class as much to serve their needs as their adolescent sadism – Fox's nephew, Henry, having his hands crippled for life by a fagmaster who amused himself by having the boy toast his bread before an open fire with bare hands.

A nursery for the establishment (one in ten pupils entered Parliament in the century before the Reform Bill of 1832), Eton was a caricature in miniature of fashionable society, the boys aping their elders in drinking, in gambling, in fighting, in hell-raising – yet always careful to observe the unwritten, yet carefully circumscribed rules of status and caste.

How Fox adjusted to his first terms of Eton is not known. They must have come hard after the indulgence of Holland House, but there were consolations, among them that as an Oppidan (fee payer) he did not have to live with the collegers (Kings's Scholars) in the Long Chamber, a rat infested dormitory of such ill-repute that even masters seldom dared to enter. More than this, Oppidans were entitled to their own private tutors and Henry Fox dispatched Dr Philip Francis (father of Sir Philip Francis, possible author of the Junius letters) to supervise his son's education within the narrow boundaries of the classical syllabus – Latin and Greek (translating and memorizing passages of, among others, Horace, Virgil, Cicero, Ovid and Homer); and oratory under the tuition of Dr Edward Barnard, Provost of Eton, and among the foremost teachers of the subject in mid eighteenth-century England.

A man whose rebellious nature cost him a bishopric under George III, Barnard inspired a generation of Etonians to treasure their language as much as they valued their independence. Always an avid reader, and already a formidable egoist, they were qualities in which Fox needed little encouragement, more especially when surrounded by youthful admirers such as the Lords Stavordale, Carlisle and Fitzwilliam. His court might be small, but its influence was far-reaching, and it more than compensated for the growing odium of his father's political reputation.

Two years had passed since Henry Fox had bettered Pitt in the contest for Newcastle's favour, and in May 1756 the first shots had been fired in what was to be a seven year war. Five months later, Newcastle fell and George II invited Fox to form a government with Pitt. The latter refused to sit in a ministry under Fox, but within the month the position was reversed, Pitt becoming effective leader of the wartime administration, and Fox languishing in the Opposition he could ill-afford. Twelve months were to pass before he was to regain office and then, as careless of his pride as Pitt was conscious of it, Henry Fox snapped up the offer of the Pay Office in his old rival's administration.

Although a political cul-de-sac, the post was as well suited to Fox's character as to his needs, for as Paymaster General he was entitled to play the markets for his own benefit with Treasury funds earmarked for the forces. Elegant in its simplicity, the system was little less than a licence to print money, Fox explaining: 'The Government borrows money at twenty percent discount. I am not consulted or concerned in making the bargain. I have, as Paymaster, great sums in my hands which . . . must either lie dead in the bank, or be employed by me.'

By his own reckoning the former was unthinkable, and during the Seven Years' War almost a third of the national debt, totalling £49,500,000, passed through Fox's hands, to net him a personal fortune. Critics were quick to compare the behaviour of Pitt, whose disregard for money was almost legendary, with that of Fox; one of the many epigrams to appear following the presentation of the Freedom of the City of London to Pitt contrasting their ambitions:

The two great rivals London might content,
If what he values most to each is sent;
Ill was the franchise coupled with the box;
Give Pitt the freedom, and the gold to Fox.

Indifferent to public opinion, Henry Fox counted his profits and consoled himself for the loss of high office with the assurance that he had secured the future of his family, while as for Pitt. . . .

In 1759, the year that saw the fall of Quebec before the dying Wolfe, that marked the inconclusive victory of Minden, that saw Admiral Hawke crush the French fleet in a November storm off Brest, William Pitt the Younger was born at the family home at Hayes in Kent. A sickly child, his upbringing was to be as austere as Charles Fox's was indulgent, though his early precocity was as marked as the man he was later to rival. In 1766, on hearing of his father's elevation to the peerage, the 7-year-old Pitt was writing to his mother: 'I am glad I am not the eldest son; I want to speak in the House of Commons like papa.'

It was to be seventeen years before his ambition was to be fully realized, in the first of his great clashes with Fox. Meanwhile, the young Etonian was fully occupied with preening his own vanity. Only recently, Dr Barnard had forecast a distinguished career for him as a parliamentarian, while on one of his visits to London, Fox was noticed concentrating intently on a debate in the Lords. 'That' said the Chief Justice, Lord Mansfield, to his neighbour 'is Fox's son, Charles, with twice his parts and half his sagacity.'

If the remark delighted the elder Fox, Charles may well have thought it no more than his due, though there may have been times when his public self-assurance disguised his private doubts. Taxed by his father to explain what he meant by saying that 'he wish'd his life was at end', Charles replied 'It is a troublesome affair, and one wishes that one had this thing or that thing, and then one is not the happier; and then one wishes for another thing, and one's very sorry if one don't get it, and it does not make one happy if one do so.'

Possibly the languor was affected, the mannerism was in fashion at the time. If not it reveals a world-weariness that contrasts, vividly, with the received impression of Fox the Eton schoolboy dominating debates; of Fox the devoted 10-year-old versifying in Latin to his beautiful, elder cousin, Lady Susan Strangways; of Fox the leading player in the amateur theatricals at Holland House, though tending to sulk at Lady Susan's absence for a Christmas performance which led his aunt, Lady Sarah Lennox, to write that he was 'as disagreeable about acting this play . . . your not being here is the reason he won't enter into it and be eager'.

The 17-year-old Lady Sarah was well qualified to comment on affairs of the heart, being widely regarded as one of the most beautiful women in England – not least by the new king, George III. As callow as Fox was precocious, the young king had proposed to Lady Sarah, to be given an ambiguous reply. When Lady Sarah finally reached her decision three months later, it was too late – a new bride had been selected for George, though not one of his choice. At 22 years of age, the king had little choice of anything, least of all a wife.

The son of Prince Frederick, known to posterity as Poor Fred, and Princess Augusta of Saxe-Gotha, George has been described as the best of a bad bunch of their progeny, the majority of whom turned out to be congenital idiots or seriously disturbed. Not that George himself was any too bright; a lumpen and apathetic boy, he was 10 years old before he could read, while he never fully mastered the arts of grammar or punctuation. And if these were not disabilities enough, they were compounded by the cloying attention of his mother, the Dowager Princess of Wales, and her confidant, Lord Bute. A Scot, and widely suspected of Jacobite sympathies, Bute attempted to educate George to a sense of destiny, and while the young prince may never have read Bolingbroke, the old Tory's precepts were implicit in much that he learned.

Having identified all political corruption as stemming from the Whigs, and more especially the Walpole ministry, Bolingbroke advanced his theory of a Patriot King:

> As soon as corruption ceases to be an expedient of government, and it will cease to be such as soon as a PATRIOT KING is raised to the throne, the *panacea* is applied; the spirit of the constitution revives of course; and as fast as it revives, the orders and forms of the constitution are restored to their primitive integrity, and become what they were intended to be, *real barriers* against arbitrary powers, not *blinds* nor *masks* under which tyranny may lie concealed.

George III was raised to the throne on the death of his grandfather in 1760 and the Whigs, whose power had been virtually unbroken since the Hanoverian succession of 1714, fancied they heard echoes of Bolingbroke in his first royal proclamation: 'Born and educated in this country, I glory in the name of Briton, and the peculiar happiness of my life will consist in promoting the welfare of a people whose loyalty and affection I consider the greatest and most permanent security of my throne.'

The grandees might smile in public at the jest that: 'Every

person brought in by the Whigs has lost his post, except the King', but in private they had little cause for amusement. There could be no mistaking the young king's target, inspired by his 'dearest friend', Bute. A lonely and neurotic figure, George clung like the child which he still resembled in so many ways to his Scottish mentor, abasing himself when Bute was displeased: 'I now see plainly that I have been my greatest enemy; for had I always acted on your advice, I should now have been the direct opposite of what I am; nothing but the true love you bear me, could have led you to remain with me so long.'

This was the George that was to write of his broken love for Lady Sarah Lennox: 'He [Bute] has thoroughly convinced me of the impropriety of marrying a country woman; the interest of my country shall ever be my first care, my own inclinations shall ever submit to it'; this the George whose mission it was to purge corruption; and this was the George that the Whigs feared – with reason. Within two years, he had ousted the Old Corps from power, and appointed Lord Bute as First Lord of the Treasury.

And this was only a beginning. Recognizing that once the king was committed to breaching the Whig position, there could be no turning back, Bute's immediate need was to demonstrate the strength of the new ministry. It was a quality that would be put to the test in steering the terms for ending the Seven Years' War with France through Parliament. The Lords posed few problems, but the Commons was a different proposition. Pitt, the architect of victory, bitterly summarized what he regarded as the betrayal of Britain's interests: 'We retain nothing, though we have conquered everything' – and although out of office, the Great Commoner still commanded a large following in the lower House.

What the Court party needed was a strong leader in the Commons, a manager without scruples to marshall the resources of the Crown against the motley of the Opposition, George III noting: 'We must call in bad men to govern bad men.' On 13 October 1762, Henry Fox abandoned the Whigs and took the post that was to earn him the title of the best hated man in Britain, rather than the earldom that he believed was his due for an act of treachery with few parallels in parliamentary history. Bute's instructions were straight-forward, to break the opposition to the peace by whatever means that were to hand – bribery, corruption, intimidation. Having nerved himself to the task, Fox pursued it with all the ferocity of an apostate attempting to expunge the evidence of this past, writing to Bute: 'Strip the Duke of Newcastle of his three Lieutenancies, then go on to the general rout, but let this beginning be made immediately.'

In the Commons, Fox was to pursue his own advice assiduously. Within the month he had bullied, bribed, or cajoled a working majority for the peace – and after the vote was taken, the butchery began. All those who had opposed the ministry, their families and dependants, were mercilessly rooted out of office. Not so distantly, these had been his friends, and while Fox's betrayal was not unique in an age of political corruption, what raised it above the common run was the sheer scale of his perfidy – though even in this, George III was to prove his equal. By the time he had safely delivered up the Treaty of Paris, Fox was almost universally loathed, writing to Bute: 'I don't care how much I am hated, if I can say to myself I did his Majesty such honest and essential service.'

The sentiment was not reciprocated. Indeed, elements of the Court party may have regarded the treaty as secondary to curbing the power of the Whigs, the Dowager Prin-cess of Wales exclaiming triumphantly when the peace was approved: 'Now my son *is* King of England.' As for George, he eagerly anticipated the disposal of his Judas, remarking to Bute in March 1763, of how he 'rejoiced whenever I can see a glimmering of hope of getting quit of him [Fox]'. He did not have long to wait.

At 58 years of age, and finally recognizing the enmity he had engendered, Fox resigned his Leadership of the Commons – expecting an earldom as a reward for services rendered. The king, however, thought otherwise. Fox had to make do with a barony, taking as his title Lord Holland. Laisser-aller; lese majesty!

In the highly politicized environment of Eton, where a significant proportion of the pupils had relatives in one or the other of the Houses of Parliament, Fox must have been well aware of the odium of his father's name, even if able to console himself with the cynical reflection that Henry Fox had simply made an art form of what formerly had been a common practice. The notion may well have appealed to the increasingly self-assertive 14-year-old, one of whose friends was writing:

What praise to Pitt, to Townshend, e'er was due,
In future times, my Fox, shall wait on you.

The compliment was not lightly won in a school that placed a premium on the oratorical skills at which Fox worked so hard to perfect, and which he studied so diligently as a spectator of the increasingly vitriolic debates in the Commons. Incensed by the loss of what they had come to regard as their political birthright, the Whig grandees opened a virulent campaign against the king and his first minister. Only fifteen years had passed since 'Butcher' Cumberland had put Stuart hopes to the sword at Culloden, and the arch-Whig publicist, John Wilkes, had no compunction about playing on Anglophile fears of Bute's imagined Jacobite connections, or in suggesting that Bute's high position resulted from his supposed affair with George's mother, a cartoon of the time featuring a tartan Jack-Bute and his mistress riding roughshod over English liberties.

The royal We was not amused, and on 15 November 1763, the young Fox was in the Commons when the government voted that Number 45 of the North Briton was a seditious libel, and ordered that it be publicly burned. Earlier in the year Wilkes, an MP for Buckinghamshire, and a man whose squint-eyed and dropsical ugliness was only matched by the ferocity of his wit, had replied to a question by Mme de Pompadour about how far press freedom extended in England: 'That is what I am trying to find out.' By the spring he had his reply.

In April, Wilkes had mounted a savage attack on the

King's Speech, in which he described George's ministers as 'the tools of despotism and corruption', warning 'They have sent the spirit of discord through the land and I prophesy it will never be extinguished but by the extinction of their power.' Within the week the government had issued a general warrant for Wilkes's arrest, and the seizure of all papers connected with the publication of Number 45. Wilkes was held incommunicado in the Tower, and appeared in Court in early May to heighten his attack on both the king and his ministers:

> The LIBERTY of all peers and gentlemen and, what troubles me more sensibly, that of all the middling and inferior sort of people, which stands in most need of protection, is in my case finally to be decided on: a question of such importance as to determine, at once, whether ENGLISH LIBERTY be reality or shadow.

The case was dismissed, to the delight of the crowd who huzzaed for 'Wilkes and Liberty'; to the fury of the king who felt himself snubbed by his own judiciary; and to the pleasure of the Whigs who were coming to suspect that there was more to the king's pursuit of the Old Corps than individual pique, that George did, indeed, have ambitions on recovering the power of the Crown at the expense of hard-won English liberties. No more than a suspicion at first, it was soon to become the bogey that haunted the Whig psyche, for Edmund Burke to inflate, for Dunning to aver that 'the power of the Crown has increased, is increasing, and ought to be diminished', and for a line of nineteenth-century historians to make the conspiracy central to their interpretation of history. It is only in the past half century that the bogey has been laid. Imagined or otherwise, however, it seemed real enough to the dispossesed Whigs of the early 1760s – and the Wilkes's case reinforced their fears.

But if they regarded Wilkes as a martyr for liberty, then George regarded him as 'That Devil Wilkes', and frustrated by the Courts he mobilized his friends in the Commons to ensure a safe majority for a proscription of Number 45. Within three months, and against the best efforts of the

Whigs, Wilkes had been drummed out of the Commons, and within the year he had been outlawed, for the *Annual Register* to note: 'This completed the ruin of that unfortunate gentlemen.' Although premature, Charles Fox may well have welcomed the news for he had little time either for Wilkes or his populist ways.

As to the former, the man represented the party that Lord Holland had betrayed. As to the latter, Wilkes's populism found little favour with the young grandee, and even less so following his first trip abroad in the summer of 1763. The date is significant. Charles and his father left for Paris, en route for Spa in May, less than a fortnight after the latter had resigned his leadership of the Commons, for Walpole to write to his erstwhile friend, Sir Horace Mann: 'Mr Fox's exit has been very unpleasant. . . . He meets with little pity, and yet has found as much ingratitude as he had the power of doing service.'

This was to be the 14-year-old Charles Fox's companion on his first trip abroad, a man as corrupted by ambition as embittered by the frustration of that ambition. Ageing now, Henry Fox had little to live for save his family, and if he made peace with his conscience by saying that what he had undertaken had been undertaken in their name, then it was almost as if he was now attempting to share his guilt with his children by sharing the spoils of his corruption with them. Stephen Fox had already developed a taste for gaming. Now Charles was to join him, being given 5 guineas a night by his father to play the tables. Like so many of Lord Holland's indulgences, the generosity may have been well meaning, but the consequences were disastrous – and for more than just the flogging that Charles is said to have received for the rakish mode of his return to Eton.

The story is apocryphal, though it is not to be wondered at, gambling having reached epidemic proportions by the mid eighteenth century. In 1754 the editors of *The Connoisseur* noted, censoriously:

> that gaming is now become rather the business than the amusement of our persons of quality; and that they are more

29

concerned about the transactions of our two clubs at White's, than the proceedings of both Houses of Parliament.

The editors were too limited. Rich or poor, virtually everyone gambled on virtually anything – on cock fighting, bear baiting, steeplechasing, cricket; on the fertility of a deacon's wife, the life expectation of a public figure, or the time taken to eat a live cat; and always, and everywhere, on cards.

In 1762 Oliver Goldsmith was writing satirically of those ladies of quality who 'stake their fortune, their beauty, their reputation, at the gaming table'; while Parson Woodforde played in somewhat less humble, if still polite society: 'Mr and Mrs Constance drank tea with us in the Afternoon with their eldest Son. After tea we all got to Loo at which I won six shillings.' Gaming, in short, was central to the way of life, and if Fox's former school-time companion, Lord Stavordale, was to loose 11,000 guineas at the tables one night, and recover it on a single hand the next to swear: 'Now if I had been playing *deep* I would have won millions', then his future patron, Georgiana, Duchess of Devonshire, was to loose a million at the tables, and bring her husband close to ruin.

Fox was not a man to carry moderation to extremes, and on his return to Eton there were few indications that within a handful of years he was to win a reputation for being the foremost rake of a notoriously profligate society. After all, 5 guineas a night at the tables was little enough, and certainly not sufficient to attract him back to Paris for Christmas: 'I am so fully convinced of the use of being at Eton, that I am afraid of running the risque of not returning. I am also resolved to stay there until Christmas twelve month, by this you may see that the petit maitre de Paris is converted into an Oxford pedant.'

Perhaps it was this note to his father that inspired Lord Holland to write to a friend, Campbell of Cawdor: 'My son Charles really deserves all that can be said of his parts . . . good sense, good nature, and as many good and amiable qualities as ever met in any one's composition. I have two sons here: the eldest bids fair for being as universally and as much beloved as ever I was hated. Thus happy in private life, am I not in the right to leave the public?'

It might well have served for Holland's political epitaph. From 1763 onwards, 'old, and abandoned by each venal friend', he spent an increasing amount of time at Kingsgate, his isolated retreat on the Kentish coast overlooking the North Foreland. A bleak and windswept shore, it was well suited to Holland's mood of rejection, a landscape to be populated with mimic ruins, as much monuments to his own career as images of the devastation to which he would have condemned London for its devotion to Wm. Pitt:

Purged by the sword, and purified by fire,
Then we would have seen London's hated walls.
Owls would have hooted in Saint Peter's choir,
and foxes stunk and littered in Saint Pauls.

The venom of Thomas Gray's lines reflected the public's mood, to refine Holland's bitterness, to heighten the isolation of his self-imposed exile, and to reinforce his dependence upon his sons. Certainly, Charles did nothing to disappoint him. In his last year at Eton, and fifth boy in the school, he was studying hard in preparation for going up to Oxford – between exercising his French on his father's political enemies: 'Longtemps du peuple Pitt favori adore/Les mesprisant toujours, en fut toujours aime. . . .'

Only one thing can have marred Charles's pleasures that summer of 1764. In April, his adored Lady Susan had eloped with a failed actor, William O'Brien. 'Why does she like him more than she likes me?' he raged at Lady Sarah Lennox, and there being no reply he took himself off to Kingsgate for a summer of cricket and partridge shooting.

*   *   *

Oxford University's reputation in the mid eighteenth century was little better than that of Eton. For Walpole it was 'that nursery of nonsense and bigotry' where the dons of Edward Gibbon's profile excused themselves from the toil of reading, or thinking, or writing 'in a round of College business, Tory politics, personal anecdotes & private scandal'. A political anachronism, the university's high Tory sympathies were still evident when Fox entered Hertford College in 1764, the Jacobite Earl of Westmorland having recently been installed as chancellor.

Hertford was then a small college with a rich clientele, Lord Malmesbury writing that the life of the gentlemen commoners of the time was an imitation of London high life with its regular round of evening card parties 'to the great annoyance of our finances'. Within the month, Fox had been tempted by the tables, writing to his father that he had broken all his good resolutions, and lost more than 80 guineas. The note ends with a new resolve 'never to play again', though qualified by a rider that tells something of Charles's doubts about his own self-control: 'I think I shall have courage enough to keep it, but cannot be sure enough of myself to give an absolute promise.'

How far he succeeded is unknown. One thing, however, is certain: Fox did not sacrifice his studies for the tables, a practice out of keeping with an age in which Oxford and Cambridge were widely regarded as finishing schools for the Quality, Lady Leicester offering her heir £500 if he agreed to travel abroad, rather than attending one of 'those schools of vice, the universities'. Indeed, the lack of information about Fox's gaming habits at Hertford contrasts, forcibly, with reports of his scholarship: 'I did not expect my life here to be so pleasant as I find it; but I really think that to a man who reads a great deal, there cannot be a more agreeable place.'

And read he did, extending his pleasures beyond the classics to pre-Restoration drama, of which he was later to claim that there was no play published in England before 1660 which he did not know intimately; to French, of which he was to write to Sir George McCartney: 'I am heartily obliged to you for your advice about French, which I will undoubtedly follow, as I am thoroughly convinced of its utility'; and into the hitherto unexplored field of mathematics, of which he remarked: 'I believe they are useful, and I am sure they are entertaining.' Indeed, the sheer intensity of Fox's scholarship soon came to trouble the Principal of Hertford, Dr Newcome, who, on being told that Fox intended to visit Paris in the spring of 1765, hastened to assure him:

> Application like yours requires some intermission, and you are the only person with whom I have ever had connection, to whom I could say this. I expect that you will return with much keeness for Greek and lines and angles. As to trigonometry, it is a matter of entire indifference to the other geometricians of the College . . . whether they proceed to other branches of mathematics immediately, or wait a term or two longer. You need not, therefore, interrupt your amusements by severe studies.

The advice was superfluous. Once in Paris, Fox had no intention of interrupting his alternative pleasures of whoring and gaming, to the alarm of the Secretary of the British Embassy, David Hume. As Hume was to write Lord Holland of his son's behaviour: 'the dissipation of this kind of Parisian life might check his ardour after useful knowledge, and loose in all appearance a very great acquisition to the public'. Lord Holland made no reply, but his wife may well have contrasted the warning with her recently formed impression of the 7-year-old William Pitt: 'the cleverest child I ever saw, and brought up so strictly and proper in his behaviour, that mark my words, that little boy will be a thorn in Charles's side as long as he lives'.

As for Fox, he was as careless of Hume's caution, as of Newcombe's counsel. Never the man for half measures, he pursued his diversions as he pursued his scholarship, with the same single-minded dedication that he was soon to bring to his career of playboy and politician. In the meantime, he returned to Oxford and the following year's study was punctuated only by the occasional visit to London to attend a parliamentary debate – and make the acquaintance of Edmund Burke.

It was a seminal meeting on a memorable occasion – the Lords debate on the repeal of the Stamp Act. Possibly the most complex, and certainly among the most controversial political figures of the eighteenth century, Burke was a late-comer to the Commons, having first had to overcome suspicions of his *petit bourgeois* Irish background and then establish a reputation for himself in Whig society. The prejudice was symptomatic of the times. For all the brilliance of Burke's intellect, it was to be a decade and more before the Whigs finally accepted the man who, together with Fox, was to lead the party for almost two decades – though never from the front, that would have been altogether too much for the proprieties of the Whig grandees.

Twenty years older than Fox, Burke was returned as MP for Wendover at the close of 1765, and made his first speech in the Commons in February 1766, to be congratulated by Wm. Pitt for his grasp of the complexities of the North American question and, more especially, the iniquities of the Stamp Act. Introduced only a year before in an attempt to meet the cost of defence in the New World, the storm of protest raised by the act reflected as much on Westminster's right to raise taxes without representation, as on the colonists' growing restlessness to manage their own affairs.

Since the leader of the Pilgrim Fathers had first prophesied: 'Wee shall be as a Citty upon a Hill, the eies of all people are uppon us', the New Englanders had tended to regard themselves a chosen people, subject to none save the Lord. After all, it was in search of the religious freedom that they were denied in England that so many of them had emigrated in the first place – and if certain of the other colonies were not quite so forward for their rights then, praise be, they would change.

And change they did. By the mid eighteenth century the Thirteen Colonies were no longer a client economy. Tough minded and independent, the settlers had opened up a New World of burgeoning wealth with a seemingly limitless western frontier beyond the Alleghenies. For all this, the colonies remained constitutionally and economically subordinate to Westminster and the City, while for friends of the Court they provided a convenient form of outdoor relief – the most lucrative posts in colonial government going to off-comers from England. Stamp Act or no, the situation was untenable; George III's intransigence merely precipitating the inevitable.

In the six years since he had ascended the throne, the king had learned something about power, but little about men. After less than twelve months in office Bute had broken and resigned, for George to write:

> Though young I see but too much that there are very few honest men in the world; as my Dear Friend has quitted the Ministry I don't expect to see it there again. I shall therefore support those who will act for me and without regret change my tools whenever they are contrary to my service.

He was as good as his word, for if the humiliation inflicted on his 'Dear Friend' incensed him, it also steeled his resolve. His short apprenticeship in kingship was over and in the next half decade George was as quick to change his tools as he was reluctant to change his measures – the more so as regards North America whose sovereignty he considered a sacred trust. As careless as he was ignorant of the new forces that were shaping the Thirteen Colonies, George insisted on the unchanged authority of the King in Parliament, and if the Stamp Act was to be annulled, then it should be replaced by a Declaratory Act: 'to make laws and statutes of sufficient force to bind the Colonies and all the people of America, subjects to the Crown, in all cases whatsoever'.

In their delight at the repeal of the Stamp Act, the colonists ignored the small print of George's intentions, and momentarily it appeared as if London's change of heart had succeeded in checking their clamour. Indeed, as John Adams, the Boston lawyer who had done so much to drum up the case of 'No Taxation Without Representation', was to write in late 1766: 'The people are as quiet and submissive to Government as any people under the sun. . . . The repeal of the Stamp Act has composed every wave of popular disorder into a smooth and peaceful calm.' Burke suspected that the calm was deceptive, but if Fox shared his views, he had little time to express them.

In the late spring of 1766, he finally quit Oxford, walking the 56 miles to London with his friend William Dickson, later to become the Bishop of Down. Stopping at Nettlebed to refresh themselves, Fox had to pawn his watch for the price of a beer. Arriving at Holland House later in the day, he tackled Lord Holland who was taking coffee: 'You must send half a guinea or a guinea, without loss of time, to the ale-house keeper . . . to redeem the gold watch you gave me years ago.'

It was a humble start to an extravagant Grand Tour. In September, the entire family, together with a retinue of servants, crossed to France on the first stage of their journey to Naples, where they wintered, enabling Charles to develop a passion for culture, and indulge his taste for gambling.

For the young grandees of the eighteenth century, the one was as important as the other, the Grand Tour serving to refine the mores of their class. After a year or two following a carefully planned itinerary through France and Italy ('A man who has not been in Italy is always conscious of an inferiority' asserted Dr Johnson, who went so far as to change his brown fustian for silk and lace on arriving in Paris), of marvelling over the ruins of the rediscovered Pompeii, of exploring the galleries of Florence and Paris, of patronizing the dealers of Naples and Rome, and of studying the gentle arts of dalliance, and the not so gentle crafts of the table, the tyro returned a dilettante, qualified to enter London society.

Fox found the education and the entertainment equally congenial. In Nice he wenched with the wife of a silversmith: 'who is almost as fair as Mrs Holmes, but not near so chaste, and she attracts me thither regularly in the evening'. In Paris, he gambled, loosing £16,000 in one ten day period. In the Alps, he explored the scenery with his friend, Lord Carlisle, to the hysterical alarm of Mr George Selwyn: 'The wild boars, the precipices, feloques, changes in climate, are all to me such things . . . that if I allowed my imagination its full scope, I should not have a moment's peace.' In Florence he wrote of his indifference to politics: 'I am very little curious about them, for almost everything I hear at this distance is unintelligible'; while everywhere he went he pursued his studies as avidly as his pleasures, writing to one correspondent:

I am totally ignorant in every part of useful knowledge. I am
more convinced every day how little advantage there is in
being what at school and university is called a good scholar;
one receives a good deal of amusement from it, but that is
all. At present, I am reading nothing but Italian, which I
am immoderately fond of, particularly of the poetry. As to
French, I am far from being so thorough a master of it as
I could wish, but I know so much of it that I could perfect
myself in it at any time with very little trouble.

The theme was a recurrent one ('Learn Italian as fast as
you can. . . . There is more good poetry in Italian than in all
other languages. . . . Make haste and read all these things
that you may be fit to talk to a Christian'), to be punctuated
by Fox's references to his enjoyment of amateur theatricals,
a powerful learning tool for the orator manqué. In the spring
of 1767, he was joined by a group of friends in Florence, to
write self-critically: 'the last time I acted I fell very short
of my own expectations'. Undaunted, however, he planned
new performances, though concerned that the size of the
company limited their productions: 'We want another actor
or two, but much more another actress. There are very few
comedies that do not require above two women.'
It was a small, elegant, and carefree world, consciously
distanced from the everyday reality of eighteenth-century
life; a world that was soon to be turned upside down. To
the young dilettanti's of Florence, with their readings of
Ariosto, their performances of *Jane Shore*, the notion may
have appeared inconceivable – though Fox himself may have
had a foretaste of things to come on his visit to the ageing
Voltaire at Ferney.
The meeting was short, Fox's companion writing somewhat petulantly that the only refreshment they received was
chocolate, but Fox himself cannot have been unaware of
Voltaire's role in the intellectual storm that was brewing
up over Europe. More than thirty years before, following
his brief exile in England for satirizing a scion of the French
aristocracy, Voltaire had written his: *Letters Concerning the
English Nation*. An encomium to the English constitution,

the work enraged the Bourbons, who rightly regarded it as a criticism of their absolutism, and in 1735 the *Letters* were burned in Paris by the public hangman.

The proscription of the work ensured its success, and in the following quarter century it helped trigger a debate among intellectuals that was to rock Europe to its foundations. Cosmopolitan, rational, free-thinking the intelligentsia challenged the established order at its very roots – spiritual and temporal, economic and scientific. Little more than a decade after Voltaire's meeting with Fox, Emmanuel Kant was to coin what could well be taken as the catch phrase of this Age of Enlightenment: *Sapere aude* – Dare to know. And the *philosophe* dared everything, not least, in their demands for freedom – the freedom from the arbitrary power of absolute monarchies; the freedom to worship how and what they chose; the freedom of speech and comment; and above all else, the freedom to reason without fear.

A subversive programme, it was to sap the foundations of received authority, and in presenting Fox with a list of his own works (*'Ce sont des livres de quoi il faut se munir'*), Voltaire may well have touched upon the subject in their brief conversation. Certainly it is unlikely that the ageing philosopher, who had warred against *L'Infame* of reaction for more than half a lifetime, would have had time for small talk as they walked in his lakeside garden. If so, then the 18-year-old Fox may have glimpsed the future, however darkly, that autumn day of 1768. Thirty years later Fox himself was to be damned as infamous for taxing Pitt the Younger with Voltaire's principles, although, more immediately, they appeared to have little consequence.

In this absence abroad, Lord Holland had secured his son a seat in the Commons, and Fox returned to England as MP for Midhurst – a duty to be shared with his time at the tables. In this, he was not unique. Although generally weighted towards the former, the divide between pleasuring themselves and meeting their inherited responsibilities at local or national level was commonplace among the nobility. Again, however, it was the demonic intensity with which Fox was to devote himself to both pursuits that was to make him exceptional, almost as if he was a character at war with himself.

Nineteen years of indulgence had led to the rebel who, it seemed, took as much pleasure in shocking society as in indulging his pleasures; the rake whose gaming was soon to become legendary; the macaroni whose reputation as a coxcomb was soon to become the talk of the town; the libertine whose exploits compared with those of the royal ancestor from whom he took his name. Yet, there was always the other Fox, the other rebel – the second son who wondered whether life was worth the candle; the Eton scholar who forewent a trip to Paris to pursue his studies; the Oxford graduate who was advised by his principal not to interrupt his amusements; and the young man who had walked with Voltaire in the garden at Ferney.

3

'The Hazard This Evening Was Very Deep'

In a moment of frankness, Lord Holland wrote of his son shortly after he entered the Commons: 'My Charles is handsome, as well as clever and good natured; but I fear he won't continue very long handsome, as he grows more like me.' At the age of 19, Fox's swarthy complexion, described by more friendly critics as Levantine, was becoming increasingly marked, to be heightened by his taste for high and rakish fashion. Whether in the House or at the table, there was no mistaking the young macaroni in his red heeled shoes, his smuggled velvet waistcoat, and cheeky little French hat.

The roughs of Covent Garden and St Giles might jeer at his fancy ways, but they were from another world, *canaille* for which he had nothing but contempt – his upbringing had seen to that. Certainly there was no escaping the rowdies who could drum up a brawl on the smallest pretext, or the harlots of the Strand who could pick one's pockets in the wink of an eye – but for Fox they were little more than furnishing of the two cities that was London in the mid eighteenth century. Hogarth's cartoons capture the place and the time exactly; a world at once elegant and uncouth where the rich and poor shared their bloodsports together (not least the hanging days at Tyburn), but very little else. The contrast never failed to astound foreign visitors, who wondered at the style of St James's and Whitehall, and recoiled from the squalor of much of the rest:

The East End, especially the quarters along the banks of

the Thames, consists of poorly built houses, on narrow, crooked, and ill paved streets. It forms an extraordinary contrast with the West End where one sees nothing but pretty houses, sumptuous squares, very straight and beautifully lighted streets, and the best pavement in Europe.

Against the folk memory of a time when Commonwealth men had proclaimed all men were equal under God, it was an unstable combination, which often flared into violence – the more so since Wilkes had taken to enlisting the mobbocracy (a word that only entered the language in the second quarter of the eighteenth century) in pursuit of Liberty. Devoted as he was to his father, Fox can hardly have forgotten the Whig publicist's pangyrics against Lord Holland in the early 1760s – the man of whom he had written that even Tories would rather have their pockets picked by that scion of Grand Whiggery, the Duke of Newcastle, than 'have their throats cut by Mr Fox'; whose appearance Wilkes had excoriated in Number 36 of the North Briton:

Another painter might, from a mistaken, transient view only of so sullen and lowring a brow which seems overhung with conceit and superciliousness, have guessed at the dark, crafty inhabitant within, and have presaged, from a most unfortunate scowl, that much deceit and treachery lurked in a black malignant heat.

And now, after five years in exile, Wilkes was back, to fight for a seat in the Commons, to beat-up the London mobs, to challenge the authority of Parliament by claiming that the liberty of the people was the keystone of the constitution. In the spring of 1768 he stood first for the City and then for Middlesex, to be elected for the latter with a clear majority. Pandemonium broke loose, and for the next two days London was in the hands of the Wilkites, causing Benjamin Franklin to declare that if the king had had a bad character and Wilkes a good one, George would have been turned off his throne.

For all the furore, the king and his friends were not to be intimidated. A month after the election Wilkes was re-arrested on the old charge of being author of North Briton

45, and committed to the King's Bench prison in St George's Fields. Where the crowd had been restive before, they were now incensed. Fearing trouble, the government increased the guard around the gaol – Scottish troops among them. The press grew thicker, tempers flared, shots were fired – and six people died. The crowd had their martyrs, though the king appeared careless of the blood on his hands, his Secretary of State for War writing: 'His Majesty highly approves of the conduct of both the Officers and Men.'

London was close to flash-point, but still the Court and its ministers pursued their vendetta against Wilkes. In June, he was sentenced to twenty months imprisonment for, among other things, the publication of the 45; while in February 1769, following the king's insistence that 'the expulsion of Mr Wilkes [from Parliament] appears to be very essential and must be effected', he was deprived of his seat in the Commons by a government majority of eighty-two.

Wilkes was delighted. His popularity soared. 'If Ministers', he wrote, 'can once usurp the power of who *shall not* be your representative, the next step is very easy and will follow speedily. It is that of telling you whom you shall send to Parliament, and then the boasted constitution of England will be entirely torn up by the roots.' On 16 February Wilkes put his name forward as candidate for Middlesex for a second time, and for a second time was returned – no opposition candidate appearing. Three times the farce was repeated, and three times Wilkes was expelled the House.

The Whig's worst fears of George's ambitions were, it seemed, finally being realized, and on 20 February a group of gentlemen meeting at London Tavern in Bishopsgate formed the Society of Supporters of the Bill of Rights. Over dinner and wine they can hardly have imagined that they were inventing an essential piece of political machinery, a school in which the secret of popular organization was to be learned.

Immediately the Society's aims were to marshall support and funds for Wilkes, but within months the membership were unanimously resolving to press for root and branch reform by shortening the duration of parliaments, by excluding pensioners and placemen from the Commons, and by demanding of each candidate for election that he 'endeavour to obtain a more fair and equal Representation of the People and . . . promote to the utmost of his Power an Enquiry into the Causes of the Troubles and Discontents which have distracted this Country during the present Reign'.

This was radical stuff, an echo of the dissent which had wracked England in the seventeenth century, which was now to be re-echoed in the North American colonies where they had already adopted Wilkes's cause as their own. Affairs in Boston, the centre of agitation, mirrored those in London, the Annual Register reporting on 'the riots and tumults of a dangerous nature' that disturbed the town which, while directed at London's ambitions on sovereignty, found a symbol in Wilkes, the Boston sons of Liberty writing to him in 1768 of their determination 'that the King of Great Britain shall have subjects but not Slaves in these remote parts of his Dominions'.

As churlish as he was intractable, George III was as quick to assert his sovereignty over his dominions as he was to continue his harassment of Wilkes. So the electors of Middlesex had snubbed his wishes three times, so a new approach was required – and Colonel Henry Lawes Luttrell, a violent man, always ready with the sword, was named as the government candidate for the Middlesex election to be held on 13 April 1769.

Early that morning a 'great breakfast' had been prepared at Holland House for the squadron of horsemen who were to conduct Luttrell to the poll. They failed in the face of a small army of Wilkes supporters. For all this, Charles's elder brother, Stephen, managed to reach Brentford to propose Luttrell's name at the hustings. The outcome was as disappointing to the king, as it was alarming to Lord Holland. Wilkes polled almost four times Luttrell's vote, while the City of London instructed its representatives in the Commons to press for a parliamentary inquiry into the conduct of Holland and, if necessary, impeach him for malpractices during his time as Paymaster General.

The threat came to nothing, but it served as a caution to

Lord Holland of his continuing unpopularity, and a further goad to the dandy that was his son to pursue the case against Wilkes. Charles James Fox made his first speech in the Commons ten days before his twenty-first birthday. His subject? The Middlesex election. Infuriated by the continuing recalcitrance of the electors, of which one MP was to assert: 'Such is the levelling spirit that has gone forth, that the people imagine that they themselves should judge us', George and his government declared the fourth election null and void and named Luttrell as the member for Middlesex.

On 9 January 1770, in the debate on the King's Speech, Sir George Savile accused the Commons of betraying the rights of the people in rejecting Wilkes, and seating Luttrell. There was uproar: Sir Alexander Gilmour raging that members had been committed to the Tower for saying less; Burke maintaining that the populace out-of-doors abhorred the present ministry, and wondering whether the Speaker did not feel his Chair 'tremble under him'; and Charles Fox coolly asserting that 'from the licence gentlemen had taken in their language that day, it seemed that the old decent freedom of debate was at an end, and they were endeavouring to establish new forms'.

As a maiden speech it was unremarkable, possibly because Fox had gambled away the previous night, though Lord North, soon to become First Lord of the Treasury, may well have noted the interjection. If not, he can hardly have failed to appreciate the drubbing that Fox was soon to administer to the Scottish lawyer, Alexander Wedderburn, who had temporarily espoused the Whig cause. The debate occurred only three weeks after Fox's twenty-first birthday, and in a brief, yet brilliant display Fox exposed the paucity of Wedderburn's case, at which 'The House roared with applause'. The following night, North visited the king to report on the state of his newly formed ministry and to emphasize, as discreetly as George's mood would allow, the need to reinforce the Treasury benches.

A staunch Commons man, North made up for his grotesque appearance with wit and personal charm – qualities that were to be tested to breaking point in the troubled years ahead.

At Eton, a tutor had remarked that he was 'a blundering blockhead, and if you are Prime Minister, it will always be the same'. Years later, North was to contemplate: 'And it turned out to be so'. He was too self-effacing. Easy going, even somnolent, he may have been, but North was both a shrewd parliamentarian and debater, while his reverence for the Crown was to provide the king with that pliant tool for which he had been searching for almost a decade. First, however, North's need was to strengthen a ministry in which talent was significant only by its absence – and there could be no question of Fox's worth.

Doubtless the man was a rake, but that was no concern of his. Inquire into their private lives, and half the Quality would be disqualified from office, which would make the difficult task of reinforcing the Treasury bench all but impossible. As it was, better have a friend than an enemy of the young cub – and on 13 February 1770, Fox was appointed Junior Lord of the Admiralty. It was the lowest rung on the ladder of preferment, and, at 21, Fox was by nine years the youngest of the seven Admiralty Lords. Lord Holland was delighted with the news, while his mother was to write from Nice: 'I hope Lord North has courage and resolution. Charles being connected with him pleases me mightily. I have formed a very high opinion of his lordship, and my Charles will, I dare say, inspire him with courage.'

He was to need it, for George and his government were as unpopular on the streets as they were in the press. The ministry may have pensioned the great Dr Johnson to write for them, but even he was no match for the barbed pen of Junius. The pseudonym still remains a mystery, disguising a writer who for four tumultuous years harried the king and his government with a contempt which, today, would be condemned as libellous. The solutions to Junius's identity are as numerous as they are imaginative, though a prime contender for the title remains Sir Philip Francis, the son of Charles Fox's former tutor, if only on the negative evidence that he never attacked Fox himself – though there were opportunities enough.

Since his return from the continent, Fox had cut a swath

through fashionable society. True, the Junior Lord of the Admiralty attended the House when the need arose, but he had other, compelling business beside – wining, dining, womanizing and, always, gaming. In 1770, Walpole was to write that Almack's had replaced White's as the club for playing deep. Soon to be taken over by Brooks, a shady wine merchant who 'Nursed in clubs, disdains a vulgar trade/Exults in trust, and blushes to be paid', Almack's was little more than a casino for the Quality, Walpole providing a delightful vignette of the scene. With as much as £10,000 in specie on the table, the players

> began by pulling off their embroidered coats, and put on freize coats, or turned their coats inside out for luck. They put on pieces of leather, such as worn by footmen when they clean knives to save their lace ruffles; and to guard their eyes from the light, and prevent tumbling their hair, wore high crowned straw hats with broad brims and adorned with flowers and ribbons; masks to conceal their emotions when they played Quinze.

Night in and night out, the young blades played for astronomical stakes, to win and lose fortunes at the turn of a card – one wretch forfeiting £70,000 and his carriages in a single night's play, at which Fox arranged to pay him an annuity from the club pool provided that he foreswore gaming in future. It was the gesture of a man who hazarded deep and often, he and his elder brother once loosing £32,000 in three nights – for Lord Holland to thank God that his time at the Pay Office had been so profitable. In the closing years of his life he had good cause to be, as Charles gambled away his patrimony, as contemptuous of his losses as he was of the moneylenders who gathered most days at his lodging above Mackie's, the grocers, in Piccadilly.

Always ready with credit, the 'Fox hunters' would crowd what he termed his Jerusalem Chamber to dunn him for his debts, to the delight of the Grub Street rhymsters:

But hark, the voice of battle sounds from far;
The Jews and Macaronis are at war;

The Jews prevail, and thundering from the stocks,
They seize, they bind, they circumcise Charles Fox.

And if, temporarily, his credit was exhausted, then there
were always his relatives, his friends, his landlord, the waiters
at Almack's, and, somewhat later, Mr Brooks himself ready
to stake his play. The full extent of Fox's gambling debts has
never been established, but the length of his credit tells as
much about his standing as it does about the character of Fox
himself, for he could have well made a good living from the
tables if he had opted for games of skill, rather than chance.

A brilliant whist player, he could have earned a comfortable income from the game, instead of which he preferred
gaming high at quinze and baccarat, playing against profes-
sionals who lived by cards. It was almost as if Fox was
tempting the fates, or re-enacting the past. Forty years
before, Lord Holland had raked about and squandered a
fortune – to spend the next quarter century recovering it,
at the expense of his reputation. Now it seemed as if his son
was bent on much the same course.

Certainly Charles visited the near-recluse at Kingsgate as
often as his pleasures allowed. Certainly he corresponded
with his father with reasonable regularity, while, in return,
Lord Holland continued to dote on his wayward son, fruit-
lessly forbidding anyone to let Charles know who was
meeting his debts, and yet . . . . At best relationships
between fathers and sons are complex affairs, and what is
true in general is doubly true of Holland and Charles Fox.

A ruthless opportunist in his public life, it was almost as
if the father was echoing Rousseau's principles and trying
to find some lost innocence in his son, yet all the while
corrupting him with indulgence – 'Let nothing be done to
break his spirit. The world will do that business fast enough.'
Nothing was, and nothing did – and for the last ten years of
his life, Holland was to pay the price of his misspent love, as
if Charles was taking a perverse revenge on his childhood,
dissipating his inheritance, and with it the memory of how it
had been won.

In his obituary of 1807, Hazlitt was to write: 'I find that it is difficult to write a character of Fox without running into insipidity or extravagance. And the reason of this is, there are no splendid contrasts, no striking irregularities, no curious distinctions to work on; no "jutting freize, buttress, nor coign of vantage" for the imagination to take a hold. It was a plain marble slab, inscribed in plain legible characters, without either hieroglyphics or carving.'

He was wrong on all counts. For the first thirty years of his life, Fox was a changeling – and never more so than during the last years of Lord Holland's life when he represented his father's Tory principles in the Commons by day, and wasted his fortune at Almack's by night. High spirited? Certainly. Capricious? Perhaps. A plain marble slab? Never. 'The gaming', Walpole wrote in 1770, 'is worthy the decline of our Empire' – and it was Fox who set the pace. Yet still Junius ignored him. The Cub was fortunate for as recently as December 1769, Junius had dared to launch a tirade against the king himself.

The progression was inevitable. Having already savaged his ministers, now only George remained: 'We are far from thinking you capable of a direct and deliberate purpose to invade those original rights of your subjects, on which all their civil and political liberties depend. Had it been possible for us to entertain a suspicion so dishonourable to your character, we should long since have adopted a style of remonstrance very distant from the humility of complaint.'

For twenty-four pages Junius developed his charge – citing George's alleged predilection for the Scots ('Like another chosen people, they have been conducted into the land of plenty'), his continuing persecution of Wilkes ('The destruction of one man has been, now for many years, the sole object of your government'), and determination to bring the dissenting colonists to heel ('They left their native land in search of freedom, and found it in a desert') – to conclude with a scarcely veiled threat:

The name of Stuart, of itself, is only contemptible; armed with the sovereign authority their principles are formidable.

The Prince who imitates their conduct, should be warned by their example; and while he plumes himself on the security of his title to the crown, should remember that, as it was acquired by one revolution, it may be lost by another.

This was the matter of Whiggism, distilled, and in the streets of London the crowds again marched for Wilkes and Liberty, while from Surrey and Buckinghamshire, Yorkshire and Essex petitions were dispatched protesting at the Middlesex election: 'the House of Commons derives its existence from the people, who never have entrusted that House with an authority to supersede the choice of the electors'.

What had begun as a personal feud between George and the Whigs had developed into a constitutional crisis which everyday promised violence, Walpole writing in March 1770: 'rebellion is in prospect, and in everyone's mouths. I, you know, have long foretold that if some lenient measures were not applied, the confusion would grow too mighty to be checked'. The son of Sir Robert Walpole, Horace was uniquely placed to observe the scene – not least, the growing disarray among the great Whig families. Where Sir Robert and his immediate successors, notably the Duke of Newcastle, had imposed some semblance of unity on the disparate elements of the party (if only by the judicious application of place and patronage), there was now dissension, with the various factions locked in bitter dispute as to how to maintain their own identity while containing what they had come to regard as the overweening ambitions of George III

In this, if nothing else, the king had been successful. Ten years previously he had determined on curbing the Whig's authority, and by 1770 they were so divided among themselves that if he had been the man they feared, George might well have developed a taste for absolutism. Then, perhaps, the Whigs would have re-united. As it was they split, and split again to form three, loose factions that devoted as much time to their internal disputes as to opposing the king himself. Claiming a direct line of descent from the Revolution of

49

1688, the Rockingham Whigs were the fiercest opponents of the king's right to choose his own ministers, and shape their policies.

Led by Lord Rockingham with the support of grandees such as the Dukes of Richmond (Fox's uncle), Devonshire and Portland, they found their mentor in Edmund Burke, who became Rockingham's secretary in 1765. Haunted by a sense of social inferiority that his party did little to allay, Burke's whole career was spent trying to reconcile the present with the past to maintain the status quo. As jealous as his masters of the Settlement of 1688, he was to spend quarter of a century of his political life attempting to adapt the Whig's inheritance to changing conditions, before acknowledging the impossibility of his task, to become the leader of reaction at the outbreak of the revolution in France. But that was for the future, and at the time that Fox joined the North government Burke was vehement in his criticism of government policy, declaring in *Thoughts on the Cause of Present Discontents*: 'The power of the crown, almost dead and rotten as prerogative, had grown up anew, with much more strength . . . under the name of Influence.'

The Whigs of the Bedford connection were of a different cast. Careless of principle, they formed a cabal 'in order to sell their conjunct iniquity at a higher rate'. And once the price was fixed, they were easily bought, in contrast to the third of the Whig factions led by Pitt the Elder. As arrogant as he was brilliant, the Great Commoner erected an altar to his own rectitude, at which he worshipped himself. Although lacking the clan following of the Rockinghams and the Bedfords, and although increasingly prone to periods of near-madness (during one spell in office, he spent two years in the room of his Hampstead home, refusing company, and being served with meals through a trap in the floor) Pitt's reputation as a populist continued to command a respect amounting to reverence – not least, from his young disciple, Lord Shelburne.

Against an Opposition riven, as it was, by personal jealousies, and depending, as it did, on the transient support of uncommitted members, the king and his Prime Minister,

North, ranged the Court party. George III may have been many things – vindictive, obstinate, boorish – but he was quick enough to learn how to work the levers of power, turning the machinery of patronage that the Whigs had used for so long, and to such good effect for their own purposes against the Whigs themselves. If the radical Tom Paine was to assert 'placemen, pensioners, lords of the bedchamber, lords of the kitchen, lords of the necessary house, and the Lord knows what besides, can find as many reasons for Monarchy as their salaries . . . amount to', then George was to exploit this venality to the full, creating a following of King's Friends schooled to follow North into the division lobbies of the House.

Allied to his traffic in clerical and military preferments, and his control of as many as thirty-two parliamentary seats, these were the 'tools' with which George was to manage affairs during the 1770s – with disastrous consequences. While Walpole's forebodings were not realized, tension still remained high when Parliament reconvened after the long summer recess of 1770 – among the first business to hand being a proposal to establish an inquiry into 'The Proceeding of Judges . . . particularly in Cases relating to the Freedom of the Press.' Again, Wilkes and the North Briton were the focus of discussion, and if the Opposition cast themselves in the role of guardians of journalistic license, then Fox had another, more personal reason, for opposing the motion.

What was it that Wilkes had once written of his father, that his 'black malignant heart' was as deceitful as it was treacherous? After seven years, the memory of the charge remained, and there were precedents enough with which to avenge it – that the debates of the House were never published, that the public seldom knew how their members voted, that while the ministry might be accountable to Parliament, Parliament was responsible to no one. And now Wilkes and his kind had set up to challenge such prerogatives, claiming it as the people's right to know something of how their representatives managed their business and, thus, take a hand in its management for themselves. To Fox the notion smacked of anarchy, for if the voice of the people was the voice of God, then the only legitimate place in which that voice could be heard was in Parliament. As for the rest, the mobbocracy had reached above itself, and needed a lesson in compliance.

Thick set, dark jowled, but as always, fashionably dressed, Fox rose to speak in the Commons on the afternoon of 6 December 1770, the words fairly chasing themselves from his mouth:

> We are told that the people are under terrible apprehensions that the law is perverted . . . that the Judges, like a dozen of Patagonian giants, either have swallowed up, or are going to swallow up both law and gospel . . . . For my part, Sir, I am not disposed to take the voice of a miserable faction for the voice of my country . . . . Such an irregular and riotous crowd are but ill-qualified to judge of their own interest. They are but unsteady guardians of liberty and property. Do you want proofs? Consult the English history, and you will find them in every page.

The trick was a neat one, and North delighted. Fox had turned the Whig's long-standing defence of parliamentary privilege – now so conveniently abandoned – upon themselves. Another half decade was to pass before Fox himself was to call up the voice of the people to redress the the excesses of the Commons, meanwhile Walpole was to write that Fox was 'the meteor of these days'. The London crowd did not share his sentiments, the more so after he harangued an angry mob with 'reproachful words' from the upper window of a Westminster coffee house. With memories of his own rough handling, Lord Holland was to warn both his sons 'to be more cautious of the mob than they are' – but Charles was indifferent to the advice. 'We have higher obligations to justice than to our constituents; we are the choosen delegates of the British electors for salutory not for pernicious purposes . . . to keep the privileges of the very freemen we represent, as much within their proper limit, as to control any unwarrantable assertion of the Royal authority.'

The reference to royal authority was significant, a fore-taste of Fox's duel with the Crown, but the crowd failed to appreciate the subtle shift in his line of attack. In mid April 1771, Walpole was reporting that 'Charles Fox again narrowly escaped with his life, a large stone being thrown at him, which passed through both windows of his chariot', while later in the month the same coach was broken up and Fox pelted with mud before being rolled in the gutter. The cub's treatment entertained the king, for he had been quick to note the sting in the tail of Fox's remarks. What might have appeared as an afterthought had dangerous implications – that Fox was as wary of regal as of populist pretensions. Doubtless, the tearaway had his uses – within months he had mastered the Admiralty brief with a thoroughness that had surprised even his friends – but he still required watching. At best, he could become an embarrassment; at worst, a menace.

As frugal as Fox was flamboyant, George deeply distrusted his junior minister. Save for his politics, the man repre-sented all he abhorred, for in an age of conspicuous consump-tion, the king was notable as much for his rectitude as for the simplicity of his lifestyle. In the first year of his reign he had issued a proclamation against profanity and immorality – and had subsequently adhered to his own precepts with a single-mindedness that marked his whole character. Others might fail, but as king he must set an example, and cartoonists delighted in satirizing the austerity of his household (as often as not, dinner consisted of a leg of mutton with caper sauce, followed by a slice of cherry pie), while the wits regaled themselves with gossip of his parsimony. Small wonder that George suspected Fox the politician almost as much as he deplored Fox the playboy.

And news of his minister's most recent exploits can have done little to reassure him. Even the gamesters at Almack's had begun to wager on his solvency (one entry in the bet-ting book reading: 'Lord Clermont has given Mr Crawfurd 10 guineas, upon the condition of receiving £500 from him whenever Mr Charles Fox shall be worth £100,000 clear of debts'), while the moneylenders were no longer willing to wait their turn in the Jerusalem Chamber above Mackie's. Now they began to press harder for the settlement of his outstanding debts, and when the Commons rose in the late spring of 1771, Fox retired to Kingsgate, no doubt relieved to escape his sundry creditors.

In Fox's memory, those summers at his father's country home were forever carefree and sun filled days; days made alive by the companionship of his elder brother, Stephen, and Lady Sarah Lennox; entertaining with the playing of a little tennis and cricket, or joining the occasional shoot; studious with the reading of constitutional history (in 1771 he was writing 'I am now reading Clarendon . . . I think that the style is bad, and that he has a good deal of the old woman in his way of thinking') and the classics. Although already growing portly, Fox the sportsman was as reckless as Fox the gambler. An erratic batsman, he frequently ran himself out in his enthusiasm to score; while as a shot, he once blew the hat of a beater to pieces, mistaking it for a flight of woodcock. The stories of the time are legion, but one remains instructive – of how a shooting party was driven home by a storm, to find Fox missing. Returning later, he explained how he had met up with a farm labourer who had views on the scientific cultivation of turnips, and how he had preferred a drenching to neglecting what might prove to be useful information.

Behind the façade of the dandiprat, there remained the ghost of the Eton schoolboy and Oxford scholar whose intellectual curiosity, allied to a retentive memory, was to take as much pleasure from his scholarship as from his gaming, who numbered among his favourite pastimes reading through the works of the Greek scholar Appolonius Rhodius in search of passages that had been plagiarized by later poets, and who was intensely proud of his membership of Dr Johnson's exclusive Literary Club. The inspiration of Sir Joshua Reynolds, and founded in 1765, the club's membership came to include Goldsmith, Burke, Gibbon, Garrick, Sheridan, Adam Smith and Boswell; as distinguished a group as ever met round a dinner table to discuss literary and philosophical affairs.

Not that such esoteric pursuits were regarded as an affecta-
tion during the age of Enlightenment, rather as the preserve
of that small, but influential coterie of intellectuals who made
a godhead of reason, and Paris their spiritual home. Thirty-
six years had passed since Voltaire's *Essays on England*
was committed to the public executioner; twenty-one since
Diderot had published the first of the seventeen volumes of
his *Encyclopedie* 'to change the way of men's thinking'; and
nine since Rousseau completed *The Social Contract* with its
resounding opening line: 'Man is born free, and everywhere
he is in chains.'

Agnostic in everything, save their belief in reason, the
intelligentsia held that 'the perfectability of man' was capable
of indefinite extension. A subversive doctrine, it was soon
to undermine the foundations of the established order – yet it
was in the Paris salons that the works of the *philosophe* found
their admirers, and the *philosophe* themselves found their
most ardent disciples. As was his custom, Fox wintered in
Paris in 1771, but there is no record that he had any dealings
either with the *philosophe,* or with their radical abstractions.
It may be that his gambling allowed little time for other, more
intellectual pursuits, or that the social round of opera and
theatre-going commanded so much of his attention that he
had none to spare to continue the discussion that he had
opened with Voltaire that day at Ferney four years before.

If so, it is out of character. At 21 years of age Fox may have
been a wastrel, a coxcomb, and much else beside, but one
thing he was not – a philistine. As such, it is inconceivable
that he was unaware of, or indifferent to the intellectual
furore that wracked Paris during the 1770s, or that being
the disputatious man he was, he would be content to stand,
quietly, on the sidelines of a debate that was to shape the
future, not least of his own career. Certainly his French was
more than adequate to make a significant contribution to
such discussions, and yet all the talk was of Fox the rakehell of whom Madame du Deffand was to write that he 'will
never form any connections except such as arise from play,
and perhaps from politics; but of politics I know nothing'.

She was too self-effacing, if only because of her long-time

friendship with de Montesquieu, whose *Spirit of the Laws* was published in 1748. As with Voltaire, Montesquieu drew heavily on the separation of powers in the British constitution ('a masterpiece of legislation') to develop his own model of government; and as with Voltaire, his work made a profound impression on the intellectuals who attended Madame du Deffand's twice weekly supper parties. Though 'now very old, and stone blind' (Montesquieu was to write her a touching letter on blindness shortly after he had suffered the same affliction), her waspish tongue continued to delight Horace Walpole, the more so with her impressions of the young Charles Fox.

After their first meeting, she was to write: 'Le petit Fox a infiniment d'esprit, mais c'est de ces esprits de tete.' In the years that followed, the contradictions within Fox's character continued to defy her French logic – at one moment, he had 'beaucoup d'esprit, mais it a pris toute sa croissance, il n'ira pas plus loin', the next 'Enfin je ne vois pas qu'il ait de la nature. Il y a du Jean Jaques [Rousseau]', while later she was to declare that 'son espirit me parait mediocre, et son caractre detestable'.

As Fox struggled to establish his own identity, his personality at once intrigued and enraged. There could be no doubts either about his talents, or his profligacy: the question was which would win out in the contest for Fox's soul? The opening months of 1772 were to highlight the conflict exactly – a period during which he played deeper than ever before, between making lightning forays in the House. At certain moments, indeed, it seemed that the two elements within his character fused, becoming a continuum, and that if Fox the gamester was playing at politics, then Fox the politician was gambling away his career.

Early in February he was sound enough, opposing a petition to the Commons on behalf of certain dissenting clergy for relief from subscription to the Thirty Nine Articles, the doctrinal mainstay of the Established Church. From his seat on the Treasury benches, the Junior Lord opined that 'religion is best understood when least talked of', and the motion was easily defeated – though Walpole noted that if Fox did not shine in debate it may well have been because: 'He had sat up playing hazard at Almack's, from Tuesday evening 6th, till five in the morning of Wednesday, 7th. An hour before, he had recovered £12,000 that he had lost, and by dinner, which was at five o'clock, he had ended loosing £11,000. On Thursday he spoke in this debate, went to dinner at past eleven at night: from thence to White's where he drank till seven the next morning; thence to Almack's where he won £6,000.'

North might be displeased, but he was in no position to complain. He was to need all the talent he could muster to steer the king's latest scheme through the House. On 21 February George had sent a message to the Commons announcing his intention to promote legislation to ensure that no future descendant of George II could marry without first obtaining the approval of the king, or his successors. As conscious of his responsibilities as he was clumsy in performing them, George had been shocked by the successive marriages of the Duke of Gloucester to Lady Waldegrave (the illegitimate daughter of a seamstress), and the Duke of Cumberland to Colonel Luttrell's sister, Mrs Horton.

George regarded such domestic anarchy as indefensible, and the Royal Marriage Bill was his answer – to the fury of the nobility who saw the measure as 'giving leave to the Princes of the Blood to lie with our wives, and forbidding them to marry our daughters'. At a stroke, George had succeeded in uniting the Opposition, while the government itself cursed both the bill and its author. As always, however, the king was inflexible and his instructions clear – North was to drum the measure through Parliament with the minimum delay. If ever there was a time when Fox's polemical skills were needed, it was then. Instead of which, he resigned.

The news caused a sensation, to be fuelled by speculation as to why Fox should have taken such a step. At first, Walpole believed that it was under pressure from Lord Holland, but this was retracted almost immediately on recalling that one of Holland's few principles was to retain office as long as one could. At Almack's the gossip was as intense as the gaming, one theory among the many being that Fox was exploiting North's weakness to obtain a better post – a theory that gained credence when it was learned that the Prime Minister had approached Fox to see whether there was not some small consideration either to Fox or his family which he had overlooked in the press of his ministerial business? The overture was rejected with contempt, and on 21 February Fox was writing to Lord Ossory from Almack's:

> It is impossible to tell you the real reason for my resigning, it is very difficult and arises from many different circumstances. I should not have resigned at this moment merely on account of my complaints against Lord North, if I had not determined to vote against the *Royal Marriage Bill* . . . . Upon the whole I am convinced I did right, and I think myself safe from going into any opposition, which is the only danger. I am convinced if you were to know the whole state of the case, I should have your approbation, which, I can assure you, would make me very happy.

Doubtless the 'different circumstances' were associated as much with the Fox family's own matrimonial exploits as with the arcana of the marriage laws. Thirty years had done little to expunge memories of the uproar caused by Lord Holland's runaway affair with Lady Caroline, or the violent row that blew up with the introduction of the Clandestine Marriage Act of 1753. In an effort to check Fleet marriages, the government of the day had introduced legislation which proposed to annul all marriages undertaken without the consent of parents, and which insisted that everyone, including Dissenters and Roman Catholics, were either married in an Established Church, or not married at all. Henry Fox was enraged, seeing the measure as a direct reflection on his own romance, and one of his tirades in the Commons provoked a member to remark that Fox's insolence was 'new in Parliament, new in politics, and new in ambition'.

And if that was history, there were always the more recent memory of the king's cavalier treatment of Lady Sarah Lennox – 'He [Bute] has thoroughly convinced me of the impropriety of marrying a country woman.' If the

Marriage Act had offended Henry Fox personally, then the Royal Marriage Act offended his son, vicariously. Four years his senior, Lady Sarah had been one of his closest companions since the childhood days of Holland House, the woman of whom Walpole was to write that 'No Magdalen by Correggio was half so lovely' – yet here was George, careless of his own youthful courtship (or possibly to revenge himself for the disappointment of it?), proposing a measure widely described as being a Bill to Encourage Royal Princes to Seduce our Wives, and Forbid them to Marry our Daughters.

At the opening of the parliamentary session of 1772, Fox himself had announced his intention of introducing a new Marriage Bill to replace the one over which his father had spent so much time and fury twenty years before – but that remained to be debated. The immediate need was to prepare his case against the new measure proposed by the king, indifferent to the charge that his resignation had been prompted by personal ambition, or that he might join the Opposition. On hearing of the resignation, in fact, Edward Gibbon had enthused: 'Charles Fox is commenced patriot, and is already attempting to pronounce the words "country", "liberty", "corruption"; with what success, time will discover.' As an historian, he anticipated history.

Fox had yet to decide where his political future lay. Fiercely loyal to his father, he had lived within the shadow of Lord Holland's political authority for twenty-three years – the authority of a man whose hostility of the Whigs had become envenomed with age. In such circumstances, to join the Opposition would have been regarded as little short of treachery. Certainly Fox's resignation over the Royal Marriage Bill did not come into that class, but the same could not be said of his passing reference to the limits of sovereign power. The thing smacked of apostasy, and may well have led his father to ponder whether the Cub was developing a political will of his own.

During the period of political flux in the aftermath of the long Whig hegemony it was no easy process, government still turning on men rather than measures; on the capacity of the small handful of grandees who dominated both Houses to mobilize a following which, in alliance with the King's Friends, would provide them with a working majority. Almost incestuous in its composition (Chatham once described the Commons as 'a parcel of younger brothers'), the ties of kith and kin frequently exerted as much, if not more influence than political principal at Westminster, and a further three years were to pass before Fox finally nerved himself to make a clean break with his father's prejudices.

Meanwhile, he regarded his defection from the government benches as a purely temporary affair, even if it was viewed somewhat differently by Lord North. On the day of Fox's resignation, the Royal Marriage Bill was brought before the House with a solemnity that disguised its odium: 'His Majesty . . . recommends to both House of Parliament to take into serious consideration . . . some new provision more effectually to guard the descendents of his late Majesty George the Second from marrying without the approbation of his Majesty.'

Within the week, the House of Lords clearly indicated what they thought of the Crown's honour and dignity by driving a debate on the bill to a narrow division, to the discomfiture of North who received a tart note from George instructing him to marshal his forces more effectively: 'I do expect every nerve to be strained to carry the Bill through both Houses with a becoming firmness, for it is not a question that immediately relates to the Administration, but personally to myself; therefore I have a right to expect a hearty support from everyone in my service, and shall remember defaulters.'

For the King's Friends, the warning was clear enough. George was a good hater. For Fox, the decision had already been made and on 9 March he launched his first diatribe against the bill, protesting astonishment that North could 'by some unaccountable fatality become the promoter of a Bill which seemed big with mischief'. It was the first skirmish of a bruising campaign during which Fox continued to harass the government 'with most amazing rapidity and clearness' – to the embarrassment of North, the fury of the king, and the delight of the Opposition. Even his best efforts, however, were of no avail, and in late March Walpole was writing: 'Never was an act passed *against* which so much, and *for* which so little, was said.'

Fox was soon revenged. A fortnight after the Royal Marriage Act entered the statute books, he tabled his own Marriage Bill aimed at amending the act of 1753. His performance reaffirmed North's belief that here was a man whom it would be foolhardy to cross. On 8 July Fox had been racing at Newmarket, where he had lost £1000, and had broken his journey back to London by drinking through the night at Hockerel. On the 9th he introduced his bill, to be opposed by North and Burke. Momentarily it appeared that Fox was indifferent to what they had to say, but then, as Walpole reports:

> Charles Fox, who had been running about the House talking to different persons and scarce listening to Burke, rose with amazing spirit and memory, answered both Lord North and Burke; ridiculed the arguments of the former and confuted those of the latter . . . . Charles Fox had great facility of delivery; his words flowed rapidly but he had nothing of Burke's variety of language or correctness; nor his method. Yet his arguments were far more shrewd . . . . This was genius – was almost inspiration.

Walpole was not alone in his opinion. The *Gazeteer* declared that Fox's performance was 'a masterly assemblage of arguments on behalf of the liberties of human nature', while twenty-three former opponents of the bill joined Fox in the division lobbies to give him a single vote majority – 'a disgraceful event for the Prime Minister' according to Walpole. North needed no reminding, the king did that effectively enough. No question, the Cub was a menace, but better to have him within the ministry than without, and for four months North worked feverishly to reshuffle his own front bench to readmit Charles Fox. By December, when the House reassembled after the summer recess, and after shifting six of the King's Friends from office to office, North was successful, George III writing on 20 December: 'I have no objection to Mr C. Fox's vacating his seat tomorrow' – and timing the note with his customary precision: '40 min pt 6p.m.'

The following day Fox rejoined the government as Junior Lord of the Treasury at £1600 a year. Lord Holland was delighted, perhaps his fears of the Cub's recusancy were unfounded after all; Lord North relieved; but the king still harboured doubts about hearing 'the rattle of the dice box at the Treasury board'. He need not have concerned himself on that score; Fox was to prove himself as conscientious at the Treasury as he had done at the Admiralty, but as for his private life and political stability . . . .

1773 was a cataclysmic year for Fox, a year in which, compelled by some personal demon, he drove his life to the extremes in an attempt to reconcile the contradictions of his character and, thus, make a whole of the trinity that was himself – Charles James Fox, the gambler, encouraged and underwritten by his father; Charles James Fox, the Tory, acolyte of Lord Holland's political canon; and Charles James Fox, the placeman, struggling to formulate his dissent. More than a century after Fox's death, the biographer John Drinkwater was to dismiss the first years of Fox's political career as irrelevant. Like Hazlitt, he was wrong. Since earliest childhood Fox had been at odds with himself, and 1773 proved a crisis year – a crazy progression of events in which one day fused with the next, each as manic as the last; of insanity in pursuit of the sane.

And all the while, Lord Holland's health was deteriorating, half a century of hard living were taking their toll at last. Possibly the two events are unconnected; possibly Lord Holland's terminal sickness had nothing to do with his son's increasingly desperate lifestyle, gambling by night and politicking by day, as contemptuous of his losses as of his parliamentary career. North may have been glad to have the Cub back on his own benches, but the relief proved short lived. Having once tasted independence, the Junior Lord was not to be denied his freedom, and within weeks of taking office he was thundering against the management of the East India Company in general, and more particularly against the hero of Arcot and Plassey, Lord Clive: 'the origin of all plunder, the source of all robbery'.

North endured the tirade in silence, but his embarrassment was acute. Surely Fox knew that Clive was the owner of at least ten parliamentary seats, and the possible purchaser of more? Fox did, but it made no difference. He had adopted India as a personal cause, with profound implications for the future. Immediately, however, there was more pressing business to hand, for during the summer it became known that his eldest brother was expecting an heir. Stephen had always been sickly, and the moneylenders quick to extend credit to Fox on the expectation that he would be the main beneficiary of his father's fortune should Stephen die. Now all that had changed. He could well be cut out of his reversionary inheritance. Above Mackie's, the moneylenders swarmed at the door, and in desperation Fox availed himself of an adventuress who styled herself the Hon. Mrs Grieve who peddled advice on emergencies at half a guinea a time.

Fox paid the price, to be told that what he needed was to marry a wealthy heiress, and that she, Mrs Grieve, knew just the woman – a certain Miss Phipps, recently arrived from the West Indies with a fortune of £80,000. The lure was attractive, and throughout the summer Mrs Grieve continued to tease Fox with the prospects of a meeting with the heiress, once going so far as to persuade him that as Miss Phipps liked fair men he should powder his face and eyebrows. Fox, it seems, complied, and still continued to pursue his elusive bride even after their first interview was postponed because the lady was said to be ill with smallpox.

Eventually, the fraud was exposed, for Walpole to exclaim: 'Had a novice been a prey to those artifices, it would not have been extraordinary, but Charles Fox has been in the world from his childhood, and been treated as a man long before season.' Society was vastly amused:

By turns solicited by different plans,
Yet fixed with none, Fox dresses, games, harangues,
Where varying fashion leads the sportive band,
And whim and folly bound it hand in hand,

Behold him ambling through those flow'ry ways,
A model macaroni, a l'Angloise.

But while Fox might protest of Mrs Grieve: 'She got nothing out of me', his financial predicament remained. In November 1773, Stephen's wife gave birth to a son – 'a second Messiah, born for the destruction of the Jews' remarked Fox, mirthlessly – and there was no longer any holding the moneylenders back. They swarmed around Fox with their promisory notes – a 1000 guineas here, 10,000 there – and when Lord Holland asked for a statement of his indebtedness, two of his old Pay Office clerks were required to establish the exact extent of his son's debts. Ten years had passed since he had first slipped Charles 5 guineas to play the tables at Spa. Now, and for the last time, he was to pay the cost, writing to his agents: 'I do order, direct and require you to sell and dispose of my long annuities, and so much of my other stock, estates, and effects, as will be sufficient to pay and discharge the debts of my son the Hon. Charles James Fox, not exceeding the sum of £100,000.'

But even that was not enough. Eventually Lord Holland was to write off a debt totalling some £140,000, at which, penitent, Fox promised to mend his ways and take up the law. It proved a hollow gesture, the blades at Almack's wagering that 'four members of the Club are married or dead before Charles Fox is called to the bar', but even then his father would have nothing said against his brilliant, yet wayward son. A dying man, lonely and embittered in his self-imposed exile, Holland was to write: 'Never let Charles know how excessively he afflicts me' – an epitaph as much to the indulgence of the father, as the egocentricity of the son.

At 24 years of age, and already out of office once, Fox pursued his political career with a frenzy that alarmed his friends, and made North wonder whether the price of his supposed fealty was worth the anxiety it caused. The memory of the Clive affair still rankled and then, in February 1774, the old question of parliamentary privilege re-emerged. The Reverend John Horne had been Vicar of Brentford at the time of the notorious election of 1769, and had made good use of his pulpit to oppose the election of the king's favourite, Luttrell. Five years on, and having inherited a small fortune and a second name from a certain Mr Tooke, the Reverend Horne Tooke again entered the lists for 'Wilkes and Liberty' with an article in *The Publick Advertiser* signed 'Strike – but Hear' in which, among other things, he accused the Speaker of the Commons of being a liar and a knave.

After Wilkes and Junius, North would have been happy to leave enough well alone. Not so Fox. The printer of the pamphlet, Woodfall, had impugned the honour of the House. The time had come to stamp out such libellous practices once and for all. There was a stir of interest on the back benches, Fox was in a combative mood, and when it was resolved that Woodfall should be placed in the custody of the House he raged that the punishment was too lenient and moved that he be committed to Newgate. The Opposition were in high spirits, the government in disarray, North disagreeing with Fox and suggesting as a compromise that Woodfall be held in the Gate House of Westminster. Momentarily it seemed that the gambit would work, but then precedents were quoted indicating it would only be proper to commit Woodfall to the care of the Sergeant at Arms.

A division was called, and the House divided on the issue of accepting the precedent – but with Fox holding North to his pledge of imprisoning Woodfall. There was chaos, with North having to advise his own supporters to vote for a measure that he, himself, was being compelled to oppose. The king was incensed, Fox had humiliated his first Minister, and on 16 February (25 pt 4p.m.) he was writing: 'I am greatly incensed by the presumption of Charles Fox in obliging You to vote with him last night . . . . Indeed, that young man has so thoroughly cast off every principle of common honour and honesty that he must become as contemptible as he is odious.'

The same day, Fox again embarrassed the government, again in pursuit of Woodfall who, he claimed, had libelled the Glorious Revolution of 1688 ('an era of liberties, of the happiness of Britain'), and within the week he was voting against the administration on a Dissenter's petition, ridiculing the notion that any 12-year-old could 'understand, relish, and swallow down the sublimer mysteries of religion'. North, as long suffering as any man, was tired of balancing patience against utility. The Cub must go, and George was happy to agree. As Fox entered the Commons on 24 February a door keeper handed him a note: 'Mr Fox, His Majesty has thought proper to order a new Commission of the Treasury to be made out, in which I do not see your name. North.' At first he took the thing for a joke, but neither North nor his master were in a joking mood – they had lived with Fox's humours for altogether too long.

Fox was out again, causing his father's old friend, George Selwyn, to remark: 'Charles for the future I shall eat salt fish on the day you was turned out. You shall be my Charles the Martyr now; for I am tired of your great-grandfather, the old one. His head can never be sewn on again; but, as yours can be, I'll stick to you.' It was a bold assertion, for in the following months Fox was to hound the government mercilessly, especially for its handling of colonial affairs. Free of ministerial constraints, he harassed North on the constitutional right to impose the Stamp Act, and on 19 April 1774, voted for the repeal of the tea duty – the first time that Fox voted with the Rockingham Whigs. Little more than two months later, Lord Holland died.

The former decision was to shape Fox's future as the latter's influence had shaped his past. In his will, Lord Holland left his son £20,000 down, and £900 a year, together with estates in Sheppey and Thanet and Kingsgate itself. Fox realized the properties immediately, while, on the death of his brother, Stephen, in November, he inherited the Clerkship of the Pells, a sinecure worth some £2000 a year – which he sold to the government in return for an income of £1700 a year for the next thirty-one years.

Undoubtedly, the realization of all he could raise was prompted, largely, by his need to settle his outstanding debts, though it is possible that there were deeper, more subtle motives at work. At best, living in the shadow of great men is never easy – and Holland made it none the easier for his son. Even at this distance, the impression is of a powerful, yet lonely man who found in his private life what he had lost in his public one, who justified his political notoriety by his devotion to his family. And within that family, Charles was his idol, the profligate product of a childhood in which he could do no wrong, in which his father indulged his every whim as if trying to atone for the public figure that he was – a man whose venality was legendary in an age when venality was the agent of politics.

No question that Holland meant well: he loved his son too much for it to be otherwise – yet Holland's love was a corrupting thing that was to sap at Fox's being for the first 25 years of his life. For love such as Holland's is not unconditional, it always has a price. Though the deed is never struck, it is implicit in the relationship itself, in the intangible ties that bind all fathers and sons and which, in the case of two Foxes, made impossible demands upon Charles – demands which, ironically, his own extravagant upbringing meant that he could never fulfil.

Encouraged from earliest childhood to be independent, to pursue his own actions and ideas, careless of constraints, the young Fox must have found it increasingly hard to come to terms with his father's politics based, as they were, on the defence of the political status quo. Ultimately the two, the man and his political heritage, were incompatible, and Lord Holland can hardly have wondered that his son became a rebel, for in challenging his father's political orthodoxy, he was asserting his own right to be free.

From the day that Charles Fox entered the Commons, thanks to his father's patronage, he had always been restless with the role which he had had to play, and for almost five years sought to reconcile the man that he was with the man that his father wanted him to be. The attempt was doomed from the outset. Sooner or later, Fox would have broken with his past, though with difficulty as long as his father lived. In July 1774, Lord Holland died – and Fox was free to become the rebel which, inherently, he always was.

4

'To Vote in Small Minorities'

Three months before Fox's resignation, the packet *Hayley* docked in Dover after a fast passage from Massachusetts. Among the papers aboard was a copy of the Boston *Evening Post* which briefly reported that on the night of 18 December 1773, a small party of Bostonians, disguised as Mohawk Indians, had boarded three ships in the harbour and dumped 340 chests of tea into the dock. George III's immediate reaction was one of concern for the welfare of the East India trade, to be followed by mounting anger at 'those damned rebels', the colonists.

The king's disquiet reflected the priorities of the time, for in London the constitutional rights of the colonists were, at best, still regarded as secondary to the welfare of trade – more especially, of trade with India. Indeed, in the mid eighteenth century the politics of the former were inextricably linked with the finances of the latter, and for ten years and more after his break with North in 1774, each was to play a crucial role in Fox's political career.

Almost three centuries had passed since Sir Thomas Roe had presented his credentials as the East India Company's first agent at the court of the Mogul Emperors. Although, nominally, an independent trading company, the fortunes of the EIC were carefully followed by successive administrations in London, for India was already widely regarded as the glittering prize of empire, a sub-continent of virtually limitless wealth to be disputed with the French at Pondicherry and Wandewash and Buxar. The battle honours of the so-called

John Company were as hard won as the corruption of the company's administration was widespread, Burke writing in the Annual Register of 1773.

> In several things the form of the Company's government stood in need of correction. Many thought that the conduct of individuals ought to be diligently enquired into, their vast wealth confiscated for the national benefit, and severe punishment inflicted, as an example to those who should hereafter be entrusted with such power, under such temptations to abuse it.

Burke's polemic against corruption disguised a more widespread concern as much with the management of India as the management of the India trade, especially that of tea. In the previous half century, the drink had become a national institution, and if the Tea Act of 1746 had lifted the Exchequer's revenue by £85,000 a year, then by 1760 it was estimated that nine out of every ten families were taking tea at least twice daily, to the disgust of Jonas Hanway who was shocked to find that 'even labourers mending the road demanded their daily tea'. And what was true of Britain was equally true of the North American colonies, where the consumption of tea had risen fourfold in the previous half century.

For the Sons of Liberty it was to prove a potent brew. In 1770, North had withdrawn all stamp duties except those on tea which, in earning the Exchequer £11,000 a year, was to cost Britain an empire, for by 1773 'the fascinating plant' of Dr Johnson had become a symbol of the pretensions of Britain to sovereignty over the Thirteen Colonies. An absentee landlord, Westminster not only continued to dictate colonial policy, but also to regulate its trade. A tough-minded people who had made an empire of a wilderness, a growing number of colonials regarded such pretensions as an insult to their liberties – the more so when the government was corrupt, and its economics venal. In 1770, a Town Resolution in Boston declared:

> A deep-laid and desperate plan of imperial despotism has been laid, and partly executed, for the extinction of all civil

liberty . . . . The august and once revered fortress of English freedom – the admirable work of ages – the BRITISH CONSTITUTION seems fast tottering into fatal and inevitable ruin.

An echo of Whig fears – of Burke and Wilkes and Junius – the suspicion was aggravated by mounting indignation at Britain's management of the North American economy. Since the days of the Founding Fathers, colonial trade had been subordinated to Britain's interests, and while a case might be made for levying taxes to help meet the costs of the Seven Years' War, the method of their imposition fuelled the colonists' belief that: 'America was the only remaining spot to which their [Westminster's] oppression and extortion has not fully reached.'

Sovereignty and trade, trade and sovereignty, there was little to distinguish between them, each living off the other, and for nine years after the passage of the Stamp Act of 1765, Westminster sought to quiet the colonists' growing restiveness, while safeguarding the dominion of the king. Once begun, however, the dispute developed a momentum of its own, both sides entrenching themselves in prepared positions – and if the trifling duty now imposed on tea, largely to assist the hard pressed revenues of the John Company, served the ends of the Sons of Liberty then so be it. What was it that the radical John Adams had written, that North America was destined for 'the emancipation of the slavish part of mankind all over the earth'?

The words had a familiar ring – 'Wee shall be as a Citty upon a Hill, the eies of all people are upon us . . .'. Almost 150 years had passed since John Winthrop had preached his shipboard sermon to the future leaders of the Massachusetts Bay Colony, and there could be no disguising his intent. If America was to become 'a by-word through the world', then there could be no compromising with liberty – and on 16 December 1773, a handful of colonists masquerading as Indians staged the Boston Tea Party.

For George it was too much. His 'damned rebels' had finally over-stepped themselves. They needed a lesson in deference. Within a month of receiving the news, the king called in General Thomas Gage, the Commander-in-Chief of British land forces in North America, then on home leave. 'His language', the king said later, 'was very consonant to his character of an honest determined man. He says that they will be lyons, whilst we are lambs; but, if we take the resolute part, they will undoubtedly prove very weak.' It was exactly what George wished to hear, and his Cabinet had devised precisely the means for taking the resolute part – to shut down Boston harbour, and starve the town of trade, until the East India Company were indemnified for the loss they had sustained.

The fateful Boston Port Bill first came before Parliament in March, and the government had marshalled its forces well – one member declaring that the tea party was in reality treason; another proposing that Boston should be razed like Carthage. Within eighteen days the bill was through the Commons, and with the notable exception of Chatham who raged that 'if that mad and cruel measure should be pushed . . . England has seen her best days', it met little opposition in the Lords. The king was delighted, writing to North at 8.35 that evening: 'The feebleness and futility of the opposition shows the rectitude of the measure.'

Authority, that was the essence of government, and if the colonists were soon to have a taste of his Royal displeasure, then nearer home the Whigs had already learned a sharp lesson in management of power. Always imperious, George's confidence burgeoned. With a 200 seat majority in the House, what better time to exploit the Opposition's weakness while driving through further legislation to make an example both of Boston and Massachusetts to discourage the remaining twelve colonies from imitating their mutinuous ways? Little more than two weeks after the passage of the Boston Port Bill, the Opposition introduced a motion for the repeal of the duty on American tea, on which Burke (from whom Fox was later to say that he had learned more than from all his books and studies) spoke for over two hours.

Although nominally directed at North, his target was the king: 'If intemperately, unwisely, fatally, you sophisticate and poison the very source of government . . . you will teach them [the people] by these means to call sovereignty itself into question. If that sovereignty and their freedom cannot be reconciled, which will they take? They will cast your sovereignty in your face. Nobody will argued into slavery.'

Fox followed Burke, but limited himself to practical considerations as to why the Stamp Tax had been laid in the first place, to conclude that it was solely to assert George's authority, in which case 'I am clearly of the opinion you will . . . force them into open rebellion.' George was deaf to the warnings, the more so when the motion was defeated by 133 votes – a sound enough majority on which to base his latest measure for disciplining is recalcitrant subjects.

Three days later a new bill was introduced in the Commons to rewrite the democratic constitution of Massachusetts, and vest virtually all power in the hands of the king. This was liberty in chains, and Fox was to his feet to mock George, his ministry, and their notion of government:

> I take this to be the question, Whether America is to be governed by force, or management? . . . I look upon this measure to be in effect taking away their charter . . . if their charter is to be taken away, for God's sake let it be taken away by law, and not be legislative coercion . . . . I consider this bill as a bill of pains and penalties, for it begins with a crime, and ends with a punishment; and I wish, gentlemen would consider, whether it is more proper to govern by military force, or by management.

Again, the government carried the day, and again George noted his delight. Now General Gage had all the legislative powers necessary to make lambs of the colonial 'lyons' – backed by the reinforcement of his Boston garrison. Elated by success, the king neglected to take two factors into account: the problem of governing Thirteen Colonies 3500 miles distant by force if they should resist his Coercive Acts, and the question of how the Opposition would react to what they continued to regard as his appetite for personal government. A year to the day after the Whigs had tabled their motion to lift the American tea duty, a column of British troops marched into Lexington en route to seizing a colonial ammunition dump at Concord. A crowd had gathered on the village green. An officer ordered: 'Lay down your arms, you damned rebels, and disperse' – and the shot was fired that was to be heard around the world.

In London the news was received first with disbelief, then with a mixture of anger and dismay, depending upon one's politics. The *Morning Chronicle* maintained that 'The Sword alone can decide this dispute.' The *Morning Post* replied that 'If conquest gives us command of America we cannot keep it by force.' In the City (already hard hit by the loss of American trade), the Constitutional Society launched an appeal for the 'relief of the widows and orphans of our beloved American fellow subjects . . . unhumanely murdered by the king's Troops at or near Lexington and Concord', while at his palace at Kew, George III was consoling himself with the thought that 'I know that I am doing my duty and therefore can never wish to retract.'

And the Opposition, what of them? Riven by private feuds, and discouraged by their years in the political wilderness, they had become a laughing stock. In 1773, one member had noted that 'Lord North has had a wonderful tide of success, and there does not seem anything likely to interrupt it. Opposition is grown ridiculous and contemptuous', and by mid 1775 the situation was, if anything, worse. In the Lords, the fighting man of the Rockingham faction, the Duke of Richmond, confessed to feeling 'very languid about the American business', holding that nothing would restore the government to sanity except the consequences that resulted from their actions.

The only consistent opposition, in fact, came from Edmund Burke and Charles James Fox, of whom Henry Grattan was later to write:'Fox during the American war, Fox on his best days, was the best speaker I ever heard.' At first, however, it was Burke who took the lead. For half a decade he had fought to provide the Rockingham Whigs with a sense of purpose that was lacking in their leader – 'the wet blanket' as Walpole dubbed him. In a torrent of notes and letters he chivied and chased them to 'come up to Town' or to 'be in their place' for important debates, but all too often his best efforts were unavailing. They had other, and more attractive business to hand, Otto Trevelyan providing a cameo of their attitude towards politics at the time:

> Rockingham and his followers loved the country; and there were few among them who did not possess plenty of it to love. Assembling for business in a November fog, and wrangling on until a June sun shone reproachfully through the windows seemed a doubtful form of happiness . . . . To haunt London when the thorns were red and white and the syringas fragrant, or the hounds were running over the Yorkshire pastures, and the woodcocks gathering in the Norfolk spinneys; to debate amidst clamour, and vote in a lobby where there was hardly space to stand, with the hope that at some unknown point in the future he might draw salary for a few quarter days – was not a career to the mind of the great landowner who seldom got as much sport and fresh air as he wished.

Against such blandishments, Burke all too often entreated in vain. The irony is inescapable, that Burke, the outsider, should have been left to articulate the interests of the Whig grandees which they were too indolent to represent for themselves; the mystery being why he never lost faith in a cause that paid him scant return. During the crisis of 1775, however, Burke had little time for introspection. American affairs pressed in altogether too hard – the disaster of Lexington being followed by the rout of Bunker's Hill. In March he had moved his famous resolution for *Conciliation with the Colonies*, appealing to the spirit of the House: 'Magnanimity in politics is not seldom the truest wisdom; and a great empire and little minds go ill together.'

Burke's eloquence was lost on the Commons. Small minded or no, the King's Friends had as little heart to alienate their paymaster as their paymaster had a capacity for magnanimity. The resolution was comfortably defeated, though one member was never to forget the polemic. Nearly twenty years later, Fox was applying Burke's views on conciliation to the issue of Parliametary Reform: 'Let gentlemen read this speech by day, and meditate on it by night; let them peruse it again and again, study it, imprint it on their minds, impress it on their hearts – they would there learn that representation was the sovereign remedy for every evil.'

In the 1790s, Burke had something to learn from Fox. In 1770s, Fox had something to learn from Burke. As always, he was a diligent pupil, and the friendship that had begun nine years before now had the makings of an alliance that was eventually to drive North to the point of begging the king to be released from what he had come to regard as the intolerable burden of office. During 1775 alone, Fox spoke a dozen times on the North American question: arraigning the government for misleading Parliament ('The Noble Lord from beginning to end has taken care to lead the House blind-fold'); taunting the ministry for its incapacity to manage the rebellion they had provoked ('Alexander the Great never gained more in one campaign, than the Noble Lord has lost – he has lost a whole Continent'); and always, by implication, indicting George for his ambitions on the constitution: 'The administration is taking advantage of the present situation to put people under martial law; all the late American acts are tending to increase the power of the Crown, and to demolish the rights of the people.'

The juxtaposition was significant. Where, previously, Fox had been concerned with the limits of sovereignty, he now began to address himself to the rights of men whom he had pretended to despise, of that 'irregular and riotous crowd . . . ill qualified to judge their own interest'. Less than a year had passed since his father's death, and Fox had begun to change. At first the conversion was hardly perceptible – he still hazarded, deeply; still womanized, passionately; still drank, heavily – but it was there, none the less.

Once free of Lord Holland, the 26-year-old Fox began to find himself, and if the rakehell remained to gamble away the nights at Almack's, then the politician no longer made a lottery of the days. The transformation was to take a decade and more to complete, but it began on that July day when he first received news of his father's death, and it was to be accelerated during the conflict for American independence.

Twelve times the issue was debated during the par-liamentary session of 1775, and twelve times the Opposition was handsomely defeated. As Burke was to write of the king in August: 'Nothing can equal the ease, composure, and even gaiety of the great disposer of all in this lower orb.' More than 1000 men, half the total force, had died storming Bunker Hill, and Washington had been appointed Commander-in-Chief of the Continental Army by the Congress meeting at Philadelphia, but George appeared unconcerned – and with the recess, Fox retired to the country as much to entertain himself with a round of cricket, tennis, and shooting, as to nerve the morale of the Whigs.

A later commentator was to write of the time that 'Fox's character, both public and private, was enough to make any man detest him. He was factious, dissolute, untrustworthy, a gambler, a voluptuary, a cynical sentimentalist, and a politician without principle of even scruple.' Yet this was the man, so recently his father's political simulacrum, who was now becoming the sought-after guest in the country homes of every great Whig grandee, the fighting man of the Opposition when the Opposition seemed close to despair.

And they had plenty to despair about, for when the House reassembled in the autumn of 1775 there was no softening of George's mood. In fact it was the reverse: he announced plans to increase both his naval and land forces and, ominously, hinted at a scheme for employing continental troops in American affairs. This was kingship as it should be, though in a small upper room in Philadelphia an expatriate stay-maker had other ideas. Late in the year, Tom Paine set down to write *Common Sense* – 'Society in every state is a blessing, but government, even in its best state, is but a necessary evil; in its worst state, an intolerable one' – which was to inspire Washington to write from his field headquarters that the logic of the pamphlet would 'not leave numbers at a loss to decide on the propriety of separation'.

Common Sense was published in Philadelphia on 10 January 1776, and the following day George III reviewed the first and second battalions of Foot on Clapham Common – after which they embarked for America. There was now a sense of inexorability about the progress of events, but the Opposition still remained supine, Walpole writing: 'What little life there was existed in the Duke of Richmond and Charles Fox. The latter bustled, tried to animate both the Duke and the Marquis [Rockingham], but neither abandoned his gaming nor rakish life. He was seldom in bed before five in the morning, nor out of it before two at noon.'

The only consolation to be gleaned from what otherwise appeared to be a hopeless situation followed a meeting between Fox and the Lord Privy Seal, the Duke of Grafton, at a Newmarket race meeting. One of the best judges of horse flesh in England, and at one time owner of a string of thirty horses, even Fox's straightened circumstances did nothing to check his zest for racing, one early biographer writing:

> He placed himself where the animal was to make a push, or where the race was most likely to be most strongly contested. From this spot he eyed the horses advancing with the most immovable look; he breathed quicker as they accelerated their pace, and when they came opposite him, he rode in with them at full speed, whiffing, spewing and blowing as if he would have infused his whole soul into the speed, courage, and perseverance of his favourite racer.

Fox was not alone with his enthusiasm for racing; it was shared by the gentry of large, not least, by Grafton. A notorious libertine, Grafton had been among the procession of George's first ministers during the 1760s, and had played a major role in formulating the king's North American strategy. That was more than six years ago, but now, over dinner, he openly criticized his own government's colonial strategy. No pledge of secrecy was asked, and none was given, and the following days news of Grafton's volte-face was the talk of town.

Shifty as always, Grafton questioned the report, and Fox hurried back from London to Newmarket to clarify the position. On hearing him out, Grafton's immediate reply was straightforward enough: 'Sir, you have repeated my words more exactly than myself', after which came the caveat 'Still, I do not desire to be thought out of humour; Lord North and his Ministers have been very civil to me. I only disapprove of all their measures' – as neat a summary of eighteenth-century political practice as can be found. Never a man to tolerate dissimulation in others, however, George demanded an explanation, and within weeks Grafton was stripped of the Privy Seal, to join the Opposition.

Beyond this, there was little to encourage the Whigs. The government machinery continued to deliver the majorities that the king demanded. The preparations for reinforcing the North American garrison continued apace, though 20-year-old Lord Pitt, eldest son of the Earl of Chatham, resigned his commission with the 47th Regiment rather than having to serve in a conflict between Britain and America. Burke continued to chivy Rockingham, but with a growing sense of frustration, and Fox, a rotund and bustling figure with seemingly inexhaustible energy, continued to harry the ministry. Careless of long nights at the table, his spirits rose as the Opposition flagged, and he redoubled his attacks on the government, to fury of the king and the embarrassment of North.

In February he was tabling a motion to inquire into 'the Causes of the Ill Success of British Arms in North America', in April delivering a broadside against the budget proposals, in June writing to Lord Ossory: 'I am still convinced that the Americans will finally succeed, whether by victories or defeats . . . . Whatever happens, for God's sake let us all resolve to stick by them as handsomely [or more so] in their adversity as we have done in their glory, and still maintain the Whig cause, however discredited by defeats, to be the only true principle of this country.'

The conversion was complete. By the age of 27, Fox had made the final, the irrevocable break with his past. His hounding of Wilkes, his contempt for the public remained to haunt him, but, with one notable exception, his destiny was fixed. Much later he was to write:'To vote in small minorities is a misfortune to which I have been much accustomed', and the rebel that was Fox was to learn the trade of Opposition in the bitter years that followed the American Declaration of Independence on 4 July 1776.

*   *   *

Drafted by Jefferson, the Declaration echoed the beliefs of those Commonwealth men who had taken up the sword against Charles I, and the principles on which the Whigs had drummed up a Glorious Revolution in 1688: 'We hold these truths to be self evident – that all men are created equal; that they endowed by their Creator with certain unalienable rights; that among these are life, liberty, and the pursuit of happiness.'

The words sounded well enough, but it was a different matter to put them into practice. Eight days after Congress made the final break with Britain, the new British Commander-in-Chief in North America, Lord Howe, inspected his forces anchored in, or encamped around New York harbour. It consisted of more than 300 vessels, backed by an army of 35,000 men. The largest expeditionary force ever to set sail from Britain, nothing could illustrate better George's determination to stamp his authority on his insurgent colonies by stamping out 'those damned rebels'. And within weeks his army was on the march, drubbing the Continental Army at Long Island, then scouring northwards up the Hudson Valley to take Forts Washington and Lee.

The king was jubilant, the Opposition in a shambles. Never a man for close combat, Lord Rockingham considered that the time was fast approaching to secede from Parliament, and to take his party with him. Possibly he regarded such a course as the only means of expressing his disapproval of the policies of an entrenched government majority; or possibly, as Trevelyan has suggested, it was because he found life more agreeable in the hunting field and on the grouse moors of his Yorkshire kingdom than he did in the corridors of Westminster. Whatever the reason, it was to further deprive the Whigs of what little influence they retained in the House.

On hearing the report, Fox was incensed. Although still unwilling to commit himself irrevocably to the Rockingham faction, Rockingham's action could only be construed as desertion in the face of an enemy that appeared as ruthless in pursuit of British as American liberties, and there is a barely concealed insolence in the letter he wrote to the Whig leader from Newmarket on 13 October 1776: 'A secession at present would be considered as running away from the conquerors . . . . Above all, my dear Lord, I hope that it will be a point of honour among us all to support the American pretensions in adversity as we did in their prosperity, and that we should never desert those who have acted *unsuccessfully* on Whig principles.'

Momentarily it seemed that his appeal, reinforced by Burke, might be successful. Rockingham came up to town for the opening of the new session of Parliament in the last week of October. In the Commons, the main thrust of Fox's attack on the King's Speech was again directed at the king, and again he amplified his concept of government: 'Sir, it has been well said that the Speech is a hypocritical one; and in truth there is not a little hypocrisy in supposing that a King . . . a common King should be solicitous to establish anything that depended on a popular assembly. Kings, Sir, govern by means of popular assemblies only because they cannot do without them; to suppose a King is fond of that mode of governing is to suppose a chimera. It cannot exist.'

North feigned sleep, but his back benchers grew restive under Fox's withering attack that scorned the notion of American liberties being secured at the point of a bayonet, liberties inherited from their English forebearers now crushed by Hessian arms.

> Such an army, employed for such purposes, for supporting such principles, would be a very proper instrument to effect points of greater, or at least more favourite importance nearer home – points, perhaps, very unfavourable to the liberties of this country.'

Edward Gibbon, who was present, was to say that he had never heard a more masterly speech delivered by Fox, and Burke was later to write: 'I never knew Fox better, or indeed anyone, on any occasion. His speech was a noble performance.' It made no difference. At the division the government won a 155 vote majority, while in the Lords the Opposition fared little better. Rockingham led the attack, to be defeated by a comfortable majority, at which he retired with his party and appeared no more in Parliament that session. As for the King, he was 'infinitely amused' by the accounts of the debates. The man was easily pleased, and usually for the wrong reasons, for if he had had the capacity to distinguish wit from witticism he would have been quicker to grasp the thrust of Fox's argument – that a standing army and a liberal constitution were antithetical. Or perhaps, as Fox suggested, he did not wish to understand.

On one thing, however, George was clear: that North should exploit every opportunity to progress his business during Fox's absences from the Commons. And he was soon to have opportunities enough. In mid November the king got wind of a tantalizing rumour, and was quick to relay it to North: Fox was soon to leave for Paris, and would not be returning until after the recess. Queen's House, 15 minutes past 8 a.m: 'I think therefore that you cannot do better than bring as much forward as with propriety can be done, as real business is never so well considered as when the attention of the House is not taken up by noisy declamation.'

For two months North had the business of the Commons to himself, Walpole noting wryly that 'As there is no Opposition, there is no Parliament', while Fox pleasured himself in Paris. Six years had passed since their first meeting, but Madame du Deffand was still struggling to explain Fox's character, and in 1776 she was as confused as ever before: 'I have seen much of Fox, but our ways are very dissimilar, our ways of thinking very different . . . . He joins together daring, generosity, and truth, but that does not prevent him from being detestable.'

Whether or not the judgement was accurate, Fox continued to fascinate Parisian society, though in this he was not alone. On the evening of 21 December 1776, Benjamin Franklin, for ten years London agent for four North American colonies, arrived in Paris, one of three commissioners appointed by Congress to negotiate with France. Simply dressed and carrying a staff rather than a sword, the 70-year-old statesman appeared as much a prophet of natural philosophy as an ideal citizen of the free world, the Comte de Segur writing:

Nothing was more astonishing than the contrast between the luxury of Paris, the elegance of our fashions, the splendour of Versailles . . . with the almost peasant clothes, the simple but proud deportment, the outspoken but honest language, the uncurled and unpowdered hair, in a word, with that air of a distant age, which suddenly seemed to transport to Paris in the middle of a decadent and servile civilisation of the eighteenth century, a philosopher of the time of Plato or a republican of the age of Fabius or Cato.

For Britain it was an alarming portent. The campaign in America appeared to be progressing well but if France, still smarting from the humiliation of the Seven Years' War, entered into affairs, it could well reverse the balance. Since the summer Lord Stormont, the British Ambassador in Paris, had been impressing on the French Foreign Minister, Comte Vergennes, the importance of France's continuing neutrality in what George III still regarded as a domestic concern. Over the months Vergennes had become increasingly non-committal, though he was said to have remarked in private that: 'If the Colonies are determined to reject the sovereignty of His Britannic Majesty, it would not be in the interest of France to see them reduced by force.'

And now Franklin was at Versailles, being entertained by Louis XVI and his Court, while Fox continued his rampage through society, apparently careless of events, Madame du Deffand remarking: 'I do not know what his plans are for the future, he never thinks beyond today.' In this, she was wrong. By late January 1777, Stormont was taxing Vegennes with news that five ships were being loaded with military supplies for the Americas 'contrary to the friendship this Court has expressed to us', and by the first week in February, Fox was back in London. North's brief respite was over, the rump of the Opposition was gathering, alarmed at reports that the government planned to bring forward a Bill for Suspending the Habeas Corpus Act in America. The rumour was no more than the truth, reinforcing Whig fears of the king and his ministry's designs on power.

Twice within a week, Fox spoke against the bill: the first

time railing against this new proscription on old and hard won liberties ('This plan . . . is nothing less than robbing America of her franchises, as a previous step to the introduction of the same system of government in this country'); the second, reporting on the mood in Paris, detailing the reception of the American mission to Versailles, and warning that 'one important truth might be gathered from the whole – that France is secretly hostile to Great Britain'.

Four years were to pass before Fox was to reveal the source of his information – Franklin.

> I remember one day conversing with him on the American war, and predicting the fatal consequences. He compared the principle of the war, and its possible effects to the ancient Crusades. He foretold that our best blood and our best treasure would be squandered and thrown away to no manner of purpose; that like the Holy war . . . while we went thither, upon the pretence of conferring temporal, not ghostly benefits, our concealed purpose was to destroy, enslave, or oppress.

Fox's time in Paris had not been misspent after all, but if North shared his fears that February day of 1777, he shrugged them off – the Opposition to the bill mustering only thirty-three votes.

The debate, and its outcome, were among a number that pressaged the future – in April Fox entered the lists on the tortured question of increasing the expenses of the Royal Household, and in May on the handling of East India affairs. The topics were diverse, but they indicated the growing consistency of Fox's policy, and his appreciation of the need for a cohesive Opposition at Westminster. In his speech on the Civil List, he briefly identified what, subsequently, was to become a key to his concept of government – that it was measures and not men that should determine politics.

The idea was not new – six years before Burke had been arguing that 'party connection' based on concerted policies was the only effective defence against executive tyranny, none the less it ran counter to established practice.

The convention was for the king to choose his ministers, and then play a significant role in determining their policies – a system that George III held sacrosanct. That the Whigs now disagreed struck at the root of his notions of government. However, where Burke was to theorize, Fox was to act, though his passing reference to measures and men provided little inkling of what was yet to come.

Meanwhile, the full extent of the rift in the Opposition's colonial policy was highlighted in May 1777, when the Earl of Chatham tabled a motion in the House of Lords. Sixty-nine years of age, wracked by gout, and leaning on a crutch, the Great Commoner made a sorry sight, though his opinions were vivid enough. In contrast to the Rockingham faction's growing recognition that only full independence would now satisfy the colonists' demands, Chatham held that the sun would set upon empire if America was lost, and appealed for peace on the basis of the unconditional redress of the colonists' grievances. The hope was illusory, but if George was to dismiss the motion as 'the specious words and malevolence of that extraordinary brain', at least one visitor to the House that day was of a different opinion.

'I cannot help expressing to you', wrote the young William Pitt to his Mother, 'how happy, beyond description, I feel that my Father was able to exert, in their full vigour, the sentiments and eloquence which have always distinguished him. His first speech took up half an hour, and was full of his usual force and vivacity. He spoke a second time, in answer to Lord Weymouth . . . . This he did in a flow of eloquence, and with a beauty of expression, animated and striking beyond conception.'

The words provide a clue to the man. At 18 years of age, Pitt the Younger was the product of an austere upbringing. Indeed, it is significant that so little has been written about his childhood, for there is so little of note of which to write. A fragile child, thin and pallid and subject to debilitating colds, 'eager little William' was educated at home on a regime of Greek and Latin texts, interspersed with Bible readings, and by the age of 11 was writing notes of such pomposity that they put pomposity itself to shame: 'I flatter myself that the sun shone on your expedition and that the views were enough enlivened thereby to prevent the drowsy Morpheus from taking the opportunity of the heat to diffuse his poppies upon the eyes of the travellers.'

At 14 Pitt entered Pembroke, Cambridge, but was so ill that he spent little time at the college during the first three years, though what time he did spend there was a model of rectitude to other students. As his first biographer, George Tomline, Pitt's tutor and later Bishop of Winchester, was to write: 'While Mr Pitt was an under-graduate, he never omitted attending Chapel morning or evening, or dining in the public hall, except when prevented by indisposition. Nor did he spend a single evening outside the college walls. Indeed, most of his time was spent with me; and exclusively of the satisfaction I had of superintending the education of a young man of his uncommon abilities and thirst for improvement, his sweetness of temper and vivacity of disposition endeared him to me in a degree, which I should in vain attempt to express.' Two decades later, Tomline was to owe his preferment to Pitt – but this was written fifteen years after his patron's death!

If the child is father of the man, then neither Fox or Pitt were to escape the conditioning of their childhood and if, on the day that the Chatham appealed for an American peace, his son was to write of his father's brilliance, then another observer was to note: 'On the day of Lord Chatham's motion in the House of Lords, a knot of members in the House of Commons, wondering at the crowd that attended, all agreed that they had heard Charles Fox as great as Lord Chatham had ever been.'

The House rose in June, and Fox retired to Chatsworth, the country seat of the Dukes of Devonshire. As with the Rockinghams and the Richmonds, the Devonshires formed a clan within the clan of Whig grandees – landed, powerful, and always sensitive of their distinction. To them, personal friendship was the essence of politics, and if Fox with his genius for friendship was once to ask: 'is it possible to be happy in acting with people of whom one has the worst opinions, and being on a cold footing . . . with all those whom one loves best?', then the Devonshire's heir, Lord John Cavendish, had the answer, wishing 'the Opposition reduced to six or seven, who could depend upon each other'. His loyalty to Fox was to be put to the test soon enough.

But if politics and the need for unity among the Whigs were high on the agenda that summer at Chatsworth, they were offset by the eclat Georgiana, the new Duchess of Devonshire, one of the great beauties of the eighteenth century, and a friend of Fox until her death. Ugly as he was with his rounding figure and saturnine features, and casual as he was becoming with his appearance, the 28-year-old Fox was a favourite with the wives of the Whig autocrats, penning verses to Mrs Crewe, and winning compliments from Georgiana: 'I have always thought that the great merit of C. Fox is his amazing quickness in seizing any subject – he seems to have the peculiar talent of knowing more about what he is saying and with less pains than anybody else – his conversation is like a brilliant player of billiards, the strokes follow one another, piff paff.'

Such skills were to be needed in the months ahead. In September, Fox left Chatsworth for Ireland, and while he bathed in the chilled waters of the Devil's Punch Bowl and made the acquaintance of the Irish barrister, Henry Grattan, Burke was reviewing his position on American affairs. It proved a soul-searching business, for on 8 October he was writing to Fox from his home in Beaconsfield that 'I now sit down with malice prepense to kill you with a very long letter' – and this from a politician with a reputation for being prolix.

After examining the character of the Opposition ('A great deal of activity and enterprise can scarcely ever be expected of such men'), and the state of public opinion ('It is far worse than I have ever known it'), Burke intimated that he, too, intended to secede, and hinted, forcibly, that the time was approaching when Fox should consider taking on the leadership of the Opposition in the Commons:

If *you* should grow too earnest, you will be still more inexcusable than I was; your having entered into affairs so much younger . . . . Do not be in haste. Lay your foundations deep in public opinion . . . because (presuming that you are disposed to make good use of power) you will want some better support than merely that of the Crown. For I much doubt, with all your parts, you are not a man formed for acquiring real interior favour in this Court or in any. I therefore wish you a firm ground in the country . . . .

Burke's advice was astonishing in its prescience – in the continuing absence of Court favour, Fox was to build a power base on public opinion – though that was for the future. Immediately there was more urgent business to hand, the Rockingham Whigs agreeing in November that the Duke of Richmond and Charles James Fox should lead for the Opposition in tabling motions in the Lords and the Commons on the State of the Nation. When Fox rose in the Commons on 2 December, London was already alive with rumours of a major British defeat in America, which is possibly why he directed much of his charge at Lord George Germain, who eighteen years before had been convicted of cowardice in the face of the enemy at the Battle of Minden, and who was now Secretary of State for the Colonies.

For the two years that a certain noble has presided over American affairs, the most violent scalping, tomahawk measures have been pursued – bleeding has been his only prescription. If a people deprived of their ancient rights are grown tumultuous – bleed them! If they are attacked with the spirit of insurrection – bleed them! If their fever should rise into rebellion – bleed them, cries this state physician! More blood! More blood! Still more blood!

North attempted to cover his minister's retreat, but Fox had not done with Germain. Almost twelve months before a bet had been struck: 'John Burgoyne wagers Charles Fox one pony [25 guineas] that he will be home from America by Christmas Day, 1777.' Within the month, Burgoyne had sailed for the New World, to take command of a British offensive out of Canada, and then link with Howe's force. In July, Ticonderoga, the northern gateway to the Hudson, fell to Burgoyne's column. On hearing the news George III burst into the queen's bedroom, elated: 'I've beat 'em. I've beat all the Americans.'

He was premature. Within six weeks, Burgoyne was in deep trouble. He had lost the majority of his Indian scouts, his supply lines were tenuous, desertions were mounting daily, there had been no contact with Howe – and he was faced by a Continental Army of 7000 under their commander, Horatio Gates, the son of the Duke of Leed's housekeeper. Twice Burgoyne launched attacks at the colonists' entrenched positions around Saratoga, the second assault resulting in total defeat. Ten days later, on 17 October, after his officers had unanimously agreed that they should treat for surrender, Burgoyne drew his sword and handed it to Gates. The Northern campaign was over.

By the evening of 2 December, the king and his ministers had a full account of the disaster, and at the following morning's levee, George decided to try and bluff the situation out, Walpole reporting that 'to disguise his concern, he had affected to laugh, and to be so indecently merry that Lord North endeavoured to stop him'. It was sound advice, for if the government intended to dissemble, they had taken no account of Fox. A close friend of Burgoyne's, 'Gentleman Johnny' had sent him a full report of the Saratoga campaign in the well justified belief that he would be made the scapegoat for the disaster.

Always a passionate man, Fox read Burgoyne's dispatch with mounting fury, to remark: 'There are passages in them which our governors will not like to make public.' In the Commons that evening Fox and the Whigs pressed Germain to confirm whether the reports of the surrender at Saratoga were true – knowing full well that they were. Germain equivocated. He believed so, but had heard nothing officially, at which he was savaged by the Opposition. 'Does the Noble Lord know the extent of his criminality?' demanded Colonel Barre; 'The obstinate wilful ignorance and incapacity of the Noble Lord calls loudly for vengeance' roared Fox, demanding an official inquiry.

Germain remained seated. There was little he could say, for as the MP Fish Crauford was to write: 'Charles spoke with great violence, but the House for this time went along with him. We were not shocked at his talk of bringing Lord George to a *second trial*, nor were we shocked at being asked if we could patiently continue to see this country disgraced by him in *every* capacity.' George III might dissemble, punctuating conversation with a nervous patter of 'What? What? Hey? What? What?', North might feign sleep on the government front bench, but there was no disguising the fact that the situation was deteriorating, and on 2 February the full weakness of the ministry was finally exposed.

The date set for Fox's motion on the State of the Nation was the social occasion of the season. On the floor of the House, members notable mainly for their absence from parliamentary business jostled to find a place, while both the titled (including Georgiana, Duchess of Devonshire) and the untitled pressed in at the doors, and swarmed through the galleries. A motion was made that the House be cleared, and the gentlemen withdrew; followed by a second that 'if the motive of clearing the House was to keep the state of the nation concealed from our enemies, then there was no reason to indulge the ladies . . . with the arcana of state'. The ladies withdrew, and Fox rose to speak.

Two hours and forty minutes later, he was finished, having demolished the government's North American policy, to conclude:

> On the whole, Sir, it appears to me that if gentlemen are not blind, they will see that the war is impracticable, and that no good can come from force only; that the lives that have been lost, and the treasures that have been wasted, have been wasted to no purpose; that it is high time we should look to our own situation, and not leave ourselves defenceless upon an idea of strengthening the army in America when [following Saratoga] it will be less strong than it was last year

– a year which produced nothing decisive, not in the least degree tending to complete conquest.

The passion was there, but it was carefully contained. This was a new and altogether more mature Fox, a politician who preferred logic to histrionics to build a case that raised politics above party in the national interest; that appealed as much to the Opposition as it troubled the consciences of certain Tory back benchers. Almost brusquely at the close, he moved that 'no more of the Old Corps be sent out of the Kingdom'. The Chamber was silent. No one rose to reply. Slumped in his seat close to the Speaker's chair, Fox watched and waited while, opposite, the King's Friends grew restless, deserted by their leaders. And still no one spoke, neither North, nor Germain, nor Wedderburn who had been taking notes throughout the speech. Seemingly they had nothing to say, then an unknown MP shouted 'Division', and the House retired to vote.

It was a personal triumph for Fox, single-handed he had silenced the ministry, and if the government won a 94 vote majority, 165 members voted for the motion, including a number who had previously been sound for the ministry. At 10.40 that night, the king was writing cryptically to North: 'I trust that when the next Committee on the State of the Nation is resumed, Gentlemen will be more willing to speak', and by the week's end the press were loud with praise of Fox: 'Ministers chap-fallen . . . to one of the most able speeches delivered in a popular assembly' *(Gazeteer)*; 'Mr Fox's speech was masterly, forcible and expressive . . . the most striking proof of judgment, sound reasoning, and astonishing memory' (*London Chronicle*); while after comparing Fox with Chatham, the indefatigable Walpole noted that his speech was 'really unanswerable, for not one of the Ministers knew what to say, and so said nothing, and that silence cost them many votes'.

The Whigs were as euphoric as North was dispirited – and worse was to come. On 6 February France signed a treaty of peace and commerce with the new-born United States. The news was slow to reach London, Horace Walpole being among the first to hear of it from his cousin, Tom. As they distrusted Burke, and feared 'the childish fluctuations of Rockingham', they agreed that the man to tell was Fox. He put it to devastating use. Eleven days after the treaty was signed, North announced in the Commons plans to dispatch commissioners to America to negotiate a settlement of the war on conciliatory terms. His back benchers were stunned. The thing smacked of defeatism, and 'a dull melancholy silence for sometime succeeded this speech'. Then Fox rose to reply.

Conciliatory himself at first, he welcomed the proposals on behalf of the Opposition, noting that they bore close resemblance to those tabled by Burke three years before. Whereas those were timely, however, these were too late for now America was in alliance with France – or was the government unaware of the news? The House was incredulous. One moment the Prime Minister talked of peace; the next a leader of the Opposition intimated an extension of the war. Momentarily North was silent, then in response to furious cries of 'Answer. Answer' he confessed that he had heard something of the sort, though the reports had still to be authenticated by our Ambassador in Paris. Whatever the news, however, surely it was better to treat with the Americans than face the possibility of fighting on two fronts? The House agreed, the commission sailed, to be snubbed by Congress and the American leadership. Fox was right. The time was passed for conciliation.

Yet again North and his master had been humiliated. Yet again, Fox was the toast of the Whigs, and yet again the papers hailed the success of 'this new champion come among us', though Fox himself was altogether more modest. In a letter to his long-time friend and brother-in-law, Richard Fitzpatrick, he reflected:'People flatter me that I continue to gain, rather than lose my credit as an orator, and I am so convinced that this is all I shall ever gain (*unless I chuse to become the meanest of men*) that I never think of any other object of ambition . . . . Great reputation I think I may acquire and keep, great situation I can never acquire, nor if acquired *keep without making sacrifices that I will never make.*'

91

The precocious schoolboy, the cocksure youth, the young rakehell were fast disappearing, giving way to a man who refused to trade self-respect for a place, and thus become 'the meanest of men'. Fox spent his twenty-ninth birthday in London, and while he may have gamed that evening at Almack's (which had now taken Mr Brooks's name), he had other, more important concerns to hand. After eighteen months of war, the public mood was shifting against the government and beyond his successes in February, he was to speak five more times during the session on American affairs, refining his attack on ministerial policy and continually harrying the Crown:

> Their lives and property could only be in danger when the Crown became despotic . . . . Good God! then, could Britons with their eyes open and, sensible to the dangers arising from executive power, wilfully throw so great an addition of strength into it, as the power of appointing the officers to the government of America? . . . . Had we not appointments, douceurs, sinecures, pensions, titles, baubles and secret service money enough already? Did not the creatures of government swarm in every department, and must we add to their number?'

Small wonder that George was coming to hate him, for he was sapping at the very foundations of royal prerogative. Small wonder that North was coming to fear him, for he was playing a crucial role in the revival of the Whigs' confidence, and as their vote rose, so his own declined. For all his careful management of the King's Friends, North's majorities were being whittled away, and unknown to Fox he was already pleading with the king that 'both his mind and body grow every day more infirm and unable to struggle with the hardships of these arduous times'. George, who had written off £12,000 of North's debts only six months before, was testy: 'I should have been greatly hurt at the inclination expressed by you to retire.'

Temporarily, North was persuaded, but in return he demanded a reshuffle of the ministry – not least, the inclusion of the Earl of Chatham, his aide, Lord Shelburne, and, possibly, Charles James Fox. The king was scandalized, seeing 'the road opened for a set of men who would certainly make me a slave for the remainder of their days', but agreed. If this was the only way to retain North, and reinforce his government, so be it. In the spring of 1788 the negotiations were opened, to drag on seemingly interminably. Fox agreed that he was 'unconnected and at liberty', though he would not work with Germain; Shelburne maintained that if his leader was to come in 'Lord Chatham must be the dictator'; while the Rockinghams would have no truck with Chatham's plans for redressing the colonists' grievances rather than granting them independence.

And all the while, as the situation moved towards impasse, George worried away at North. He would rather lose his Crown than be shackled by 'those desperate men'. Equally desperately, North struggled to patch together a coalition that would relieve him of office, but the effort was unavailing. Even under the intensifying threat of war with France, the differences between the factions were too great to be reconciled, differences that could no longer be decently disguised after 7 April. On that day, Richmond had tabled a motion in the Lords calling for American independence, and Chatham determined to speak and call once more for reconciliation.

Seventy years of age, and gravely ill, Chatham drove to London, accompanied by his three sons. As he entered the chamber, his face a death mask, the House rose as a token of respect. At first his voice was so weak that he could hardly be heard, but towards the close it seemed that something of the old magic, the old fire had returned: 'His Majesty succeeded to an Empire as great in extent as its reputation was unsullied. Shall we tarnish the lustre of this nation by an ignominious surrender of its rights and fairest possessions?' Exhausted, he collapsed back in his seat, and Richmond rose reply. It was clear, however, that Chatham wished to speak again. Richmond gave way, Chatham rose, to collapse on the floor of the House, unconscious.

On 11 May 1778, William Pitt, Earl of Chatham, died at his home at Hayes, in Kent. Both Houses agreed that he should be buried at Westminster Abbey, only George III dissenting. 'This compliment' he complained 'is rather an offensive measure to me personally.' The man was as spiteful to the dead as to the living. As for North, he was at desperation point again. Three months of abortive negotiation had achieved nothing, while little more than a month after Chatham's death a squadron of twenty sail under Admiral Keppel had opened fire on two French frigates. Britain and France were at war again.

For the Prime Minister the parliamentary session which ended in June had been a disaster (at the close he was only able to muster a fifty-three vote majority against a motion calling for an end to the American war), for Fox a triumph. Four years had passed since he had quit government, four years since his father had died; in the interim, he had come to play a commanding role in the Opposition. Much of the old bragadaccio still remained, but the American question, and all it implied, had driven Fox to a reappraisal not so much of his politics, as of himself. Where, in all probability, Lord Holland would have compromised his principles for place, his son had no wish to be considered 'the meanest of men', a fellow MP writing to George Selwyn on 28 June:

> Charles eats and drinks and talks and, though he never loses sight of the Treasury, confesses it is rather distant prospect at present. I do think that it does him . . . great credit, that under all his [gaming] distresses he never thinks of accepting place on terms that are in the least degree disreputable; and I assure you, upon my honour, that he has had very flattering offers made to him more than once of late, and has never for a moment hesitated about rejecting them.

As Fox rode north to Chatsworth at the beginning of his now customary round of the great Whig houses, he may well have reflected on the irony that an impoverished rebel could afford the price of his principles – and pondered what the future might bring.

* * *

The game books of 1778 record a poor season, violent storms punctuating a prolonged heatwave, but what the Whig grandees missed in their sport was more than compensated for by the press of events, rumour and counter-rumour competing for attention. The French fleet was out; Admiral Keppel had taken six prizes. Invasion was imminent; George III was touring south coast fortifications. American privateers had been sighted off Kirkcudbrightshire; Lord Selkirk's home had been sacked. Sixty Americans had escaped goal in Gosport; the militia in Hampshire were under arms. A sign had been seen in the night sky over Shrewsbury, Hull, Worcester, Carlisle? No matter where, what did it portend? Victory? Defeat? The end of the world?

In a country where roads were little better than bridle ways, and the London–Edinburgh stage took twelve days to complete the 600 mile journey, intelligence was hard to come by, and speculation rife. As far as the Whig magnates were concerned, however, two things were certain: that the ministry's policies had proved disastrous, and that it was necessary to reverse them as quickly as possible. Always welcome for the pleasure of his company, Fox was now valued as much as the strategist as the spokesman of the Opposition. When the weather allowed, he still played a keen game of cricket, still blasted away at partridge and grouse with more enthusiasm than accuracy, but now pleasure took second place to business, and discussions raged late into the night as to the best way to curb George and his puppet, North.

To Fox, only one, feasible course lay open – to form a coalition to end the war. Throughout the spring he had pressed the matter, but without success. The grandees still harboured their doubts. Men rather than matters continued to dominate their thinking – whether Rockingham would serve with North, or it would be Shelburne who kissed the king's hand. The internecine dispute dragged on through the autumn, into winter, and on 25 November Parliament returned for yet another bellicose speech from George III: 'I hope, under the blessing of God, to derive the means of vindicating and maintaining the honour of my Crown, and the interests of my people, against all enemies.'

Fox was soon back on the attack, seconding a Commons amendment to the King's Speech – denouncing the ministry for its mismanagement of the war; ridiculing its pretension at peace-making; and excoriating George and his government: 'Have the Ministers no regard to the fame of a master who has sacrificed everything to their emolument and ambition? Will they entail infamy upon his name, after having robbed him of one half of his people?' The *Morning Chronicle* was impressed, but more important the king's parliamentary croney, John Robinson, was to write to North: 'If you get Charles James Fox it may do for a while, but otherwise you are at your last gasp.'

Robinson anticipated events, though in January 1779, a new and unlooked for crisis was wracking the unhappy ministry. In the main, senior naval appointments were still largely dependent on an officer's political persuasion, and Admiral Augustus Keppel, a distant cousin of Fox, and Commander of the Channel squadron, was as staunch a Whig as his subordinate, Sir Hugh Palliser, was a Tory. In July of the previous year, Keppel, with twenty-two ships of the line, had engaged a French fleet of thirty-two sail off Ushant, but any chance of winning a decisive victory was lost when Palliser, commanding the rear, disobeyed a signal and refused to give chase to the retreating French fleet.

On returning to port, the Whig *General Advertiser* accused Palliser of failing to obey his superior's commands, for Palliser to round on Keppel in the Tory *Morning Post*, and demand that he be court martialled. The First Lord of the Admiralty, Lord Sandwich, was happy to oblige, and the hearing began on 7 January 1779. For once, the Whig patricians were united. One of their own was to be tried for his life, and five dukes, a bevy of lesser nobility and Charles James Fox posted down to Portsmouth to support the accused – and raise the cost of living in the town to unprecedented heights. The trial dragged on for almost a month, but when it was learned that all references to the disobeyed signals had been torn from the log of Palliser's ship, the prosecution collapsed.

Keppel was free, a hero. The news reached London on 11 February, and that night the town was en fête. The streets filled with crowds roaring Keppel's triumph, burning Palliser in effigy, and driving North into hiding on the roof of his house. In the early hours Lord Derby, Major Stanley and Fox sallied forth from Brooks's into an orgy of window breaking – a drunken Tory, the Duke of Ancaster, rampaging with the best. Combining forces, the crowd made first for Lord Germain's, then for the Admiralty where, after forcing the gates, they broke every window within range of a brick as 'Lord Sandwich, exceedingly terrified, escaped through the garden with his mistress, Miss Ray, to the Horse Guards, and there betrayed manifest panic'.

Fox may have dined out on the story in the following weeks but he was quick to recognize that the Keppel affair was simply a diversion from the business of Westminster. True, it had animated the Whigs, briefly. True, it had further embarrassed North, but otherwise it was no more than a side-show in the game of power. Even before the House had reconvened, Fox had been urging Rockingham to enter government and put an end to the war: 'Believe me, my dear Lord, I certainly disapprove of some things you have done, and many things you have left undone yet . . . the Salvation of this Country must ultimately depend upon you and your friends.' Damned by indecision, Rockingham sent an equivocal reply and two months later, on 24 January 1779, Fox made his own position plain:

What you considered as a step of the most dangerous tendency to the Whig party, I looked upon as a most favourable opportunity to restoring it to power and influence which I wish it to have as earnestly as you do . . . that power (whether over a people or a king) obtained by gentle means, by the goodwill of a person to be governed . . . . In short, our difference of opinion is quite complete. You think you can best serve the country by continuing in fruitless opposition. I think that it is impossible to serve it at all but by coming to power, and go even so far as to think it irreconcileable with the duty of a public man to refuse it.'

The tone of the letter must have come as a shock to Rockingham. This was not how he was accustomed to being addressed. In a carefully mannered age, Fox had abandoned the niceties of dissimulation, and was introducing a new and altogether more astringent note into Whig affairs. The trouble from Rockingham's standpoint was that Fox now commanded a small but growing following of his own in the Commons. The consistency of his policies, allied to the power of his speeches had seen to that. Five years previously he might have been 'the Cub', but now he was virtual leader of the Opposition in the House – a man to be wooed, in his own right, by North, and to be treated with circumspection, if not respect by the Whigs.

As a member of the family, the Duke of Richmond was recruited to draft an avuncular reply: 'You have many of those social virtues which command the love of friends . . . You have abilities in abundance, and your conduct of late years has done much to regain the public confidence which is so necessary to a public man. By steady perserverance you may accomplish so essential an object.' Allied to Burke's persuasion, the note achieved its purpose. Fox abandoned his pursuit of a coalition, in favour of harassing the beleaguered ministry – with Sandwich as his chosen quarry.

In March, he proposed a vote of censure on the Admiralty, raking the government front benches with detailed charges of incompetence, and hinting that he intended to press for Lord Sandwich's removal. After a nine hour debate, a division was called and in an unusually full House the government only achieved a thirty-four vote majority. North was alarmed, George infuriated. For all the best efforts of his friends, the ministry was inexorably losing ground, while Fox continued to reinforce his position.

Not that he was any longer content to restrict the debate to Westminster. Nine days after the Admiralty debate the first issue of *The Englishman* appeared, the brainchild of Richard Brinsley Sheridan. Wit, raconteur, and the leading playwright of the eighteenth century, Sheridan had long been a favourite at Devonshire House, Lord John Townshend writing of their first meeting:

'Fox told me after breaking up from dinner that he always thought Hare, after my uncle Charles Townshend, the wittiest man he had ever met with, but that Sheridan surpassed them both; and Sheridan told me the next day that he was quite lost in admiration for Fox, and that it was a puzzle to him to say which he admired most, his commanding superiority of talent and universal knowledge, or his playful fancy, artful manners, and benevolence of heart.'

With his sense of the dramatic, his Whig connections, and his friendship for Fox, it was almost inevitable that Sheridan would be drawn into the politics of the day. In 1775, he had succeeded Garrick as manager of the Drury Lane Theatre, but by 1779 he was already contemplating trying to find a seat in the Commons. In the meantime, there was *The Englishman* to produce, the first issue being devoted to an encomium of Fox, and a detailed analysis of the emoluments of all those who had voted against him on 4 March – 'nephew to a Lord of the Admiralty', 'brother to the Lord of the Bedchamber', 'brother-in-law to the Secretary of the Treasury'.

The thing had a familiar ring. Only the year before, Fox had been declaiming against the creatures of government 'swarming in every department', and now here was Sheridan echoing his own sentiments on the corruption of 'ministerial borough interests, Jobbs, reversions, private Douceurs, Lottery Tickets, Places in Trust, Couplings and Quarterings, Commissions for Children, Curacies for Cousins, and etc'. This was the essence of the ministry's power, and in the following months the king struggled to rally his fairweather friends against Fox and the Whigs. In mid April, Fox tabled his promised motion for the removal of the Lord Sandwich from the Admiralty; in May he spoke three times in an inquiry into the American War, intimating that a time might come when it would be necessary to call for the impeachment of North for his misconduct of affairs; and in June was supporting the ministry's proposal for doubling the militia, while damning any suggestion that the Opposition might join forces with the ministry to prosecute the war:

What! enter into an alliance with those very Ministers that have betrayed their country; who have prostituted the public strength, who had prostituted the public wealth, who had prostituted what was still more valuable, the glory of the Nation! The idea was too monstrous to be admitted for a moment.

The vehemence of Fox's denial stood in sharp contrast with his policy of six months before, which may have been due as much to changed circumstances as to political gerrymandering. Twelve months previously the danger of invasion was largely illusory. Now it was very real. By the end of the parliamentary session, Spain had allied itself to France, and Fox's fears of the ministry's incapacity to manage the war were redoubled. They had bungled the American campaign, botched their preparations for a European war – and by July a combined fleet of sixty French and Spanish sail were off Plymouth, with 50,000 troops and 400 transports in reserve.

England was in greater danger than at any time since the Armada, the Channel fleet consisting of only thirty-six ships of the line, the army consisting of only 10,000 regular troops, and Plymouth itself virtually undefended. There was no time for partridge shooting that season, Fox hurrying down to Saltram to extract a promise from the captain of the *Foudroyant* that if he sailed, then Fox should sail with him. Through July and into August, the tension mounted, and on the 27th Fox was writing to Fitzpatrick:

> The fleet today was a most magnificent sight. It was formed in order . . . and faith, when one comes to look at it, and thinks that there is a possibility of its coming to action in a day or two, *on se sent emu beaucoup*. If somethings were otherwise at home, and the fleet commanded by Keppel, one should feel very eager indeed, when even in the present damned state of things, who can help feeling something at the sight of it?

For a further month, the combined enemy fleet continued to shadow the English coast, only withdrawing to Brest on the outbreak of smallpox. Unbeknown to England, the threat of an invasion was over, but North's nerve had been badly shaken. Again he pleaded with George to accept his resignation, again George refused, and again North toyed with the possibility 'to admit into his confidence and service any men of public spirits and talents . . . provided it be understood that *every means are to be employed to keep the Empire entire*'.

The Whig leaders were contemptuous. It was not so much that the terms were unacceptable, more that there was a growing sense of unity among the Opposition which, allied to the disastrous progress of the ministry, must eventually bring the government down. For almost ten years they had been denied office, why should they now share the odium of ministers with whose policies they had no truck? If George viewed the matter differently, complaining of their 'cold disdain' and writing 'to obtain their support, I must deliver up my person, my principles, and my dominions into their hands', then he had best remember his own behaviour over the past decade.

Parliament reassembled in late November, and the King's Speech made no mention of American affairs, where Clinton, who had replaced Howe as Commander-in-Chief, had all but abandoned the Northern Colonies in favour of campaigning in the Carolinas. The Opposition were quick to exploit the omission, though one Whig, William Adam, announced that he intended to vote with the government, declaring that the king had men in his Cabinet 'fully adequate to the task of saving their country'. Fox, in reply, listed the ministry's inadequacies to flay the recussant mercilessly: 'Begone! begone wretch! who delightest in libelling mankind, confounding virtue and vice . . . .'

That was on Thursday evening. Two days later, Fox received a note from Adam asking for a public apology for his remarks in the Commons. Fox refused, and on Sunday afternoon Adam demanded the satisfaction of a duel. The time and place were fixed for the following day – Hyde Park at 8 o'clock. Fitzpatrick agreed to act as Fox's second, and on their way to the park he advised his principal to stand sideways to reduce the target area, for

Fox to reply with a laugh: 'Why, I am as thick one way as another.'

Save for the duellists and their seconds there were no other witnesses. After charging, then inspecting the pistols, Fox and Adams each walked the statutory seven paces before turning to fire. Adam invited Fox to fire first, Fox answering 'Sir, I have no quarrel with you, do you fire.' Adam fired, and Fox replied. Apparently neither man was hit, and the seconds asked Adam if he was satisfied. He wasn't, demanding that Fox declare that 'he meant no personal attack on my character?' Again Fox refused, saying that this was no place for apologies, and Adam fired his second pistol without effect, at which Fox discharged his pistol in the air. The duel was over, Fox assuring Adam that he meant him no more offence than either of the seconds present, Adam replying; 'Sir, You have behaved like a man of honour.'

It was only then that Fox mentioned that he had been wounded though, on inspection, it proved to be a minor injury. Within days he was back at Brooks's, to be ribbed that as the shot had lodged in his groin it could well ruin his future pleasures, and on his feet in the Commons levelling new charges at the ministry for their incompetent handling of Irish affairs. With its Parliament subordinated to Westminster, and its Lord Lieutenant a Crown appointment, Ireland had long chaffed at English domination, the more so as its trade was regulated by London and its largely Catholic population was not only disenfranchized, but also excluded from holding military rank, practising law, or entering a range of other professions.

In short, the country was little better than a satellite state, to be managed at London's whim. A proud people, they had followed events in America closely, especially as it was for many of them a sanctuary from the poverty and distress they knew at home. Since the Declaration of 1776, a force of 40,000 volunteers had been organizing, nominally as a defence against invasion, in reality to defend their own interests if and when the opportunity arose. For three years of war the North ministry had ignored the threat but then, in October 1779, the Irish Parliament presented an address to the throne:

> The associations and people at large, full of anger and jealousy, manifested strong apprehensions of duplicity on this side of the water; have suffered the discontents in that kingdom to rise to such a height, as evidently to endanger a dissolution of the constitutional connections between the two kingdoms.

Finally alert to the dangers, the government offered trading concessions to Ireland to avoid a repeat of the American crisis, giving Fox the opportunity to review the disasters of the past twelve months – the French war, the Spanish war, the troubles in Ireland – and trace their ultimate cause to a king and his ministers who claimed to rule for the general good but in fact served only their particular ends:

> The Irish Associations had been called illegal; legal or illegal he approved of them. He approved of the manly determination which, in the last resort, flew to arms to obtain deliverance. When the last particle of faith in men was exhausted, they would seek in themselves the means of redress, they would recur to first principles, to the spirit as well as the letter of the constitution . . . truth, justice, and public virtue, accompanied by prudence and judgement, would ever bear up good men in a good cause, that of individual protection and national salvation.

At first glance it was just another speech to bolster the Opposition and torment the government, one among a succession in which Fox exposed ministerial incompetence for political ends. Collectively, however, Fox's speeches in the previous half decade had shown a growing consistency. On American as much as on Irish affairs, he had pursued a common theme that ultimate sovereignty rested with the people, and that those entrusted with power who neglected this contract between the rulers and the ruled abrogated their right to power itself. Where, six years before, he had denied the right of the people (a term to be employed with contempt) to have any part in the management of their own affairs, Fox now stood for open government. Where, six years before, in the shadow of his father, he had railed that the crowd out-of-doors were ill-qualified to judge their own interest, Fox was learning the language of those he had formerly condemned.

What was it that Voltaire had written almost half a century before: 'The *English* are the only people upon earth who have been able to prescribe limits to the power of Kings by resisting them . . . . Where the People share in the government without confusion.' And now? Now deeds mocked the words. How did the American Declaration have it, that: 'We hold these truths to be self-evident, that all men are created equal.' And now? Now George's contempt for the principle had cost him half an empire. And what was it that Burke was now proposing, a plan for economical reform.

Ten days before Christmas 1779, the Member for Bristol rose in his place to outline his proposals for reforming the administration of government finance in an attempt to eliminate the 'old corruption' that had long been at the root of executive power. Possibly the plan did not go far enough, possibly more was needed, but it deserved a welcome none the less:

> I hope that for the sake of the public, for the sake of all public men, for the sake of the Crown, and for the sake of the King upon the throne, that my honourable friend will add perseverance to the diligence he has already employed in his plan for lessening public expenses and reducing the ruinous influence of the Crown.

When the House rose for Christmas the following day, Fox can hardly have foreseen where his championship not only of Burke but of a more general public interest would lead. Ten years had passed since he had first entered the Commons, as much a political tyro as a gamester. The years between had been tumultuous – the death of his father, the breach with Lord North, the American war – but now the long apprenticeship was over. While Fox the gambler still remained, Fox the rebel had found his cause – the prosecution of arbitrary power wherever he found it, at home or abroad.

5

'The Contest is Now Become Personal'

The Christmas recess of 1779 provided a brief but welcome respite from his ministerial duties for Lord North, a man whose 'pleasant, affable, and recommending sort of wit' had been tested to the uttermost during his ten years as George III's first minister. In fact, there were good grounds for his reply to a member of the Commons who had recently complained that he slept during debates – that it was hard to be grudged such a natural relief from such considerable suffering. For considerable suffering there was. The American war was going badly. The government was inexorably giving ground to the opposition. The king became more tetchy by the day, and on 30 January 1779, some 200 gentlemen of 'weight and influence' (including eight peers and seventeen MPs) convened a meeting at York to petition for parliamentary reform.

Eleven years had passed since the Society of Supporters of the Bill of Rights had first met in a London tavern to drum up support for Wilkes and press for 'a more fair and equal Representation of the People', for George to dismiss their ambitions as fanciful. Now, however, things were very different. If Wilkes had made a principle of liberty, then the colonists had put it to the test, to expose how little it meant in England itself. The crowds that huzzaed for Wilkes might call themselves free-born, but the practice mocked the word. As Fox himself had noted, there was much to be learned from America, and if a slowly awakening political consciousness was not enough, there was always the rapid decline of trade

105

and the precipitate increase in taxes caused by four years of war to give focus to the discontent.

The gentlemen of York had little taste for root and branch reform. Their ambitions were altogether more modest: to curb ministerial corruption for 'notwithstanding the calamities and impoverished condition of the nation, much public money has been improvidently squandered, and that many individuals enjoy sinecure places . . . to a large and still increasing amount'. Burke was delighted ('Your Yorkshire meeting does not admit of much amendment. It is well, very well' he enthused to Rockingham), the more so when supporting petitions began to flood in from towns and counties throughout England and Wales.

Fox was impressed. For three years and more he had used the American experience to play on the Commons' fears of the growing influence of the Crown, yet here was evidence of a more widespread concern. Once, and not so distantly, he might well have dismissed the petition movement as one more instance of the inability of the public 'to judge of their own interest' – to be rolled in the gutter by the mob for his sentiments. And now? Now the colonists' lesson, and the lesson he had learned from the colonists, had to be learned closer to home – though his critics were to make much of the volte face.

In late January 1780, Fox shared a platform in Wiltshire with Lord Shelburne (the Great Commoner's protégé), to deliver his first speech outside the Commons, and assert 'that though much used to Public Speaking, he had never addressed an assembly as that then present, for he had never before spoken to an uncorrupt Assembly', while the following week he presided at a mass meeting in Westminster Hall to canvass support for the Yorkshire petition. Three thousand people were present, among them the Duke of Portland, Lord Temple, Burke, and Fox's old antagonist, John Wilkes, to hear Fox declaim:

> You must be the ministers of your own deliverance. . . . Your brethren in America and Ireland show you how to act when bad men force you to feel. Are we not possessed with equal

veneration for our lives and liberties? Does not the blood flow
as freely in our veins as in theirs? Are we not as capable as
they of spurning at life when unaccompanied by freedom?

The past was forgotten. This was a new Fox, Fox the man
of the people, and as the crowd roared their approval he
was proposed as candidate for Westminster at the next
general election. The irony of the situation was not lost
on the opposition, the *General Evening Post* remarking
that 'Truly Fox has changed his opinion and his conduct
as much as any man.' It was a charge that was to haunt Fox
for the remainder of his life – a charge of inconsistency that
smacked of opportunism – and possibly it was true. As leader
of the Opposition in the Commons, it is possible that Fox was
trimming to public opinion to further embarrass Lord North
and, in the process, was developing a taste for the plaudits of
a public that he had so recently despised.

All is possible, if the evidence of Fox's political development is ignored. At 24 years of age, he had still conformed,
if uncomfortably, to his father's views. Six years later he
had learned the lesson of American independence, and the
irony would have been if he had not applied it to England.
Then the charge of inconsistency would have held. Instead
of which. . . .

Six days after the Westminster meeting, Sir George Savile
presented the York petition in the Commons, requesting an
investigation into 'the gross abuses of public money', and Fox
was to his feet tormenting the government with the wit for
which he was already famous:

> I will put the controversy between the Ministry and the
> gentlemen on this side of the House, on the same issue on
> which the wisest of men, Solomon, rested the determination
> of the dispute between the two women, each of whom claimed
> the living child. We say to the Ministry, you misapply public
> money – nay, you do worse, you apply it to bad purposes.
> Ministry say to us, you want our places, and thus the charge of
> corruption is given and retorted. Come now, let us see whose
> Child corruption is. Opposition are willing, are desirous, that

it should be sacrificed; Ministry have often made similar professions. The time is come to prove the sincerity of both. See who will now acknowledge, see who will father this dear but denied child: Corruption.

The House ordered the petition to lie on the table, but there was no deferring Burke's plans for economical reform which he presented in a three-hour speech on 11 February. Aimed at rooting out 'the corrupt influence which is itself the perennial spring of all disorder,' his proposals included the abolition of a range of government offices and the publication of the Pension List, measures which, collectively, would save the Exchequer £200,000 a year. Even North commended Burke, and did not press for a division – in contrast to the treatment meted out by the Lords to a bill tabled only a couple of days before by the Duke of Richmond.

Its intent was straightforward, to restore 'the natural unalienable and equal right of all the Commons of Great Britain . . . to vote in the election of their representatives in Parliament', while its fate was as immediate (the bill being rejected without a division being called) as its significance was far-reaching. The Opposition was already dividing against itself on the nature and extent of reform, Burke going only as far as his innate conservatism would allow, which was not far enough as far as radicals such as Richmond were concerned. In the years ahead the difference, as much a matter of temperament as of politics, was to play a crucial role in the final disintegration of the Whig party – though there were few indications of the danger that February of 1780.

All through the month, the ministry was in retreat. A clause to abolish the Secretary of State for the Colonies was lost by only seven votes, one to disqualify MPs from being government contractors was won by an equal number, while there was an eight vote majority for the abolition of the Board of Trade – to the dismay of Edward Gibbon. Only once, in support of Fox's 1778 motion against sending further troops to the Americas, had he voted with the Opposition, but that once had been enough to secure him a seat and £800 a year on the Board, for Fox to write:

King George in fright
Lest Gibbon should write
The story of Britain's disgrace,
Thought no way so sure
His pen to secure
As to give the historian a place.

Gibbon was entertained. The verse was a hit, a palpable hit. No question, he disagreed with Fox's politics, but he still delighted in his company none the less, and two years later, while still treasuring Fox's friendship, Gibbon's £800 a year was forfeit, victim of a new mood in the Commons which the king was to attribute to its loss of reason. And if George had fears for the sanity of the Commons in February, then they were to be redoubled in April.

On the 6th, the House was as crowded as it ever had been for the presentation of forty petitions from counties and boroughs throughout England and Wales – 'Vast parchments subscribed by thousands of names.' After the title of each had been read, John Dunning, the principal lawyer of the Opposition and a follower of Shelburne, rose to propose the motion that: 'The influence of the Crown has increased, is increasing, and ought to be diminished.'

There was uproar. For once Lord North's temper gave and he raged that the Opposition meant to destroy the constitution. Helplessly the Speaker called for order as charge and counter-charge were hurled across the floor of the House. 'Am I to be charged as the author of our present misfortunes?' roared North, to be answered 'You are. You are' – and when the division was called, Dunning's motion was carried by 233 votes to 215.

Ten years had passed since North had kissed the king's hand on becoming his first minister, and at two in the morning on 6 April he wrote to George III to plead, once again, to be allowed to resign. Unruffled, the king replied that it was clear against whom the vote was *personally levelled*, adding 'It would be madness not to call a new Parliament as soon as we have hobbled through the present session.' Contemptuous as he was of the Opposition, it was no longer possible to disguise their growing strength, and since the previous autumn he had been laying plans for a snap election to check their advance.

As early as 16 October 1779, he was writing to North: 'If the Duke of Northumberland requires some gold pills for the election, it would be wrong not to satisfy him' – and it would be 'gold pills' that would secure his ministry's re-election. If Burke and his petitioners railed against jobbery, then they would learn what jobbery meant. What was it that Burke had once written, that all honours, emoluments, every sort of gratification to vanity and avarice lay on the side of the Court, while on the other there was nothing, not even the price of a place.

But if rooting out corruption was Burke's prime concern, what of Richmond and his nephew, Fox, who on the day of the Dunning motion had led a march to Westminster Hall behind a banner proclaiming: 'Annual Parliaments and Equal Representation'? To George III, Fox's villainy was doubled-dyed. First he had befriended England's enemies, and now he was touting his democratic principles closer to home.

A product as much of historical accident as caprice, the entire electoral system was a shambles. In England and Wales, only 214,000 people out of a population of some 6 million were entitled to vote in the 513 constituencies – 130,000 electors returning 92 county members; 84,000 electors returning the 421 members who sat for cities, towns, and universities.

The whole, archaic edifice was fashioned for corruption; seats being rented and bought 'as standings in a fair', and if Junius was to write in 1769 that 'the Duke of Bedford bought and sold more than half the representative integrity of the nation', then Sir Philip Francis was later to describe his election for Appleby in Yorkshire: 'I was unanimously elected by one Elector to represent this ancient Borough in Parliament . . . there was no other Candidate, no Opposition, no Poll demanded, Scrutiny or petition. So I had nothing to do but thank the said Elector for the Unanimous Vote with which I had been chosen.' At which Sir Philip quit the town, vowing not to return for another seven years.

In the spring of 1780, this was the system that Burke wished to ameliorate, Fox to redress, and George to exploit to secure his own ministry – but first it was essential to forestall Dunning's motion until Parliament was dissolved. Burke was already tiring of his efforts to drive through his bill for economic reform 'inch by inch, clause by clause, line by line', while on 14 April Dunning tabled a motion that the House should not be prorogued until the influence of the Crown had been diminished, and the abuses listed in the petitions corrected.

Whether or not the Fox had word of the king's intention, he made the Opposition's position clear: that no ministry would dare advise the king to dissolve Parliament when the Commons had requested him not to do so. He was too optimistic. Two weeks before, North had lost control of the House. The mistake was not to be repeated. The ministry whipped-in every member capable of reaching Westminster, and the motion was defeated by a comfortable fifty-one votes. Fox, incensed that the principle accepted on 6 April had been betrayed, rose to savage what he regarded as political turn-coats:

> It was a scandalous, treacherous, and disgraceful vote. . . .
> It was shameful, it was base, it was unmanly. The gentlemen
> he alluded to surrounded him, they sat on his side of the
> House. . . . No man who held those who were at the devo-
> tion of the Minister in more contempt than he did; they were
> slaves of the worse kind, because they had sold themselves.

North, on the Treasury benches, smiled. It was rare to see Fox in a pet. The opportunity was too good to miss. Interjecting, he teased Fox for his spleen at having found himself in the minority after having 'for a short moment of his life' been in the majority, reminding him, sardonically, that he was ill-advised to be so hasty for some day he might find himself in the majority again!

The minister had every right to be pleased. Little by little the government was recovering lost ground. Holland might be supplying the French with arms, Russia showing growing sympathy for the neutrals, but it appeared that General Clinton had finally managed to stabilize the North American campaign, while in early June the Gordon Riots occurred, a week of mayhem of which Dr Johnson later wrote: 'The late Riots have done for the Ministry what the Rebellion did for the House of Hanover; established their authority and made their government popular.'

The cause of the troubles was deep laid: the age old fear of popery combined with a suspicion that the government was abandoning its proscription of Catholics. In the previous half decade Parliament had passed a series of measures extending relief to Catholics, and in the spring of 1780 petitions inveighing against the imagined spread of papist influence began to flood into the Commons. Lord George Gordon, a Protestant zealot, adopted the cause as his own, and on 2 June addressed a crowd of between 50,000 and 60,000 people at St George's Field. The meeting itself was well ordered, but during a march to Westminster to present a further petition to Parliament sections of the crowd got out of hand. By evening, large parts of the city and Westminster were ablaze.

Primed by bigotry, soon to be reinforced by drink from looted wine cellars, the mobs raged through London, putting Catholic chapels and schools to the torch, sacking Newgate gaol, besieging the Bank of England and threatening the House of Commons. Initially, the government was paralysed; the Guards contenting themselves with digging trenches in Hyde Park, Lord North watching the mayhem from the roof of his Mayfair home, and Fox and Burke mounting guard at Rockingham House, from where Burke was to write: 'There are no men in the country June 7th, 1780, in what was London.'

He forgot to mention Fox, who would occasionally sally forth to arrest a rioter. With the mob in savage mood, it was a foolhardy occupation, but then he could never resist a hazard. At 31 years of age, and for all that he was slowly learning to curb his hot-headedness, traces of the vaunty gambler still remained, whether in the House or at the gaming tables. By temperament, always a high risk player, he continued to follow the horses at Newmarket, and to stake funds he no longer possessed on the turn of a card, relieving two young blades who had had the temerity to establish a bank at Brooks's of 4000 guineas in a single night, to remark: 'So should all usurpers be served'.

But even here there were intimations of change. In 1780, Walpole noted: 'My old game faro, is lately revived' – though another six months were to pass before Fox himself decided to exploit the vogue by 'joining the hounds rather than the hounded'. Meanwhile, he and Burke mounted guard at Rockingham House, while George III grew impatient with the 'great supiness of the civil government' and determined that 'examples must be made' of the mob. On the fifth day of rioting, he called a meeting of the Privy Council and ordered the troops into action. Within 24 hours, and with more than 300 dead on the streets, London was calm, for the reckoning to begin – 29 rioters (mostly children) going to the gallows.

George had the examples he felt essential to discourage other 'designing men from using [the riots] as a precedent for assembling people on other occasions' – not least, the county associations and their spokesmen at Westminster. Within two months of the passage of Dunning's motion, it seemed that authority was once again in the saddle, and the opposition in retreat, though Fox was not to be intimidated by either the king or the mob. That they shared a common cause in their intoleration made it none the more defensible, and within days of the ending of the riot, he was opposing a motion for the Repeal of the Bill for the Relief of Roman Catholics, pleading for toleration and 'against everything that had the least tendency to bridle and restrain liberty of conscience'.

To their credit, the Ministry also opposed the motion, possibly in the knowledge that they could afford the indulgence with the Whigs in despair, or possibly because their plans were more deep laid. Since fortune had first turned against them in the early summer, George and his ministers had been laying their trap for the Opposition. Now it was sprung. Recognizing their current weakness, an approach was made to Rockingham to establish whether his party would be willing to join a comprehensive ministry, knowing that if the proposal was rejected a contingency plan was already in place to dissolve Parliament a year short of its seven-year term.

Save for the radical Richmond, the king took no serious exception to the personnel proposed by Rockingham. Burke was there, 'a real acquisition' according to George, as were Keppel, Townshend, a couple of Whig Dukes, and Charles James Fox. 'As to Mr Fox', the King wrote, 'if any lucrative, but not ministerial office can be pointed out for him, provided he will support the measures of government, I shall not object to the proposition, he never having had any principle can certainly act as his interest may guide him'. The omissions from Rockingham's list were as significant as the inclusions – Shelburne and Dunning and all of Lord Chatham's former following.

The old rivalries remained, and having tested the weakness of the Opposition, and calculated his own strength, George had no hesitation about going to the country. On 1 September 1780, Parliament was suddenly dissolved, the news coming like a 'clap of thunder' according to the *Annual Register*. Fox, making a leisurely progress to Bath to take the waters on the orders of his physician, was totally unprepared, though North had already noted: 'If Mr Fox stands we shall have much trouble and more expense.'

He was right on both counts. Fox was elected at a cost to the king in electoral expenses of £8,000 – £3,000 more than he spent in any other constituency to secure the return of his friends. In agreeing to stand for Westminster, Fox recognized the risk he was taking. Malmesbury, his old seat, was as safe as the thirteen electors in the town allowed, whereas Westminster represented what the eighteenth century regarded as a real test of democratic opinion, with some 14,000 electors on the rolls. It was this vote that George hoped to buy for his nominees – the ageing Lord Lincoln, and the absentee Admiral Rodney.

For almost three weeks the polling continued, the count for each candidate being announced each night. 5 September: Fox 296, Rodney 243, Lincoln 150. The Foxites were elated. 16 September: Rodney 4594, Fox 4223, Lincoln 3460. There was rioting, and an attempt made to destroy the poll books. 23 September, and the polls closed: Rodney 5298, Fox 4878, Lincoln 4157. Rodney and Fox were returned, for the latter to be carried from the hustings and triumphantly chaired past the great Whig homes of Westminster – the constituency he was to represent for the rest of his life.

While George was disappointed with the Westminster result, and the poor return he had received from his investment, he had little to complain of elsewhere. Although he was later to write to North: 'As to the immense expense of the General Election, it has quite surprised me; the sum is at least double [£80,000] what was expected of any other General Election since I came to the throne', his calculations had proved correct. The ministry was returned with a safe majority, though the final outcome in the Appleby constituency may have given him pause for thought.

In June, Pitt the Younger was called to the Bar, and after a brief period on the Western Circuit, was offered the seat by its borough monger, Sir James Lowther. At 21 his childhood ambition was fulfilled, and he took his seat in the House for the first time on 23 January 1781, Burke remarking of his first speech: 'He is not a chip off the old block, he is the old block itself.' For the king, it raised the ghost of Chatham; for Fox, it was a reminder of the remark made by his mother fourteen years before: 'Mark my words, that little boy will be a thorn in Charles' side as long as he lives.'

Not that Fox was troubled. On the contrary, he entertained high hopes not only of enlisting Pitt's friendship, but also his political support. Meantime, however, he had more immediate concerns. In the new Parliament the Opposition continued to play the old tunes – the war with the colonies, the war with France, the war with Spain, and always, the malign influence of the Crown – while as for Fox himself, Walpole was writing: 'Mr Fox is the first figure in all the places I have mentioned, the hero in Parliament, at the gaming table, at Newmarket. Last week he passed twenty-four hours without interruption at all there.'

The old demon still haunted him, and the moneylenders still pressed him to the point that he considered the idea of travelling England as an itinerant punter. However, while he once considered that if life's greatest pleasure was to win, and its next greatest pleasure to lose, he was beginning to learn that discretion was the better part of hazard.

Faro was again in fashion, and in the spring of 1781 Fox and two companions opened a bank at Brooks's with the backing of Mr Brooks himself. The venture was the talk of the town, an astonishing success. Where Fox the gambler had lost a fortune, Fox the banker now made one – to the delight of his sundry creditors. They had held off long enough, knowing that they had little to gain, but now he was in funds they closed in for the kill.

It was a spectacle not to be missed, and those two ageing gossips, Horace Walpole and George Selwyn hurried down Arlington Street to see 'two carts at Charles' door filling by the Jews with his goods, clothes, books, and pictures'. Fox, however, appeared unconcerned, Walpole reporting that when he returned home: 'whom should I find sauntering by my door but Charles? He came up and talked to me at the coach window, on the Marriage Bill, with as much *sangfroid* as if he knew nothing of what had happened.'

But then, why should he worry? The bank continued to win, and if his house was going 'to rise like a phoenix from the flames . . . with certain precautions to keep his furniture *a l'abri de ses creanciers*', then Fox was to astonish his friends for, having settled his debts, he proceeded to give presents, being *'magnifique avec une abondance de richesses'*. Selwyn was impressed. Seemingly, Fox was finally changing his ways. Why, in contrast to his former slovenly habits, he now had 'a new hat, frock, waistcoat, shirt, and stockings' – the frock in blue, and the waistcoat in buff, the colours worn by the colonial troops. And the man himself? Early in the parliamentary session of 1781, a new member wrote of Fox:

His features, in themselves dark, harsh, and saturnine, like those of Charles II from whom he descended in the maternal line, derived a sort of majesty from the addition of two black and shaggy eyebrows, which sometimes concealed, but more frequently developed, the workings of his mind. Even these features, however, did not readily assume the expressions of anger or enmity. They frequently and naturally relaxed into a smile, the effect of which became irresistible, because it appeared to be the index of a benevolent and complacent disposition. His figure, broad, heavy, and inclined to corpulency, appeared destitute of elegance of grace, except the portions conferred on it by the emanations of intellect, which at times diffused over his whole person, when he was speaking, the most impassioned animation.

This was the gamester who for six years had hounded the king and his ministry, the profligate who had animated the Opposition when Rockingham and Burke despaired, though by the summer of 1781 even he seemed to be tiring of the game. The House rose in June, following yet another fruitless debate inspired by Fox on the progress of the North American campaign, and in September he was writing to his friend Fitzpatrick of his contempt for the king and his despondency that those 'who expected to play some part upon the stage of the world . . . to heal the wounds made by others' should be in the power of George III. Surely the 'blockhead' couldn't hold all the cards, yet that is how it seemed. Once, perhaps, it was otherwise. Once, perhaps, there had been the hope of breaking the man and his ministry – after the débâcle of Saratoga, following the Keppel trial, when Dunning carried his motion – but now? Now George and North cosseted their majorities, and there seemed little prospect of a break in their power.

Unbeknown to Fox, a change was already in the making. Since the summer General Clinton, with his headquarters in New York, had reinforced his campaign in the Carolinas, and detached a force to invade Virginia. Aware of the danger of over-extending his position, however, Clinton's field commander, Cornwallis, decided in August to consolidate his position on the peninsula of the Chesapeake, at the mouth of the York River. The choice was a shrewd one, providing, always, that the fleet retained command of his seaward communications. For a month all seemed well, but in early September the British squadron of nineteen sail was driven off by the French under Admiral de Grasse, while Washington was closing in from the north with a Continental Army.

By early October, Cornwallis's command was ringed by an army of 14,000 men, while the French fleet lay off the Chesapeake headland. For a week Washington bombarded the British positions, and then on 17 October, and regarding the situation as hopeless, Cornwallis requested a parley. Two days later he surrendered his force of 7000 men. The siege of Yorktown was over and as the British marched out of the town, the band played 'The World Turned Upside Down':

> If buttercups buzzed after the bee,
> If boats were on land, churches on sea,
> If ponies rode men and grass ate the cows,
> And cats should be chased to holes by a mouse,
> Then all the world would be upside down.

The war was to drag on for another year, but to all intents and purposes it ended that October morning when Brigadier Charles O'Hara, deputizing for Cornwallis, surrendered his sword to Washington. The news of the disaster reached London two days before Parliament reassembled, for Lord North to react 'As he would have taken a ball in the breast', pacing his room and exclaiming 'Oh God, it's all over; it's all over.' The king, however, remained phlegmatic ('A good end may yet be made to this war'), and in his speech from the Throne he reasserted his right to American sovereignty:

> No endevours have been wanting on my part to extinguish that spirit of rebellion which our enemies have sound means to foment and maintain in the colonies, and to restore to my deluded subjects in America that happy and prosperous

condition which they formerly derived from due obediance to the laws.

The world was turned upside down, but George was hard pressed to notice the difference. It was left to Fox and a newly revived Opposition to tell him. The speech smacked of despotism ('despotic monarchs were the most tenacious of their rights') in pursuit of a policy that had led to much misery ('Much has been lost, much blood, much treasure has been squandered') and achieved nothing but disaster ('To the influence of the Crown we must attribute the loss of the army in Virginia. To the influence of the Crown we must attribute the loss of the thirteen Colonies in America'), while all the while the king and his ministers blamed everyone, save themselves.

Fox's amendment to the Speech from the Throne was supported by Burke, Sheridan (newly elected for Stafford) and William Pitt, of whom Fox was to say that he no longer lamented the death of Chatham, for all his talents were living in his son. At the division, the government won a eighty-nine vote majority, but for the first time serious rifts were appearing in the Cabinet, not least whether George Germain and the Earl of Sandwich (First Lord of the Admiralty) should remain in their posts. The one was a branded coward, the other a notorious profligate, and together they had carried much of the responsibility for the American campaign. To Fox, always quick to exploit the ministry's troubles, they offered a natural target. He would impeach Sandwich and call Germain as a witness.

As at Minden twenty-two years before, Germain's nerve broke and he resigned his post as Secretary of State for the Colonies, leaving Sandwich undefended. In early December, the Opposition tabled a motion for ending the American war which showed the growing weakness of the ministry, and on 20 December Fox signalled his intention of prosecuting the First Lord: 'a man who in their hearts they [the Ministry] believed to be unfit for the office which he held'.

The Christmas recess of 1781 must have been a cold comfort to Sandwich, and when the House returned on 24

January 1782, Fox's proposal to conduct an inquiry into 'the gross mismanagement of His Majesty's naval affairs' was carried without a division, Lord North supporting the motion, which causes one Member to remark that 'Sandwich seems to be abandoned by all persons, and many members who constantly support the Government are ready to join in a Vote for his removal.' A fortnight later, the forecast proved correct. For three hours a relay of clerks read through the papers relevant to the inquiry, then Fox rose to speak. Briefly he listed five charges against Sandwich which, he claimed, rendered the minister 'highly criminal' and which, if carried, could lead to the First Lord's impeachment.

Only six months before, North had thought himself secure. Now 'the Rats were Very Bad' according to a note to the king. Even George was perturbed. The ministry and its support was collapsing by the day, and the Opposition pressed hard on their weakness. On 22 February North only achieved a single vote majority on a motion tabled by General Conway to end all offensive warfare in the colonies. When pressed, Conway explained that he did not mean military surrender, simply the abandonment of any idea of subduing the colonists by force. Within the week, Conway re-tabled the motion which, despite intense activity by the ministry, was carried by nineteen votes.

The end was near, very near. George, however, still clung to the coat tails of power, careless of North's advise that 'Your Majesty's affairs grow worse by every hour that my removal is delay'd.' London might ring its bells to celebrate the likely end of the war with America, and Fox might be drawing up lists of the new government, but through the last week of February and into March the king struggled frantically to avoid having to form a ministry of men whom he regarded at best as rogues, at worst as traitors. And if all else failed, the Royal Yacht was standing by to take him back to Hanover!

On 8 March Fox spoke on a vote of censure on the ministry: 'when the House should become so lost to all sense of duty, and so far gone in corruption to abandon the rights of the people . . . then it might be justifiable for the people to revert to the original principles of the constitution, and to resume the direction of their own affairs'; on 15 March on a motion for Withdrawing the Confidence of Parliament from the King's Ministers, he was on his feet again: 'The offices of government had been for some weeks past in most shameful disorder. Surely it was time for some Ministry to be established, for a bad government was better than none', and on Wednesday, 20 March. . . .

North was in despair, On Monday he had tendered his resignation. On Tuesday it has been refused, though with the promise that he would hear further from the king the following morning. Through the night, Fox had been in a frenzy of activity, drumming up votes, and the House was packed when the Speaker called 'Order, Order'. Lord North rose – he had information that would make any further proceedings unnecessary. There was chaos, and above shouts of 'No adjournment' he continued that his time on the Treasury benches was ended, the king had come to the 'full determination to change his Ministers'. Charles James Fox had won.

The night was cold, with a brush of snow, and members who had expected a long session crowded the lobby at the door of the House waiting for their carriages. Only North's coach stood outside, and as he moved through the press he chuckled genially: 'You see, gentlemen, the advantage of being *in the secret*' – then disappeared into the night.

Twelve years had passed since he first took office, not so much as a minister more as a lackey of the king; twelve disastrous years. As Dr Johnson, as good a Tory as any man, was later to write of North's ministry: 'Such a bundle of imbecility never disgraced a country.' America was lost and, however ill-found, the fear of arbitrary government had again been unloosed in England. Between his time celebrating at Brook's that night, Fox may well have considered what he had learned from the one, but can hardly have foreseen where his championship of the people would lead.

* * *

121

In June 1762, George III had what the eighteenth century regarded as his first bout of madness, which has since been diagnosed as porphyria, an inborn metabolic disorder. Henry Fox, then at the Paymaster's Office, took the matter seriously for 'the law of England made no provision for government when no King or minor King exists' – a consideration that was to cast a long shadow across much of the remainder of George's reign. Three years later, in January 1765, there was another attack, and in the spring of 1782 there were once again symptoms, albeit slight ones, that George might be heading for another breakdown.

Now 44 years of age and already growing portly, he felt himself 'drove to the wall.' His ministry was gone. He was mocked by his subjects, and would soon be in the hands of men he had so long reviled – profligate men, and traiterous too. Near desperation, he drafted a note of abdication in favour of his son, George, Prince of Wales: 'His Majesty therefore with much sorrow finds He can be of no further Utility to his Native Country which drives Him to the painful step of quitting it for ever.'

For whatever reason, the message was never delivered, and within a week of North's resignation the new ministry was in place, headed by Rockingham with Shelburne and Fox as his Secretaries of State and Burke (for all his contribution to the party, still stigmatized as a *parvenu*) in the comparatively lowly office of Paymaster General to the Forces. Virtually all the old names, all the old faces had gone, George writing that there was 'a more general removal . . . than I believe was ever known before. I have to the last fought for individuals, but the number I have saved except for my Bedchamber is incredibly few'.

But it was measures as much as men that troubled the king, that he had been deprived as much of determining policy as choosing his own ministers. For seven years the Whigs had bitterly opposed both his domestic and foreign policies and now, as Pitt and Burke prepared to revive the question of parliamentary reform, Shelburne dispatched an emissary to Paris to open peace negotiations with Benjamin Franklin – a move that was soon to exacerbate the hostility that already existed between the two Secretaries of State. Quarter of a century before, Henry Fox and Pitt the Elder had fought for the spoils of power, Now their successors were to re-open the feud – and Shelburne was well cast for the role.

A disciple of Chatham, and twelve years older than Fox, Shelburne had already won a Machiavellian reputation, though no one could doubt his abilities. An intellectual in the Age of Enlightenment, he was a patron of free-thinkers such as Joseph Priestley, Richard Price, and the father of philosophic radicalism, Jeremy Bentham. For all this, his compliments rang false, and it could have been with this in mind that Fox noted at the making of the ministry that it consisted of two parts – the five members of his own bloc, and the four members of Shelburne's faction. At the best of times, it would have proved an uneasy alliance. With a weak leader such as Rockingham, understrapped by powerful figures such as Fox and Shelburne, in a ministry committed to a radical programme, it proved a formula for disaster.

The *London Courant* might eulogize that 'Now Chatham is no more, Fox is the man to whom the people should look as their *avenging angel*', and the *General Advertiser* assert that the government needed to be 'the most powerful that was ever established in this country', but they neglected the traditional rifts which, for two decades, had turned the Whigs against themselves, and within days there were the first signs of a falling out in Cabinet. Shelburne's representative, Oswald, was already in Paris, and now Thomas Grenville was nominated to represent Fox – a duplication of effort on a sensitive mission that could only lead to confusion.

The appointment represented, exactly, the divide as much of ministerial responsibilities between the two rivalrous Secretaries of State, as between the two factions in the ministry, though in Fox's case there may have been more to it than this. His father had once labelled Shelburne 'a pious fraud', and the suspicion remained, Fox writing to Fitzpatrick in April: 'He affects the Minister more and more every day, and is, I believe, perfectly confident that the King intends to make him so.' All too soon, his suspicions were confirmed.

In the meantime, there was more than enough business to occupy Fox. Abandoning Brooks's to the disappointment of members who had paid up their arrears in subscriptions to rub shoulders with a Secretary of State, he was already winning a powerful reputation for diligence, Walpole writing that: 'He shines as greatly in place as in opposition. He is now as indefatigable as he was idle.' Never a man for half measures, the business of implementing a radical programme demanded all his attention.

In Ireland, his old friend Henry Grattan was pressing hard for improved Irish representation, with 40,000 volunteers to reinforce his case; while in the Commons there was growing dissension among the government over the exact nature of parliamentary reform. On Ireland, Fox's position was clear – 'Unwilling subjects were little better than enemies' – and in May he introduced a four point programme to redress Irish grievances which passed through both Houses in a day, and was greeted with delight in Dublin.

On reform, there was growing chaos. Burke, although bitter at not having been appointed to a Cabinet post that his merit deserved, was determined to press ahead with his plans for economical reform which, for Rockingham, was quite far enough. Pitt, however, disagreed. Equally bitter at being overlooked by the new administration, he pressed for more equal representation which, for Rockingham, was altogether too far.

Again the Whigs were split. Before the debate on Pitt's motion to inquire into the state of representation, Fox persuaded Burke to stay away from the House, but spoke himself in support of the proposal. Ten days later, on a bill brought forward to shorten the duration of parliaments, Fox was less fortunate. Both he and Pitt spoke for the measure, but then, in a grotesque outburst of temper, Burke 'attacked William Pitt in a scream of Passion, and swore Parliament was and always had been precisely what it ought to be, and that all people who thought of reforming it wanted to overthrow the Constitution.'

Twelve years had done much to change Burke. Then he

had railed against the encroachment of executive power – 'Where popular discontents are very prevalent; it may be well affirmed and supported, there has been generally something found amiss in the constitution.' – whereas by the spring of 1782 he was already alarmed at where his former rhetoric might lead. Now no one questioned the need for a modicum of reform, but to ask for more was to threaten the whole, delicate fabric of government.

So much for the ministry's unity, and while Fox struggled to maintain its sense of purpose, Shelburne and the king progressed their intrigue against Rockingham. Even before the new ministry was in place the two were conniving, Shelburne drafting a memorandum of their discussion on 21 March: 'His bad opinion of Ld. Rockingham's understg. His horror of C. Fox. His preference for me compared to the rest of the opposition', and by April he was firmly established as George's agent within the Cabinet.

The situation was an impossible one, and grew worse by the day. Through May and June, the ministry was locked in a series of internecine wrangles, the king using Shelburne to exacerbate the divide that existed between the factions, first to the frustration and then the mounting anger of Fox. Over America, over reform, over political appointments (where Shelburne exploited the king's influence to nominate his own friends), the man dissembled, sapping the grounds on which the ministry had been formed.

Unless the position was clarified, Rockingham's administration would be hard pressed to last out the parliamentary session, and at a meeting of Westminster electors Fox delivered a clear, if coded message to Shelburne to quit his devious games:

If the present Administration . . . which must be called the Administration of the people, should at any time fly from the principles which they had adhered to, or declared themselves to adhere to when out of place, they ought to be branded as the worst sort of men. The influence of the Crown has been one of the great grounds on which the present Administration opposed the last. If they . . . should now make use of it, they would deserve to be charged with having deceived their constituents and the public.

It made little difference. Shelburne continued to take George's part at the expense of his Cabinet colleagues. Towards the end of June, Rockingham was taken gravely ill, and at a meeting on the 30th Fox decided to force a decision from the Cabinet on the issue of American independence. Shelburne was later to write to the king that the Cabinet came 'to no final Resolution', but even here he misrepresented the case. After a protracted meeting, Fox had been out-voted on his plan to grant immediate and unconditional independence to the colonies, and had resigned – though agreeing to defer the announcement in view of his chief's illness. On the following day, Lord Rockingham died.

Weak as he was, the man had done much to provide the Whigs with some semblance of unity, but now, after twenty years in Opposition and little more than three months in office, he was gone, Fox having written what could have well been the epitaph for his ministry: 'Provided we can stay in long enough to have given a good stout blow to the Crown, I do not think it much signifies how soon we go out after.' The very existence of the Rockingham administration had been a severe blow to the Crown, but now the brief and bloody in-fighting as to who should succeed to office began.

The Foxites, as the largest group in Cabinet, claimed the right to nominate the new Prime Minister – and asked Shelburne to recommend the Duke of Portland to the king. George was delighted. By employing his confidant, his enemies were doing his business for him. It was not so much that Portland was a nonentity, rather that he regarded the Whigs' claim to appoint their own first minister as totally unconstitutional. Instead, he invited Shelburne to form the new government.

George's decision placed Fox in a quandary: whether or not to serve under Shelburne, an issue on which his friends were happy enough to proffer advice, though no two of them agreed. The Duke of Richmond said one thing, Burke another, and Gibbon reported that all was confusion. For two days Fox havered, balancing political expedience against his suspicions as much of Shelburne as all that he represented. The man was the agent of George rather than Parliament, Fox remarking to Lord Grafton on Rockingham's death that Shelburne was as 'fully devoted to the views of the Court' as Lord North. It was a system, an occult tyranny depending on the king's facility to manage his ministers, that Fox had opposed for almost a decade and he did not intend to compromise with it now. On 4 July Fox had a brief interview in the Closet, and resigned his seals of office.

The king was delighted, writing to Lord North: 'The contest is now become personal and he indeed sees it also in that point of view', adding to his confidant Robinson: 'Every honest man must wish to the utmost to keep him [Fox] out of power.' Perhaps he had finally seen the last of the man. As for Fox, he wrote to Lord Ossory on 3 July: 'I have only time to write a line to beg you to come to town to see the *denouement* of this farce, whether the title of it ought to be *Les Dupes*, or *Honesty the Worst Policy*, or what I cannot tell; but the last scene has certainly come.'

Seemingly the hopes of the Foxites were to be buried with Rockingham, and when Shelburne formed his ministry, with the 23-year-old Pitt as Chancellor of the Exchequer, absentees from his lists included the Duke of Portland, Lord John Cavendish, Sheridan and Burke. What once had been a rivalry based as much on personalities as a niggling interpretation of policies, had developed into a struggle for the soul of Whiggery, Gibbon remarking caustically: 'Three months of prosperity has dissolved a phalanx which had stood ten years of adversity.' Fox needed no lessons in politics, and having played high, and lost, he returned to the gaming tables.

There is an element of fatalism in every gambler, a sense that fate has a stake in the game, and Fox was philosophical enough to know when he held a losing hand. Certain of the party might blame him for not making more of a showing, but they were inclined to forget the principles involved and, unlike Shelburne, he did not have a king to play – though there was always the royal knave! On 4 July, Fox dined with the Prince of Wales, after which the two men gambled through the night at Brooks's.

George Augustus Frederick, eldest son of George III by Charlotte of Mecklenburg–Strelitz, had already won an extravagant reputation for himself when he first met Fox. From early childhood he had been restless of the disciplined upbringing of Windsor and Kew and his father's austere ways. Pious, frugal and sober, the king's lifestyle held no attractions for his son, with his well-known 'love of dissipation', and what began as a childish rebellion was soon to harden into outright hate.

The situation was not peculiar to George III. The reverse. For two generations the heirs apparent had been at loggerheads with their parents, to be used by the Opposition as stalking horses to mount attacks on the Crown and its ministers – and Prinny proved no different. By his mid-teens he was showing open contempt for the king, encouraged by his uncle, the Duke of Cumberland, who had already turned the prince's apartments into a combined gambling den, pawn shop and brothel. When he was 16, George took the lovely young actress Mary Robinson for his mistress. At the time she was playing the role of Perdita in *The Winter's Tale*, and she was later to write of their first meeting:

> A few words, and those scarcely articulated, were uttered by the Prince, when a noise of people approaching from the Palace startled us. The moon was now rising, and the idea of his royal highness being seen out at so unusual an hour, terrified the whole group. After a few more words of the most affectionate nature, uttered by the Prince, we parted. The rank of the Prince no longer chilled into awe that being who now considered him as the lover and the friend. The graces of his person, the tenderness of his melodious, yet manly voice, will be remembered by me, till every vision of this changing scene shall be forgotten.

The affair was to last four years, by which time the prince had tired of both Perdita and the Duke of Cumberland. If he was to play the profligate, then it would be played with style and his uncle, who had lately taken to calling him Taffy, was little better than a noisesome boor. In Charles James Fox, he was to find an altogether more amiable companion, Walpole writing: 'The Prince of Wales has of late thrown himself into the arms of Fox, and this in the most undisguised manner.'

There is no record of when or where the two men first met, possibly at Brooks's, possibly at Newmarket, or possibly at Fox's apartments in St James's Street. Here Fox held his levees, and entertained his disciples: 'his bristling black person, and shaggy breast quite open, and rarely purified by any ablutions, was wrapped in a nightgown, and his bushy hairy dishevelled. In these cynic weeds, and with epicurean good humour, did he dictate his politics, and in this school did the heir to the crown attend his lessons and imbibe them'.

It was the beginning of a close and prodigal friendship, even if not entirely detached on Fox's part, for he was quick to appreciate the advantage of a political connection with the heir to the throne. Initially, however, politics were secondary to more domestic concerns – not least, the Perdita affair. In the early days of their infatuation, the prince had settled a bond of £20,000 on his mistress to be redeemed when he reached his majority. The gesture was typical of the man whose extravagance was rarely matched by the means – and £20,000 was a considerable sum. Near desperation, he approached the king for help, and in August 1781, George was writing to Lord North:

> My eldest son got last year into a very improper connection with an actress and a woman of indifferent character. A multitude of letters past which she threatened to publish unless he, in short, bought them off her. He made her very foolish promises which, undoubtedly, by her conduct to him, she entirely cancelled. I have thought it right to authorise the getting them from her (and now learn she will return them) on receiving £5,000, undoubtedly an enormous sum; but I wish to get my son out of this shameful scrape.

Considering the poisoned nature of their relationship, it was a magnanimous settlement, but twelve months later the prince was still paying the price of his 'scrape', Fox having to negotiate further annuities of £600 a year for Perdita and £200 for her daughter. Admirable as it may have been, the arrangement was not entirely disinterested, for by September 1782, Fox had inherited the prince's mistress, his cousin Lady Sarah Napier writing: 'I hear Charles saunters about the streets, and brags that he has not taken a pen in his hand since he was out of place. Pour de desunnuyer he *lives* with Mrs Robinson, goes to Sadler's Wells with her, and is all day figuring away with her. I long to tell him that he does it to show he is superior to Alcibiades, for *his* courtezan foresook him when he was unfortunate, and Mrs Robinson takes *him* up.'

Conveniently for Fox, Perdita's apartment commanded a fine view of Shelburne's town house, and on being reproached by his friends for his absence from Brooks's he was able to retort: 'You see, I have pledged myself to the public to keep a strict eye on Lord Shelburne's motions.' And so he did.

* * *

Rockingham was dead, the Whigs divided, Shelburne in place, but Fox's discouragement was short lived, and by the autumn he was back to the cockpit of Westminster. The new First Lord of the Treasury provided a moving target – shifty and evasive – but on one ground, at least, he was vulnerable – the American peace. Immediately the new ministry was formed, the House was prorogued, and for the next five months Shelburne struggled to patch together a treaty that would command a parliamentary majority, one observer laconically reporting on the state of the parties: 'Ministers 140; Reynard 90; Boreas 120; the rest unknown or uncertain.' Unless Shelburne could dislodge either Fox or North, his success in concluding the peace negotiations would be a close run thing.

Parliament met on 5 December and at first sight the King's Speech offered little about which Shelburne's critics could complain: it appeared placatory on the American issue, firm on the need for further economic reform. On closer inspection, however, doubts began to arise. As with so much of Shelburne, fine words disguised equivocal intentions. When Fox rose to reply he was in a deceptively affable mood. He welcomed the speech, and would propose no amendments, but would be grateful for clarification on a couple of points.

In the first place, did he understand aright that the king had only issued instructions for the cessation of all offensive operations in the colonies *after* Rockingham's death? If so, some mistake had been made. Surely, the order had gone out *before* Shelburne took power? The imputation was clear, that once again Shelburne was economizing with the truth, and from the government front bench Pitt rose to deny the charge, for Fox to accept in honeyed tones that while this might not have been the government's intention, that is how it appeared.

The doubt was sown, and Fox was quick to exploit it. Both he and the House were largely ignorant of the details of the peace proposals, but if the ministry was intent on bartering peace for independence, or of playing France as a pawn in the negotiations, then he could only oppose it. And his reasons for such opposition? On the one hand, that it would be unmanly not to accept America's immediate and unconditional independence; on the other, that the granting of independence should divorced from negotiations for a peace with France.

But again, perhaps he had misunderstood all that he had heard, and then, in open tones of savage irony, Fox continued:

The independence of America was acknowledged by his Majesty's ministers; and though it had been said that 'whenever this should happen, the sun of England would set, and her glories be eclipsed for ever', yet he was of the contrary opinion, and would defend the Earl of Shelburne against any peer who should hold such language. He had set his hand to sign the independence of America, although it had insidiously been said that 'it would be the ruin of his country, and he would be a traitor who should do it.' But if any peer should dare to impeach the Earl of Shelburne for having done this, he [Fox] would stand up his advocate . . . and pledge myself that the recognition of the independence of America shall 'not be stained with the blood of the minister who should sign it.'

Three times Fox quoted Pitt the Elder, Shelburne's master, while Pitt the Younger sat silent on the Treasury benches. Three times he exploited the past to reinforce doubts about Shelburne's veracity, and while the House agreed the king's address without a division, the ground had been prepared for Fox's assault on the new ministry. What may have seemed a pleasing prospect to Shelburne in July was already turning sour, and seven days before Christmas 1782, Fox was back to the attack, charging the minister with duplicity ('The noble Lord had drawn up a case of conscience, and submitted it to a casuist') over reports of the peace negotiations, and demanding clarification of the details. The motion was heavily defeated, largely because North was unwilling to commit his forces, but Shelburne read the portents well enough – either he reinforced his position or he was doomed.

Shelburne's choice was limited – North or Fox – and the dangers considerable, that failing an arrangement with either, he would unite the opposition against him. However, it was a risk that had to be taken, and in January 1783, a tentative approach was made to North to explore the possibilities of his support. Although his faction consisted of what the Duchess of Portland dismissed scornfully as 'shabby People', the overture was rejected outright.

Now only Fox remained, and Pitt was dispatched to St James's Street to sound him out. It was not a happy choice. Briefly, the long standing breach between the two houses appeared to have been repaired when the 21-year-old Pitt took his seat in the Commons, but by 1782 Fox was already beginning to doubt the sincerity of his support: 'I wish I could say that I was quite as well satisfied in regard to the other person, he is very civil and obliging, profuse of compliment in public, but he has more than once taken a line that has alarmed me.'

Understandable as it was, Pitt's alliance with Shelburne alarmed Fox even more, and the meeting between the two men was short. Told that whatever the outcome of the talks, Shelburne intended to remain as First Lord of the Treasury, Fox remarked: 'It is impossible for me to belong to any administration of which Lord Shelburne is the head', Pitt replying: 'Then we need discuss the matter no further. I did not come here to betray Lord Shelburne.' It was the last recorded interview between Fox and Pitt, and while George III might have delighted in the outcome ('I am not in the least surprised at Mr Pitt's interview with Mr Fox having ended as abruptly as the hastiness and impoliteness of the latter would naturally lead one to suspect'), Shelburne must have realized that his game was pretty well up.

At the end of January, the provisional treaty with the United States, and the preliminary articles of peace between Britain and France had been laid before Parliament, and 17 February was the date settled to debate them. Three days before, Fox and North met and, seemingly, there was much common ground between them. Both agreed to oppose the peace settlement, while North tacitly accepted Burke's proposals for the reform of a system which he had managed for more than twelve years, asserting 'the appearance of power is all that a King of this country can have'. What Shelburne feared most, a union of the Opposition, was in the making.

For the next 72 hours, the two parties were in a frenzy of activity – meetings arranged, emissaries dispatched, detailed proposals drafted and rejected and drafted again – and it was not until five in the morning of 17 February that the final arrangements were agreed. Eight hours later, when the Speaker called the House to order, Fox and North sat side by side on the Opposition front bench. What their critics were quick to dub 'the unnatural alliance' was in place, and the debate that followed turned as much on the peace proposals as on the coalition between the minister who had waged unconditional war on the colonists and the man who had most consistently opposed him.

It was after midnight when Fox rose to challenge what

he termed 'a peace more calamitous, more dreadful, more ruinous than war could ever be', and to answer 'the most heinous charge . . . of having formed a junction with a noble person, whose principles I have been in the habit of opposing for the last seven years of my life'. The House tensed. North shifted, uneasily, in his seat. Pitt appeared languid, but concentrated intently:

> I can see no reason for calling such a meeting an unnatural junction. It is neither wise nor noble to keep up animosities for ever. It is neither just nor candid to keep up animosity when the cause is no more. It is not in my nature to bear malice, or to live in ill-will. My friendships are perpetual, my enmities are not so . . . . I disdain to keep alive in my bosom the enmities which I may bear to men, when the cause of those enmities is no more. When a man ceases to be what he was, when the opinions that made him obnoxious are changed, he is then no more my enemy, but my friend.

The defence was an elegant one, and appealed to the House. North relaxed. Now Shelburne could say what he liked, while in reply even the young Mr Pitt could do no better than to consider such apostasy as being 'among the wonders of the age'. At 7.30 on the morning of the 18th the Commons divided, and the ministry was defeated by sixteen votes. Four days later came a second defeat, with a slightly increased Opposition majority. Less than twelve months had passed since Fox had broken North. Now he and North had broken Shelburne, for George III to despair: 'I am sorry it has been my lot to Reign in the most profligate Age and when the most unnatural coalition seems to have taken place.'

Certain of Fox's friends and the majority of the press agreed, the *Morning Post* among others highlighting what they regarded as his inconsistency by quoting his old speeches against him: 'What! What! Enter into an alliance with those very Ministers who have betrayed the country. Gentlemen must have forgotten their principles and have given up their honour before they could approach the threshold of an alliance so abominable, so scandalous, so disgraceful.' That was

Fox in 1779, yet here in 1783, the alliance was fixed – but were the principles forgotten?

While the peace terms were the trigger for Fox's decision, it is probable that North's guarded acceptance of the need for reform was of equal, if not greater importance. Since 1774 Fox had been unwavering in his criticism of the Crown's malign interference in political affairs. He had spoken on the point ('Kings, Sir, govern by means of popular assemblies only because they cannot do without them; to suppose that a King is fond of that mode of governing is to suppose a chimera'); had written on the point ('There are two parties, that of the Court and that of the people'); and had refused a place in Shelburne's Cabinet on the grounds that he considered the man and his ministry as little more than tools of the king.

For three months of the sixteen years he had sat in the Commons, Fox had served in a ministry committed to curbing sovereign power; for the rest George had chosen the men, then determined their measures. The system ran counter to a constitution of which the jurist Blackstone had recently written: 'every branch of our civil polity supports, and is supported, regulates and is regulated by the rest'. Unless the defect was corrected, Fox's principles were of as little worth as the time he had spent expounding them.

To his critics, Fox's defence of the coalition smacked of casuistry ('Our party is formed on the principle of Confederacy; ought we not, then, to confederate with him who can give us the greatest strength?'), but to Fox it was the constitution itself that was at stake. With memories still fresh of Shelburne's behaviour during Rockingham's short-lived administration, the over-riding question was: Who ruled? – and in the spring of 1783, he was to put all that he had earned to the test, not least his hard won reputation out-of-doors.

Only two years had passed since Burke had counselled him to put his trust in the people rather than the king, but now he was to risk the one to curb the other. As much a mature politician who knew the Commons, as a gambler who knew the odds, it is inconceivable that Fox did not think the game worth the hazard, writing to Lord Lauderdale many years later: 'After all that can be said, it will be difficult to show when the power of the Whigs ever made so strong a struggle against the Crown, the Crown being thoroughly in earnest and exerting all its resources.'

On 2 April 1783, North and Fox formed their coalition ministry, with the Duke of Portland as its titular head, North as Secretary of State for the Home Department, and Fox as Secretary of State for Foreign Affairs. Once, years before, Henry Fox had been keen to impress his son with the maxim: 'Aspire to the first employments, and *never* trust as I did.' In thirteen years of politics, Fox had shown little inclination for the former – but the full meaning of the latter still remained to be learned.

6

'Under the Wand of the Magician'

George III was again close to abdication. In the five weeks between Shelburne's fall and the formation of the new ministry he had done everything in his considerable power to avoid leaguing himself with what he regarded as 'the most daring and unprincipled faction that the annals of this kingdom ever produced'. Twice he had approached the 23-year-old Pitt with the idea of forming a ministry, and twice he had been disappointed ('I am clear that Mr Pitt means to play false and wants I should again negotiate with the coalition') and finally, having abandoned a plan for apologising to Parliament for his conduct since 1760 and then retiring to Hanover, he accepted the inevitable. North and Fox came in.

At the formal ceremony, first Portland and then North kissed the king's hand, but when it came to Fox's turn George 'turned back his ears and eyes just like the horse at Astley's, when the tailor he had determined to throw was getting on him'. The metaphor was apt. George had already determined that he would unseat the coalition as soon as the opportunity arose, declaring publicly that 'It was impossible that he could wish that such a government should last. I hope many months will not elapse before the Grenvilles, the Pitts and other men of ability and character will relieve me.'

In this, if nothing else, the king and the people were as one. Fox was the man of the people no more, having forfeited much of their sympathy by his alliance with North. Ignorant of the principles that motivated him, it seemed

Plate 1 The Mask – featuring Fox (left) and Lord North, when they formed their coalition government in 1783. (Sayer, 1783)

138

that the coalition was a betrayal of the democrat who had so recently raged 'You must be the ministers of your own deliverance.' Then they had lionized him, but by April 1783 a growing number agreed with the verdict that the new ministry had 'the vices of both parents; the corruption of the one, and the violence of the other', to echo the doggerel of the *Public Advertiser*:

> Quoth N   to F   , 'You've got your Ends,
>   In spite of all your foes!'
> 'I'd have' says F   , 'See how my friends
>   I do lead by the nose.'
> 'I see't' says N   again; 'such Blocks
>   Prove Country's Good a Farce is;
> So we're broad bottomed' – 'Right' says F   ,
>   'We bid them kiss our   .'

Even if Fox was unaware of the new public mood at the formation of the ministry, he was soon to learn what he had sacrificed. Following the practice of having to stand for re-election on being appointed a minister, Westminster went to the polls on 7 April. The temper on the streets was hostile, Sir Samuel Romilly reporting: 'The populace received Fox with hisses, hooting, and every sign of displeasure', though it made little difference. It would have been a triumph if the Court party had been able to oppose Fox on his own ground, but they had been unable to drum up a candidate, and he was returned unopposed to take up the post he had quit only nine months before.

With the king in opposition, Fox was quick to recognize that new ministry could succeed only by success, and that this would not come easily. From the outset, it was clear that North had little inclination for office, and even less for his ministerial duties. At 52 years of age, the new Secretary of State for Home and Colonial Affairs had had enough of government, and if he had hurried into the coalition he was now to repent at leisure, devoting his time to arranging pensions for officers' widows and pardons for felons, while leaving the major decisions to Fox.

It may have been that North was unconsciously revenging himself for the slights that he had received from Fox over the past decade, pleasuring himself with the irony of watching Fox struggling to hold the coalition together as, so recently, he had struggle to hold together a ministry under Fox's withering assaults. Whatever the reason, North played an inconspicuous part in the life of the short-lived ministry, while Fox was not only left with the problems of renegotiating the provisional peace terms with the United States, France and Spain, but also affairs closer to home.

And affairs pressed in hard, to be exploited with demonic skill by Pitt. Both North and Fox had urged him to remain with the new ministry as Chancellor, and equally forcibly he had declined. After little more than two years in the Commons, Pitt had developed a political instinct which was to serve him well in the years ahead, and was quick to grasp not only the fundamental weaknesses of the coalition but also the dangers of being associated with what, from the outset, was an unpopular administration. Beyond which, there was always Fox. Answering critics of the new Secretary of State for Foreign Affairs on his first, and only visit to Paris, Pitt accepted the licentiousness of Fox's character, but added the rider that they had never been 'under the wand of the magician'.

As austere as Fox was extravagant, as friendless as Fox was companionable, and as conscious of Chatham's inheritance as Fox was haunted by the memory of Lord Holland (as late as June 1783, the question of settling his father's accounts as Paymaster was raised in the Commons) the two men were at heart incompatible, Pitt riding ambition like a Newmarket breaker, Fox playing it like the gamester he was. The stakes were high, but, as Walpole perceived, it was Pitt's character that would eventually win out, though 'Had not Pitt so early aspired to be his rival, Fox would have cherished Pitt as his friend and disciple.'

By the spring of 1783, the opportunity had long gone, and Pitt only waited his chance to make his first play against the new ministry. In the Lords, Shelburne's leadership of the Opposition was failing, but in the Commons on 7 May Pitt opened up the divide between Fox and North. Twelve months before he had tabled his proposals for parliamentary reform, now he returned to the question, as much to expose fragility of the unnatural alliance as out of conviction. His plan was threefold – to prevent bribery at elections, to disenfranchise any constituency convicted of 'gross and notorious corruption', and to add a further 100 seats to the House – and while Fox spoke for the motion, North and his faction opposed it. At the division, Pitt's proposals were rejected by 144 votes, a damaging blow for both Fox and the ministry.

And worse was to come. In June 1783, the Prince of Wales reached his majority, and came into his establishment. Only two months had passed since George III had decided against abdication, in part because he could not bear the thought of seeing his son on the throne, the more so because of his growing attachment to the profligate Fox. Alone, they were trouble enough. Together they were quite impossible, especially since their circle at Brooks's had taken to gambling on the duration of his reign. The thing was intolerable, yet the word was that Fox had promised to secure the prince a £100,000 settlement when he came of age, for the prince himself to approach the queen with the same proposal.

Briefly, George was tempted to expose the chicanery of a ministry that preached economy while practising extravagance, while Fox struggled to extricate himself from a trap of his own making. If the king were to go to the country on the question of a six figure settlement on the Prince of Wales there could be little doubt about the outcome, Fox writing on 16 June 'there is great reason to think our Administration will not outlive tomorrow'. For a further two weeks the ministry sought to find a compromise solution; George eventually agreeing to make a £50,000 annual payment to his son from the civil list, together with the income from the Duchy of Cornwall and £30,000 down.

It had been a close run thing, and if the king remarked that every morning he wished himself 'eighty, or ninety, of dead', then he would see the coalition buried first. The prince's settlement had offered a powerful temptation to break the ministry, but there were better opportunities still to come – though Fox had yet to grasp the extent of George's enmity when the House rose for the summer recess. His Majesty might still be tender at the loss of Shelburne, and his refusal to allow the new ministry to bestow any peerages certainly created difficulties, but on 16 July Fox was writing: 'The King continues to behave with every degree of civility and sometimes even with cordiality; cependant il faut voir.'

Another five months were to pass before George was to unmask his true intentions, and reveal himself for what he was. In the meantime Fox had abandoned both his rakehell ways and Perdita Robinson, the former to the press of ministerial business, the latter for Mrs Armistead.

Two years older than Fox, Liz Armistead had established herself in London society in her mid twenties. In 1778, after three years as mistress to the Duke of Dorset, the MP James Hare was writing to George Selwyn: 'Derby is gone into camp near Winchester, and has built a kitchen and a stable for twelve horses, while Lady Derby is living away at Brighthelmstone. He does not think, however, his establishment complete without a declared mistress, and he is therefore to take Mrs Armistead from Lord George.'

In 1782, she had had a brief affair with the Prince of Wales, and then she met Fox. It was the beginning of a relationship that was to transform his life. For ten years and more Fox had been in search of himself, attempting to make a whole of the disparate elements of his character. True, he was coming to terms with a political philosophy, but much remained besides, and it may have been that during his pursuit of escapism he occasionally recalled a remark once made to his father that life was a troublesome thing for 'one wishes one had this thing or that thing and then one is not the happier . . . '. The years between had borne him out. Much of what he had wished, he had had (a fortune to gamble with, a reputation to stake), but rather than making him any happier it seemed that once begun there had been no satiating expectations. They had lived upon one another – until he met Liz Armistead.

A notable beauty, who sat for Reynolds at least four times,

she was to provide Fox with what he had not yet found – a stable relationship that allowed him the time and tranquillity in which to find himself. Since 1778 Mrs Armistead had owned the small property of St Anne's Hill, 2 miles south of the Thames at Chertsey, and for the last twenty years of his life Fox was to call it his home. However, the summer recess of 1783 allowed Fox little time for country pursuits – the House was to reassemble in November with the new peace treaties before it.

For all the bombast of the previous winter, Fox and his agents had done little to improve what he had then termed the 'calamitous' terms negotiated by Shelburne, the definitive treaty with the US being ratified in August, and with France in September. George III deplored both settlements ('It is no wonder that our enemies, seeing our spirit so fallen, have taken advantage of it'), but was quick to recognize their potential for embarrassing the coalition.

All too soon Fox's early hopes that the king would remain neutral were to be exposed for what they were – illusory. Since the summer George had been corresponding with the former Lord Chancellor, Thurlow ('old Hurlo Thrumbo'), and Lord Temple, who as far back as April had written that nothing might 'delay the hour of your Majestys's deliverance from that thraldom that bears so heavily upon you'.

A scheming couple, the one was as devious as the other was covetous. For more than a decade, Thurlow's progress had been determined by the degree of his obsequience (from Attorney General in 1770 to Lord Chancellor in 1778), and it was only with the formation of the coalition that Fox insisted on his dismissal from office, maintaining that 'No man was ever so wise as Thurlow looks.' He was right in everything, except the limits to which Thurlow would go to unseat him. And in this, George Grenville, Lord Temple, proved an unscrupulous ally.

For all his inheritance as the head of one of the most powerful political clans in the kingdom (Pitt the Younger was his cousin, and his two younger brothers sat in the Commons), Temple was a grandee who still craved grandeur, careless of its provenance; Walpole writing that he combined many 'disgusting qualities . . . with a natural prospensity to avarice'. When Shelburne fell, Temple quit the office of Lord Lieutenant of Ireland in high dudgeon, and spent the autumn of 1783 planning his revenge on Fox.

Individually, George's enmity, Thurlow's hatred and Temple's ambition were formidable enough. Collectively, they were to prove a lethal combination, though when Parliament reassembled there were few outward signs of the impending confrontation. True, there were fresh disturbances in Ireland where the Volunteers were still under arms, and from where the Lord Lieutenant was warning that '*a secret hand*' was attempting to undermine the government. As Fox had already noted, there could be no catchpenny solutions to the Irish question.

Otherwise, however, it seemed that the coalition was reasonably well found, the King's Speech going so far as to hope that now peace had broken out it would be possible 'to keep the calamaties of war at a great distance'. Only one short passage referring to the affairs of the East India Company aroused interest, and that took second place to the debate on the definitive treaties signed with the United States and France.

Nine months had passed since Fox and North had turned Shelburne out on the issue, yet the final terms differed little from the original articles. Pitt was scathing, berating the ministry for hyprocrisy and implying that he only supported the treaties because they were of Shelburne's making. Fox spoke briefly, and by six in the evening the debate was over, for Germain to note that 'The present Ministry have opened the session with all the appearance of support they could have wished for.' He was as unaware as Fox that George and his cronies had already chosen their ground on which to break the coalition.

The troubles with the East India Company were deep-rooted. Established by royal charter in 1601, the agents of the company had long since become laws unto themselves, distanced as they were by a sixteen-week sea voyage from the Court of Directors in London. Throughout the mid eighteenth century, and for all the wealth of their dominion, the company was in almost continuous financial difficulty, a situation compounded by the corrupt and corrupting nature of Indian commerce, the internecine rivalries of Indian politics, and the Anglo-French power struggle that had made a battleground of the sub-continent. By 1770, Britain's hegemony was virtually assured, but the corruption remained, India having become a fortune hunter's paradise, for Walpole to lament 'What is England? A sink of Indian wealth filled by Nabobs.'

Almost everyone agreed that the government of the sub-continent could no longer be left to commercial interests, and since 1781 a select committee of the Commons had been reviewing the administration of a Company which Burke believed had betrayed their chartered rights for 'it is of the very essence of every trust to be rendered *accountable*, and even totally to *cease* when it substantially varies from the purpose for which alone it could have lawful existence'.

The source of much of Burke's information was Sir Philip Francis, the son of Fox's old tutor at Eton, the probable author of the Junius letters, and since 1773 a member of the Supreme Council of Bengal. An implacable opponent of the Governor General, Warren Hastings, with whom he fought a duel in 1780, Francis's acerbic comments on the management of Indian affairs provided Burke with the material required for drafting the India Bill that Fox introduced in the Commons on 18 November 1783.

Its central proposal was straightforward (that for five years Parliament should appoint seven commissioners to rule India, the appointments then reverting to the Crown), and from the outset Fox appreciated the risk of the venture, writing to Liz Armistead at St Anne's Hill:

'They are endeavouring to make a great cry against us, and will, I am afraid, succeed in making us very unpopular in the City. However, I know I am right, and must bear the consequences . . . . I know that I never did act more upon principles than at this moment, when they are abusing me so. If I had considered nothing but keeping my power, it was the safest way to leave things they are.'

North agreed, though on more practical grounds. On the morning of the first reading of the bill, he dispatched a note to Fox: '*Influence of the Crown and influence of party against Crown and people* are two of the many topics which will be urged against your plan.' He was not alone in isolating the danger. As Fox resumed his seat in the Commons, Pitt was to his feet fulminating against this dangerous increase in ministerial power, while at St James's the king calculated the odds and bided his time, a royal confidant writing to Thurlow: 'the King sees in the Bill all the horrors that you and I do'.

To the vested interests in the city, in Westminster, and at Court 'horrors' was hardly too strong a word. If the directors of the largest of London's great trading companies could be dispossessed of power, then what of the other and lesser chartered corporations – and what, moreover, of the principle of private property so precious to Whig memory? In fact, the bill was widely regarded as a naked extension of legislative power, the most famous cartoon of the period caricaturing Carlo Khan (Fox) riding a bemused elephant (North) down Leadenhall Street, led by an Indian herald (Burke).

Sayer's image captured the mood exactly, conveying the suspicion that the new board appointed by the coalition would continue to ride to power on the back of Indian patronage, and that even if turned out by a combination of George and his friends such patronage could still be employed to offset the influence of the Crown at the hustings. Small wonder that Fox feared the Opposition would make a 'great cry' against a bill which Pulteney asserted would give him 'a power of five or six years continuance, independent of the Crown, over all the Eastern Empire', and that he attempted to hustle it through the Commons.

Only a week was allowed to pass between the first and second readings, and Fox was in a pugnacious mood when he rose to speak. He knew that the Opposition was gathering: Pitt and his ally, Dundas, were both in their places, and the East India Company and the City of London had both tabled representations against the bill. He knew that the king was already conniving with Thurlow and Temple, and he knew that the charge that the measure would make him the most powerful commoner in England was already being levelled against him. Twenty years before Lord Holland had been hungry for power – and he was his father's son. The stigma, it seemed, was indelible, for all he had done to expunge it.

> 'Whenever I rise up in this House to present a broad and comprehensive scheme of policy to the nation . . . I shall always consider what I say in its support as an argument in my own defence; because I shall always consider my character, my situation, my rank in the country, as at stake on every measure of state which I shall presume to undertake . . . [however] I have something better than my own defence in view, because the present bill is something greater than my own advantage; it is a bill which I from my soul believe to be necessary to the deliverance of empire.'

For the next two hours Fox proceeded to catalogue the charges against the East India Company and its agents – of fraud, corruption, peculation, murder, rape and 'wars of horror and devastation' – to close as he had begun, staking his reputation on the propriety of the bill:

> 'He knew that in doing so, he put his own situation, as a Minister to the hazard; but where upon a great national ground he could establish a measure at once salutary and useful, likely to rescue the natives of India from oppression, and save the country from disgrace, he little cared how great the personal risks were that he was to encounter . . . . If he should fall in this, he should fall in a great and glorious cause, struggling not only for the company, but for the people of Great Britain and India, for many, many millions of souls.'

The echo was of the American debates of half a decade before, but Pitt had little patience either for Fox's principles or for an eloquence 'that would lend a grace to deformity'. On the contrary, Pitt argued, the whole case turned on whether, in relieving oppression abroad, the bill would enforce it nearer home. On this, he had no doubts: it would be inimical both to the constitution and the liberties of England, the relief of India being 'grounded on violence and injustice in Europe'. This was the issue on which all the rest turned, and after thirteen hours of debate the House divided to give the ministry a 109-vote majority.

Fox, however, was far from happy. Whatever his intentions, they appeared suspect, and in the coffee houses and taverns of The Strand they remembered his handling of Wilkes. Whatever his motives, they appeared specious, and in the salons and gaming rooms of Mayfair they recollected his hostility towards the king. Whatever his principles, they recalled the Man of the People, and jested that the new India board would be the People of the Man. The world, it seemed, was closing around him, though he could still rely on his friends. What was it that he had once remarked, that happiness was acting with those and loved best – and for all the enmity that he now aroused, Fox still commanded friendship.

He was soon to need, as never before, the devotion of men such as Sheridan and Cavendish and Burke. On 1 December, the House went into committee to examine the bill. Towards the close Burke rose to speak as much in defence of Fox as of the measure which he, himself, had such a significant hand in preparing. It was to be regarded as one of the greatest orations of one of the greatest parliamentary orators:

> He [Fox] has put to hazard his ease, his security, his interest, his power, even his darling popularity, for the benefit of a people he has never seen. This is the road that all heroes have trod before him. He is traduced and abused for his supposed motives. He will remember that obloquy is a necessary ingredient in the composition of all true glory . . ... He is now on a great eminence, where the eyes of mankind are turned on him. He may live long, he may do much, but here is the summit. He can never exceed what he does this day.

But if this was the present, Fox himself was to touch on the future not simply of India, but of government itself. For the first time, the moral implications of the bill were highlighted ('What is the end of government? Certainly the happiness of

148

the governed.'), and then, in response to a critic, he mocked the notion of the independent man, above party, to assert:

> 'I have always acknowledged myself to be a party man. I have always acted with the party in whose principles I have confidence; and if I had such an opinion of any Ministry as the gentleman professes to have of us, I would pursue their overthrow by a systematic opposition.'

For almost a decade the notion had been in the making, and Fox was to make it the capstone of his political philosophy. Where, previously, government turned on men, it was now to turn on measures. Where, previously, opposition had turned as much on personal attachments as on principles, it was now to develop a rational, a consistent response to legislation. And where, previously, the Crown determined men and been party to their measures, Parliament was now to be its own master. This was Fox's credo, though there was still the king to take into account.

The committee stage of the bill went well enough, the ministry winning a 114 majority at the division, but that evening, and unbeknown to Fox, Thurlow delivered a memorandum from Temple to the King. If its opinion was crushing (that the India Bill was 'a plan to take more than half of the Royal power, and by that means disable His Majesty for the rest of the reign'), then for all of Temple's persiflage, its recommendation was explosive: that the King make his personal opposition to the measure clear to the Lords. Recognizing the constitutional dangers involved, George hesitated. Like it or not, the ministry was his ministry, and if he was seen to be plotting against it, the consequences could be disastrous, and yet . . . .

While the king remained undecided, Temple and Thurlow were undeterred. By the first week of December they had extended their cabal to include Pitt, Dundas, the maverick Duke of Richmond, Lord Clarendon, Richard Atkinson (a proprietor of the East India Company), Charles Jenkinson (one-time Secretary of War), and the king's long-time confidant, John Robinson. Although their personal goals varied (Pitt, for instance, demanding the Treasury if he was to be party to the plot), they were unanimous in their intent – to break Fox on his own bill – and on 3 December Atkinson was writing 'Everything stands prepared for the blow if a certain person has the courage to strike it.'

Yet still George hesitated, determined to know the voting strengths of both Houses if there was to be a change of government and Pitt should take office. Robinson's calculations reassured him. Pitt and his friends would be in a minority until an election, after which, and by careful management of Crown influence, a new ministry could hope for a working majority of 180 seats.

No more was needed. The plot was hatched. On 9 December the India Bill came before the Lords, with rumours already abroad of royal concern over the passage of the measure. In public, Fox feined unconcern, but in private he had growing doubts, writing to Portland: 'I have heard of so many defections tonight that the thing appears to me to be the more doubtful than ever I thought it was.' Six days later his suspicions were confirmed. On the 11th, Temple had had an audience with the king, and received a written statement that:

> 'His Majesty allowed Lord Temple to say whoever voted for the India Bill was not only not his friend, but would be considered by him as an enemy; and if his words were not strong enough, Earl Temple might use whatever words he might deem stronger and to the purpose.'

The king had abandoned what constitutional scruples he still possessed. For too long he had tolerated Fox. Now he would break the man for good. On 15 December, the bill was debated by the Lords for a second time, for Richmond to read a newspaper extract reporting that, following the king's opposition to the measure, his government had resigned. The story was a lie, though it contained one truth – that Temple was the messenger of George's disfavour. Challenged on the issue Temple resorted to evasion, while hinting that he was, indeed, privy to the king's counsel. Always conscious of royal favours, it was enough to nerve their Lordships to defer further discussion of the bill for forty-eight hours.

Fox was incensed. By interfering in the affairs of the legislature the king was again trying to re-establish his system of government by favourites. Two years before, George had remarked that his conflict with Fox had become personal. Now the clash between them turned on the altogether more fundamental issue of whether England was to be ruled by royal prerogative or by Parliament, and Fox placed his trust in the Commons. Even if the coalition fell no other ministry could be found to manage affairs for 'we shall destroy them almost as soon as they are formed'. It was an error of judgement that was to cost him more than two decades in opposition.

On 17 December both Houses met, the Lords to debate the India Bill, the Commons a motion that to report the king's opinion in order to influence the outcome of a bill was a high crime and a misdemeanour. As to the former, the result was a foregone conclusion. Temple had done his work well, and where the king's writ did not go far enough he had no hesitation about using whatever words would suit the purpose, Fox's long-time friend Richard Fitzpatrick noting dramatically: 'The Bishops waver, and *the Thanes fly from us.*' At the division, the ministry were defeated by nineteen votes.

And all the while in the other chamber, Pitt and Fox disputed the constitutional issues involved. Although well aware of the content of George's message to Temple, and of the use to which it was being put, Pitt maintained that the whole charge turned on 'The monster, public report, which daily and hourly fabricates every species of the grossest absurdities and probabilities.' As such, the motion itself was a slur on Parliament and, dismissing the rumours of secret influence, he demanded the ministry's resignation.

Fox was to his feet. The whole question turned on the rights of Parliament and then, pulling a copy of George's note to Temple from his pocket, he challenged the Opposition to deny its authenticity. Here was the evidence of secret influence. Here was the infamy of a secret faction whose principal object was power and place.

If, however, a change must take place, and a new ministry is to be formed and supported, not by the confidence of this House or the public, but the sole authority of the Crown, I, for one, shall not envy the gentleman [Pitt] his situation. From that moment I shall put in my claim for a monopoly of whig-principles. The glorious cause of freedom, of independence, and of the constitution is no longer his, but mine. In this I have lived. In this I will die.

The alternatives were clear-cut – either Fox and the Commons, or Pitt and prerogative – and all that remained was the vote. At the division, the motion was carried by a seventy-three majority, though it did little to change the eventual outcome. The defeat of the India Bill in the Lords was a resigning matter, and that evening Fox wrote to Liz Armistead: 'We are beat in the H. of Lords by such treachery on the part of the King, and such meanness on the part of his *friends* . . . as one could expect either from him or them.' For 24 hours, George waited at Queen's House to receive the Seals of Office, and then at 43 min. past 10 p.m. on 18 December, he drafted a note to North:

Lord North is by this required to send me the Seals of his department, and to acquaint Mr Fox to send those of the Foreign department. Mr Frazer amd Mr Nepean will be the proper channel of delivering them to me this night; I choose this method as audiences on such occasions must be unpleasant.

To the last, he was sensitive only to his own feelings. North was in bed when George's messenger arrived, to be told on insisting that he deliver the note personally 'if you see Lord North, you will see Lady North too'. After handing over the key of the cupboard in which he kept the seal North settled to sleep again, having delivered his last speech as a minister.

The following afternoon, 24-year-old William Pitt kissed the king's hand, and took office as First Lord of the Treasury and Chancellor of the Exchequer – on the strength of the votes of nineteen peers. It was a bold stroke, and a dangerous one. The cabal might have broken the coalition, but could it retain its power against a Commons majority managed by Fox?

Fox himself was confident that Pitt's administration could not survive ('The confusion of the enemy is beyond all description, and the triumph of our friends proportional'), resting his case on the authority of the Commons, but he underestimated the king's and Pitt's resolve. If they had been none too scrupulous about ousting him, then they were to be none too fastidious about preventing his return. At 35 years of age, and having served little more than thirty-seven months in office during his fifteen years in the Commons, Fox again crossed the floor of the Commons to take his place on the Opposition benches where he was to remain until 1806.

Once he had made the passage with all the bravado of the rakehell he was, jesting at the loss of office, and wagering on his return. Those had been good days, wild days, to be played out with elan. Even then, however, there had always been the other Fox, the diffident guest at Dr Johnson's table, the student of Appolonius Rhodius and Virgil, the politician of whom Walpole could say that in Charles James Fox was discovered 'the phenomenon of the age'.

A decade later, the gambler remained, though tempered by experience, and not only at the tables. America. India. Ireland. England. For Fox they had fused into the single question of who ruled whom, and how, which drove him to his hazard against the king. The issue was, indeed, personal, though there was now much more to it than what Dr Johnson regarded as ' a struggle between George the Third's sceptre and Mr Fox's tongue'.

1783 was a constitutional watershed. By its very nature the coalition had offered a direct challenge to George's arcane system of government, and in plotting its destruction the king became party to the polarization of loyalties between the Crown and the Commons which, eventually, was to lead to the extinction of royal prerogative. Immediately, George prevailed,but the future was against him. In the meantime, Fox consoled himself with the thought that he had 'a natural partiality to what some people call rebels', and set about deploying his forces against Pitt.

7

'A Kingdom Trusted to a Schoolboy'

The GREAT FISH, as George III was called by the *Morning Herald*, had escaped again. Twice in as many years he had thwarted Fox's challenge to his authority, though his new ministry under Pitt was a fragile thing, a makeshift of principles as much as of talent (Dundas, a deserter from the North camp; Richmond, the former Rockinghamite; and Thurlow, as always, trading in fealty), expeditiously united by their opposition to Fox. The Whigs might laugh at the motley, and applaud performances of *The Alchemist* in which Pitt was cast as the Angry Boy (an epithet later adopted by Sheridan in the Commons), and Shelburne as Subtle, but they underestimated the political resolve of George's new first minister.

The whole of Pitt's short life had been directed to one end – the management of power – and during his first months in government he had few scruples about how he retained it. An MP for four years, and a sound member of the Court party, Nathaniel Wraxall, was soon to write a chilling description of Pitt's character: of a man cold in manner, severe in conversation, contemptuous of amusement, and ruthlessly dedicated to 'the functions of office'. This was Pitt at 24 years of age, already the consummate political machine, and while Wraxall may have exaggerated, the description stands in sharp contrast to his profile of Fox: convivial by nature, generous in friendship, rich in talent, and yet:

> He is inferior in only one requisite [to Pitt], an opinion of his public principle, generally diffus'd among the people.

When to this great and inherent defect, is super-added the unquestionable alienation of his Sovereign, both to his person and his party, we may lament . . . that abilities so universal and so sublime are left unemployed, and are permitted to waste their sweetness in the desert air.

Not that Fox was despondent, or Pitt sanguine that Christmas of 1783. In Brooks's and at the great Whig houses the betting was that the enfeebled ministry would not last out the winter against the Opposition's majority in the Commons, and while George contemplated that 'on the edge of a precipice every ray of hope must be pleasing', Pitt had no illusions about the vulnerability of what many had already come to regard as little better than a caretaker government.

Within four days of the coalition's defeat, he had persuaded the king to sacrifice his pride and countenance an approach to Fox to join the new ministry. The reply was contemptuous – 'Why don't they advise us to pick pockets at once' – but within a fortnight, the overture was renewed. With only five days to the return of Parliament after the Christmas recess, the Prince of Wales hosted a meeting between Fox and Richmond at Carlton House. Fox must have delighted at the irony that, having so recently broken his government, the king and Pitt were now reduced to employing his uncle as their emissary in suing for terms, though they got no further than discussing the preliminary articles. On being told that no place could be found for Lord North, Fox left the room without saying a further word.

On 12 January 1784, the Commons reconvened, with Fox confident of his majority, and Pitt aware that his only prospect lay with the Crown. Less than a month had passed since Fox had laid claim to the Whig inheritance, and now the partisan *Morning Chronicle* was to amplify his case:

The contest which has been carrying on by the Whigs since the beginning of the present reign, against secret influence, opposed to the spirit of the constitution is now at public issue . . . . The points to be decided on are, whether the Crown, by privately issuing forth its mandates, can crush every measure it chooses to disapprove, and whether the sense of the House of Commons is to have any further weight in the great scale of government.

In the weeks ahead, these were the grounds on which Fox was to harry Pitt into a series of humiliating defeats. Pitt introduced a revised India Bill, and was out-voted at the division, but refused to resign. Fox tabled a motion that the Ministry did not have the confidence of the House, and carried it through the lobby, but Pitt remained unabashed. Thomas Coke moved against 'The Continuance of the Present Ministers in their Offices', and won a nineteen-vote majority, but still Pitt endured, confident in the support of the king. Fox might rage on about constitutional precedents, but Pitt's was the constitutional power, and he would never 'consent to march out of it, with a halter around my neck, change my armour, and meanly beg to be re-admitted as a volunteer in the army of the enemy'.

Fine words, but they disguised the reality that effective government was grinding to a halt. Britain, again, was facing a constitutional crisis, and while Lord Cornwallis might assert that 'Pitt rises every day in character and estimation', the Duchess of Clermont feared that 'there will be a revolution, and Fox will be king.' Twenty years had passed since Lord Holland had drummed up prerogative; eight since Chatham had declared 'either the Parliament will reform itself from within or be reformed with a vengeance from without', and twelve months since their sons had voted for reform. Now, however, it was very different. Now Pitt rode power and was quick to grasp that Fox's influence would diminish the longer he remained in office – and commanded the Crown's patronage.

He was right. Through January and into February, the opposition's majorities fell, first slowly, then at accelerating pace with the defection of the Northites. Under Fox's leadership, however, the Whigs held firm. For three months he fought the case, in the Commons and out-of-doors:

The true simple question of the present dispute is, whether the House of Lords and Court Influence shall predominate over the House of Commons and annihilate its existance, or whether the House of Commons, whom you elected, shall have the power to maintain the privileges of the people, to support its liberties.

The echo was of those Parliament men who had challenged Charles I, to speak in the name of the Commonwealth against arbitrary treason. George III, however, placed a different interpretation on events. Confident that his cause was 'that of the Constitution as fixed at the Revolution (of 1688) and to the support of which my family was invited to mount the throne', he pledged himself 'to oppose this faction . . . to the last period of my life' – or, failing that, to abdicate. As careless of his own constitutional jerrymandering of only two months before, as he was convinced that ultimate constitutional power lay with Crown, his support for Pitt was unswerving. And Pitt himself? As he said, it had pleased His Majesty to command his services and, with his support, he would ride out the crisis.

In the meantime, the public were fast tiring of the inter-necine feuding at Westminster. This was not so much government, as government by default, and in late January fifty-three independent Members met at St Albans Tavern and agreed to make an approach to Pitt and Portland, still nominally the leader of the Opposition, urging them to open negotiations 'to rescue the country from its present disastrous state'. Neither leader welcomed the initiative. The time for reconciliation had passed, but for appearances' sake some gesture had to be made, and at Fox's suggestion Portland's opening gambit was to accept in principle the idea of a coalition but to demand, as a pre-requisite, the resignation of the ministry.

Inevitably, Pitt refused. It was not so much that Fox's majority in the Commons was now down to single figures, more that he saw nothing to be gained by compromise. Again the gentlemen of St Albans Tavern pressed for conciliation; again Fox insisted that Pitt should acknowledge the authority of Parliament by resigning before forming a new administration; and again Pitt refused. The deadlock was total, to the king's relief. Since the Commons had returned, he had feared for his ministry, but by mid-February it seemed that Pitt's position appeared secure – though tempers in London still ran high.

On his return from the Grocers' Hall where he had received the freedom of the city, Pitt's coach was attacked by a mob armed with bludgeons, outside Brooks's. Always quick to inflate a promising story, gossip soon had it that Fox was involved in the affray, to be discountenanced by the assertion that he was in bed with Mrs Armistead at the time! As for Fox, he was shouted down by the crowd at a meeting of Westminster electors celebrating the fourth anniversary of his selection as their candidate, a cartoon of the event showing him branded with Cromwell's ambition, Catiline's abilities, and Machiavelli's politics. So much for the Man of the People. In less than two years he had dissipated what Burke regarded as his greatest asset, public trust, and by the first week of March Fox realized that the game was pretty well up.

He had staked everything against Pitt, but by doing little more than doing nothing the Angry Boy had called his hand, and on 8 March Fox made a last, desperate play. Three days before he had only succeeded by a narrow majority in deferring debate on the Mutiny Bill (the final sanction that the Opposition could use to turn out the government) and at four that Thursday afternoon he moved a Representation to the king in the House. Although couched in uncharacteristically subdued terms, it was a damning indictment of what Fox regarded as Pitt's and his master's abuse of power:

> It did not become the King's ministers to be entirely dependent upon the Crown yet this, it seemed, was now the fashion . . . . Those ministers who pleased their master were safe. Those who did their duty were damned . . . . It became the Commons not to see such men disgraced and foreaken . . . . Better to be a courtier in France than in England, for there the King's favour was the sole object . . . Here Ministers played the double part, enslaving the Commons into obedience to the Crown . . . . The thing was big with

danger to the freedom of the constitution . . . . Thus he was warranted in moving the resolution 'that he was an enemy to his country, who should advise his Majesty to continue his present administration'.

Confident that he had beaten Fox, Pitt did not trouble to reply, and at the division the Representation was approved by only a single vote. Eleven weeks had passed since Pitt had kissed the king's hand and Fox had marshalled a 124 majority against the new minister; eleven weeks in which the small world of Westminster had been turned upside down. The constitutional crisis was over. Fox had hazarded, and lost. Now all that remained was for the Commons to vote in supplies, then prepare for the dissolution.

Whatever the mood at Brooks's that night, Fox may well have been entertained by the irony that for all his defence of the Commons, he was now widely abused by the public, while Pitt, as agent of the Crown, was idolized by the mass out-of-doors. The only consolation to be gleaned from the events of the previous three months was that, in their pursuit of prerogative, the king and Pitt had succeeded in uniting the Whig Party where previous attempts had so often failed. In the set piece debates between Fox and Pitt following the fall of the Coalition, it was not only the line of future constitutional debate that was drawn, but also the future shape of party government.

For Fox, however, this may have proved cold comfort. What had he written only four months before, at the first reading of the India Bill?: 'If I had considered nothing but keeping my power, it was the safest way to leave things as they are.' His critics, remembering Holland's axiom, may have mocked at the notion. Fox, a man of principle? Absurd. Yet in the breaking of his government, and the making of Pitt's, they were to expose their own principles for what they were worth – while Fox was to spend all but five months of the rest of his life in opposition.

* * *

159

George III dissolved Parliament on 24 March relying on Robinson's prediction that an election would provide a comfortable majority for Pitt. That night the Great Seal was stolen from the Lord Chancellor's house, and word went abroad that this was the work of Fox and his friends, their final, wild throw to make dissolution impossible – a story assiduously promoted by their enemies. Whether or not the king was taken in by the fabrication was of no consequence, it merely confirmed him in the belief that the country's affairs had been in confusion for too long, and that all too often Fox had been party to the mischief – the turmoil of North's last months; the destruction of Shelburne's ministry; the odium of the coalition. The need now was for the smack of firm government, and if golden pills were still needed (the much be-titled Duke of Northumberland was to collect a further barony for safely returning his six seats), the assumption was that much of the electorate would agree.

Fox, however, had still to learn how deeply the performance of his party over the previous two years had alienated the country – or that part of it entitled to vote. It would take more than a month for the extent of the débâcle to be revealed, meanwhile he offered himself for a third time as a candidate for Westminster. Only six weeks had passed since he had received a rough handling from the electorate, and Fox must have realized that his seat was by no means secure – not least, since the government candidates were the naval hero, Lord Hood, and a defector from his own back benches, Sir Cecil Wray.

The Westminster polls opened on 1 April for an election that has since become legendary as much for its violence as for its outcome. From the first day there were pitched battles between the rival factions, a 'gang of fellows, headed by naval officers, and carrying His Majesty's colours' (this according to the Foxites) clashing with 'Irish chairmen and pick pockets' (this according to the government party). After three days Fox was trailing the poll by fifty-two votes, but he remained confident – 'I think I feel that misfortunes, when they come thick, have the effect rather of rousing my spirits rather than sinking them.' By the 5th, and having lost more ground, he was not so sure – 'I have serious thoughts, if beaten here, of not coming back into Parliament at all.' The temptation was Mrs Armistead and the peace of St Anne's Hill, but as long as the election continued he would continue to fight, and by the close of the first week Georgiana, Duchess of Devonshire, and her sister, Lady Duncannon, had rallied to his support.

By eighteenth-century standards their canvassing methods were virtually unique, Georgiana allegedly kissing a butcher in return for his vote, to the delight of the electorate (one labourer remarking 'Were I God Almighty, I should make her the Queen of Heaven') and the fury of the government agents who launched a barrage of abuse against her:

Arrayed in matchless beauty, Devon fair
In Fox's favour takes a zealous part.
But, oh! Where'er the pilferer comes – beware!
She supplicates a vote and steals a heart.

The scurrility of the campaign mounted by the day, causing Lady Rockingham to write of the 'vile methods of giving out the idea that *Mr Fox aim'd* at being *king*', though it made little difference. The civil list might spend tens of thousands annually sweetening the Westminster electorate, but from the 11th onwards Fox gained progressively on Wray, and by the 22nd had overtaken him. There were still twenty-five polling days to run, but now the Fox bandwaggon was running strongly, Perdita Robinson soliciting votes, the Prince of Wales appearing with a badge of laurel leaves surmounted by a fox's brush, while a burlesque based upon *The House that Jack* built, and possibly written by Sheridan, featured Fox as 'the Cat that Killed the *Rat*', Thurlow as 'the *Bull* with the crumpled horn', Dundas as 'the *Scot* by all forsworn', and Wilkes as 'the *Cock* that crowed in the morn'.

Polling closed on 17 May, and Hood (6694 votes) and Fox (6234 votes) were returned. Dissatisfied with the result, however, Wray demanded a scrutiny, and the High Bailiff refused to declare Fox elected until it was complete. The decision was to have far-reaching consequences, though momentarily it made no matter. Fox and his principles had been redeemed, and chaired by his supporters the triumph began – Fox being preceded by a squadron of horsemen in blue and buff uniforms beneath the standards 'THE RIGHTS OF THE COMMONS' and 'THE MAN OF THE PEOPLE' and followed by the state carriages of the Portlands and Devonshires under the banner 'SACRED TO FEMALE PATRIOTISM'.

The celebrations continued deep into the night, and the following day Prinny held a fête that lasted from noon until six. The mood may have been festive, but as the king passed Carlton House on his way to the opening of the new Parliament he may have smiled at the thought that Fox was attending his own wake. Robinson had been right. The coalition had lost some 160 seats in the country, Fox's Martyrs including the Lord John Cavendish and the ageing General Conway, and Pitt was comfortably ensconced in power.

For Fox the irony was ineluctable, the *Morning Herald* reporting that through the artifice of the Court 'the people have been completely blinded, and the more ardently Mr Fox supported their rights, the more they reviled him'. For George, he had a man, a ministry and a majority to his taste for the first time in two years. At last he could begin to relax, and while he continued to take an active interest in the business of Westminster, it was to be less as a player, more as a spectator of affairs.

The king's retreat suited Pitt admirably. If Wilberforce once noted that he was not a man for friendships, then he was to prove a good hater as far as Fox was concerned. Throughout the election Pitt had concentrated his attention on Westminster, sardonically remarking on one occasion that the polling went well 'in spite of the Duchess of Devonshire and *the other women of the people*', and he was as disappointed at Wray's defeat as he was bitter at Fox's success, describing the outcome as 'forty days' poll, forty days' riot, and forty days' confusion'.

The only consolation was the High Bailiff's decision to grant a scrutiny – a stratagem that Pitt was to employ in a malign attempt to debar Fox from the House. For nine months the Angry Boy deserved his epithet, devoting almost as much time to the vendetta as to parliamentary affairs. The High Bailiff informed the Crown Office of the scrutiny in May, and excluded as the Member for Westminster, Fox got himself returned *ex abundante cautela* for Orkney. On the 24th, it was moved that the High Bailiff make an immediate return, which was heavily defeated by the irregulars on Pitt's back bench. The following day, Fox tabled a motion for his return, to have it withdrawn, and on 8 June it was moved for a second time that the High Bailiff make his return, the Member for Orkney rising to speak in his own defence.

Two years before a young German visitor to the Commons had written his impressions of Fox the orator:

> It is impossible for me to describe with what fire and persuasive eloquence he spoke, and how the Speaker in the chair constantly nodded approbation from beneath his solemn wig; and innumerable voices called Hear him! Hear him and when there was the least sign that he intended to leave off speaking, they no less vociferously claimed, go on; and so he continued to speak in this manner for nearly two hours.

Half a century later, Lord Brougham, for twenty years an MP and among the most perceptive critics of oratory in an age of great orators, rated Fox's speech on the Westminster scrutiny among the finest that he ever delivered. Aware that he faced a hostile audience across the floor of the House, he opened with a direct challenge to their prejudice: 'I have no reason to expect indulgence, nor do I know that I shall meet with bare justice in this House.' The taunt produced a mutter of protest, and to heighten the impact, Fox repeated it, substantiated the remark, and then repeated it again:

> There are in this House, Sir, many persons to whom I might on every principle of equity, fairness, and reason object, as judges, to decide upon my cause, not merely from their acknowledged enmity to me, to my friends and to my politics, but from their particular conduct on this particular occasion.

Secure in his majority, Pitt settled back on the government front bench, as Fox developed his argument. For almost three

163

hours he reviewed the case, answering the charges of his critics and dismissing the need for a scrutiny, to conclude with a warning to Pitt not to over-reach his power:

> Let him weigh well the consequences of what he is about, and look to the future of it on the nation at large. Let him take care, that when they see all the powers of his administration employed to overwhelm an individual, men's eyes may not open sooner than they would if he conducted himself within bounds of decent discretion . . . . There is a principle of resistance in mankind, which will not brook such injuries; and a good cause and a good heart will animate men to struggle in proportion to the size of their wrongs.

The inner consistency of the case, of the rights of the individual against insolent power, had an illustrious history, and Fox was to make it the touchstone of his policies in the troubled years ahead. Pitt, however, was dismissive in reply. It was all very well for Sheridan to rant on about the 'severity of epithet, redundancy of egotism, and pomp of panegyric' that entangled the government's case, he did not command a majority, though at the division there was a significant drop in the ministry's vote. Blinded by vindictiveness, Pitt continued to pursue Fox for another nine months, as his majorities continued to fall from eighty-seven June, to thirty-nine in February 1785, to defeat by thirty-eight votes on 3 March 1785. As for the scrutiny, the High Bailiff finally subtracted 107 votes from Fox, 106 from Hood, and 103 from Wray, for Fox to win a £2000 action for damages which he distributed among the charities of Westminster.

It was small comfort for the magnitude of the Whig's defeat the previous spring, and though Fox was in the House to support Pitt's budget in June 1784, and to oppose the new India Bill in July, he had growing doubts about his future. Writing to Portland he complained that he was tired out in mind and body ('I cannot express to you how fatigued I was with the last day's attendance, and how totally unequal I feel myself in spirits to acquit myself as I ought to do'), while by August George III was peddling rumours that Fox was intending to retire altogether from active politics.

If so, Liz Armistead and St Anne's Hill certainly offered powerful counter-attractions. Years later, Fox was to write to his nephew, Henry ('Dear Young One'), of the time spent at St Anne's: 'I am perfectly happy in the country. I have quite resources enough to employ my mind; and the greatest resource of all, literature, I am fonder of everyday; and then the Lady of the Hill is one continual source of happiness to me. I believe few men, indeed, ever were so happy in that respect as I.' With the arrival of the summer recess in 1784, he was to need what happiness he could find. Since 1782 he had fought three elections for Westminster, and twice in as many years he had been in and out of government, and now
. . . .

Now Fox entertained himself – though not just with Mrs Armistead's charms. By the autumn stories were circulating of Fox's escapades in the newly fashionable resort of Bright-helmstone, a favourite retreat of the Prince of Wales, but while something of the old gambler still remained it was now tempered by discretion. At 35 years of age, Fox was no longer the fast man, even if he was sometimes given to his old enthusiasms, once alarming a party of friends by bursting into a room roaring 'Great run! Great run! Finest thing you ever saw. Pay the Jews! Pay 'em all! Great run', then dashing out again.

For all the defeats and disappointments, for all of Pitt and the king, there was no stifling the old ebullience. A little more portly, a little more heavily jowled, he still retained that zest for life that had made Walpole wonder at his seemingly inexhaustible energy. Yet while Fox loved idleness 'so much and so dearly that I have hardly the heart to say a word against it', there was still something due to 'one's station in life, something to friendship, something to the country'. At times, he may have longed for 'Dear Home', but there was no escaping the trinity of his faith (his responsibilities, his friendships, his country), and by the New Year Fox had returned to what was to become his station in life (a seat on the Opposition front benches close to the Speaker's left hand) holding that there was still work to be done.

Not that the previous six months had been entirely wasted.

In May 1784, when the party's fortunes were at their lowest, the Whig Club had been formed, and Fox had enrolled William Adam among its first 100 members. In the five years since they had fought their duel in Hyde Park, the two men had become firm friends, and now Adam set about organizing the party on professional lines, a new and significant development in English politics. Where, previously, political management had largely turned on piecemeal arrangements, the Whigs now established a fund and appointed agents to fight elections, and subsidized newspapers and pamphleteers to promote their case. Their only problem was to determine exactly what case they should represent, and how it should be represented.

Momentarily, the Westminster scrutiny had revealed Pitt's vulnerability. None the less, he continued to command an awesome majority in the Commons, and while Fox doubted that the election results were as much a vote for the new ministry as against what remained of the coalition, there was no escaping the need for the Whigs not only to regroup but also to reappraise their parliamentary strategy. In the meantime, they could only pick off single issues – defeating the government on an Irish Commercial Bill and plans for the fortification of Portsmouth and Plymouth – all the while testing their policies against Pitt's more substantive legislation.

Their first opportunity came soon enough. Only a month after the scrutiny, Pitt again introduced a bill for parliamentary reform. Almost two years had passed since he had pledged himself to the issue, asserting that he would support it 'on every seasonable occasion', while in December 1784 he assured a visitor to Downing Street that he would 'put forth his whole power and credit, *as a man* and *as a minister, honestly* and *boldly* to carry a plan of reform'. On 18 April he put his pledges to the test, though his proposals for change were puny and only to be introduced gradually.

Thirty-six rotten boroughs each returning two members were to be disenfranchised, with a million pounds being set aside to compensate electors for the redistribution of their seats among county and metropolitan constituencies.

Careless of his recent shabby treatment at Pitt's hands, Fox supported the principle of the bill at the division, though voicing his reservations about the clause covering compensation.

> 'The very idea of purchasing from the majority of electors, the property of the whole was inequitable . . . against the true spirit of the constitution . . . . There was something injurious in holding out pecuniary temptations to an Englishman to relinquish his franchise . . . . The right of governing was not a property, but a trust.'

The notion may well have horrified the old guard of the Whigs, including Burke, for it struck at the very heart of their belief in property. In the years ahead, Fox's apostasy was to have far-reaching implications, though when the House divided Burke and his cause were safe, the bill being defeated by seventy-four votes.

For all his previous undertakings, it was Pitt's last attempt at reform. The heir to Chatham's populism, and the favourite son of the reformists, he quickly lost his taste for the enterprise once established in power, much to the king's relief. From the outset George had opposed the bill, contemplating in March that it was unfortunate 'that he [Pitt] had early engaged himself in this measure', though Pitt's willingness to press the issue indicated his growing independence of the king. Always jealous of power, Pitt was as happy to assume authority as his master was to relinquish it, and by the close of 1784 the Angry Boy was firmly in the saddle of government – while George had other worries.

At 23 years of age, the Prince of Wales continued to behave more like the heir to perdition than the heir to the throne. Dilettante and rake, he remained the talk of the town, and now there were rumours that his latest affair had carried him into the arms of a Catholic, Maria Fitzherbert. The king's concern was not that she was six years the prince's senior, and already twice widowed, rather with her faith. The anti-Catholic provision of the Act of Settlement was quite specific, yet his son seemed quite indifferent to where his latest infatuation might lead. The prince appeared mad, quite mad. Why, there was even talk of the prince attempting his own life on having his advances refused.

Ruse or no, Maria Fitzherbert later left her own account of the event, dictated to Lord Stourton:

> Keit, the surgeon, Lord Onslow, Lord Southampton, and Mr Edward Bouverie arrived at her house in the utmost consternation, informing her that the life of the Prince was in imminent danger – that he had stabbed himself – and that only her immediate presence could save him.
>
> She found the Prince pale and covered with blood. The sight so overpowered her faculties, that she was deprived of almost all consciousness. The Prince told her, that nothing would induce him to live unless she promised to become his wife, and permitted him to put a ring round her finger. I believe the ring from the hand of the Duchess of Devonshire was used upon the occasion, not one of his own. Mrs Fitzherbert being asked by me, whether she did not believe some trick had been practised, answered in the negative.

The following day, Maria Fitzherbert left the country, protesting that she had not been a free agent to what had taken place. The prince was distraught, and between pressing the king to allow him to go abroad spent time with Fox and Mrs Armistead at St Anne's Hill. Inconsolable, he would weep by the hour, tear his hair, roll on the floor banging his head, all the while swearing 'he would abandon the country, forgo the crown, sell his jewels and plate, and scrape together a competence to fly with the object of his affection to America'. His friends were sympathetic, though less so in December 1785 when Mrs Fitzherbert returned to England.

Fox's concern was straightforward, that the prince was going to take 'the very desperate step (pardon the expression) of marrying her at this moment', and he warned, passionately, against such a move, reminding the prince that marriage to a Catholic would exclude him from succession, while under the Royal Marriages Act of 1772 the marriage, even if performed, would not be a real one. The prince's reply arrived within hours, assuring Fox that there were no substances to his suspicions: 'there not only is, but never was, any grounds for those reports which of late years have been so malevolently circulated'.

The prince lied. Four days later he married Mrs Fitzherbert in the drawing room of her house on Park Street, paying the Anglican priest who performed the ceremony £500 for his silence. Even his 'Dear Friend' was not party to the secret, with damaging consequences. If it was to be another sixteen months before Fox learned the truth, however, it was impossible to disguise the growing crisis in the prince's financial affairs from him. The extravagances of Prinny's lifestyle – not least the cost of maintaining Carlton House, and of creating his palatial folly at Brighthelmstone – had far outstripped his allowance of £60,000 a year, and by the spring of 1786 he was in debt to the tune of some £200,000.

Where, recently, he had been so cavalier with Fox's trust, he was now exhorting his friendship as the only man who could possibly persuade Parliament to increase his allowance under the civil list. Privately, Fox sounded out opinion, but it was far from encouraging. It seemed that the prince's friends could no longer afford the price of his ways, while Pitt disclaimed all responsibility for his affairs, and in June Prinny was forced to break up his establishment in an attempt to pay off his debts. The *Morning Post* was much amused – between reporting the more serious business of Warren Hastings.

Appointed Governor General of Bengal in 1773, Hastings symbolized for Fox and the Whigs all the chartered repacity of the East India Company – any doubts that they harboured being dispelled by Philip Francis, a member of Hasting's council of four. For almost as long Francis had been providing Burke with waspish accounts of the management of Indian affairs, and for almost as long Burke had been building his case against Hastings, and while the India Bill of 1784 had taken the civil government of the sub-continent out of the hands of the Company, the man and all he represented remained.

Now in his late fifties, and for almost twenty years the unacknowledged mentor of the Whigs, Burke had come to regard the prosecution of Hastings as a personal crusade, a test of his humanist principles at a time when his interest in party was waning. But if Burke regarded impeachment as a moral issue, Fox viewed it altogether more pragmatically, recognizing that the prosecution could be developed to party advantage by forcing Pitt to take a stance on a potentially embarrassing issue. True, Pitt had only recently pushed through his own India Bill, but not before ensuring that it safeguarded the Company's management of commercial affairs.

Through the late winter and into the spring of 1786 the Whigs prepared their case against Hastings, all the while probing Pitt's position on the issue in the Commons, while on 1 May, Hastings himself knelt at the bar of the House to refute the growing number of charges being brought against him. His appearance was a failure, and a month later Burke rose in his place to advance the first of twenty-two charges against the former Governor General – that in defiance of orders, Hastings had come to an agreement with the Nabob of Oude that, in return for payment to the East India Company, the Company's troops should be provided 'for thoroughly extirpating the nation of the Rohillas'. Dundas replied for the ministry, to win a majority at the division, but Pitt remained silent. The Hastings party were elated. Momentarily it seemed as if there would be no case to answer.

Thirteen days later, all that had changed. On 13 June Fox brought the second charge against Hastings – that he had fixed an unreasonable fine on the prince of the independent state of Benares, Cheyt Singh, and that in return the Cheyt Singh had paid Hastings, a bribe of two lakh (then worth approximately £20,000). In what, for him, was a comparatively short speech, Fox summarized the case against Hastings, ending with an appeal to the Commons to set an example to Europe that 'there were Englishman who did not to avow those principles which had originated in the corrupt heart of a most corrupt individual'. The House waited for Pitt's reply, and it proved decisive. The fine was unjust and tyrannical, Hastings was guilty of a 'very high crime'. For whatever reasons, Pitt had abandoned Hastings, and the charge was carried by a 119 majority. Impeachment was now certain.

Before any further charges could be laid, however, the Commons rose for the summer recess and Fox retired to St Anne's Hill. The more sceptical among his friends might continue to doubt this transformation in his character. No question, Liz Armistead was an intelligent and a beautiful woman, but how long would that serve to satisfy the firebrand that was Fox? Two years, or three? They wagered on the outcome, underestimating both Fox's need for love and the capacity of Mrs Armistead to provide it. Since his childhood days, Fox had commanded friendship and admiration in equal parts, but love had been as much a stranger at Holland House as at Brooks's. All else was there, the extravagance and the self-indulgence, but not the one quality that he needed most, and for twenty years Fox, a passionate man, spent his passions at the tables before meeting with his Dear Liz:

> I feel every day how much more I love you than *I* knew. You are *all* me . . . . Indeed my dearest angel the whole happiness of my life depends upon you. Pray do not abuse your power.

She didn't. At St Anne's Hill she made a home for Fox that he had never had; a place where he could hunt and swim and play whist and chess, and enjoy the quiet world of the countryside only 20 miles distant, yet so far removed from the frenzy of Westminster. For the remainder of his life, Fox's loyalties were to be divided between the one and the other – between his private and his public worlds – and when the new session of Parliament opened in January 1787, he was back in his seat in the House.

The King's Speech contained proposals for only one major measure – a treaty of commerce and navigation with France. A student of Adam Smith's free-trade principles, Pitt held that France was a natural market for British goods even if her economy was close to bankruptcy. The American war had cost France some 2000 million livres that her treasury could ill afford, and by 1787 the cost of handling the public debt totalled 300 million livres annually – all of which had to be raised by taxes, the bulk of which fell on the peasantry. The nobles and clergy were exempt from direct taxes levied by the *taille* (a 'cut' of all production) and *capitation* (a tax on income reckoned in terms of production), while indirect taxes on such necessities as salt (the *gabelle*) and shoe leather (*marque de cuir*) also discriminated heavily against the poor.

The country was in an ugly mood, and the Anglophobes among the French had already begun to denounce the treaty as a further cause of their economic plight. Fox was equally critical, though for different reasons. The family compact between France and Spain had long been directed against Britain, yet here was Pitt drumming-up a commercial treaty in the pretence that it would consolidate 'the good harmony' which existed between Britain and France. The notion was absurd. What was needed was a closer understanding with the northern powers (Russia and Prussia), and on 12 February he was reminding the House: 'France is the natural political enemy of Britain . . . . Past experience shows that whenever France sees this country weak, she seizes the opportunity and aims at effecting her long desired destruction.'

Within two years Fox's words were to be used against him, careless of the caveat that: 'One reason to distrust France is the amiable character of her king, celebrated for his love of justice, for his desire to serve his country, and his wish to aggrandise her name.' Members appreciated the irony (Hear him! Hear him), for if Louis XVI had little time for justice he had a keen sense of power, the British Ambassador in Paris, Lord Dorset, having written some months before: 'The spirit of intrigue which Versailles is endowed with is more dangerous to the balance of power than all the mighty armies of Louis XIV; and if we do not watch him close, we shall be in a most unpleasant situation.'

Dorset can have had little idea of how prescient he was to be proved, while in London, obsessed once again by the Warren Hastings affair, there was little grasp of how fast the situation in France was deteriorating. In February, Sheridan laid the third charge against Hastings – the despoilment of the Begums of Oude. The subject lent itself exactly to the dramatist in Sheridan, and he spoke on it for six hours in what has since come to be regarded as the consummation of English oratory. At the close, members were so moved by his eloquence that for the first time in history Parliament was adjourned without further debate, Fox later enthusing that 'all he had ever heard . . . dwindled into nothing' in comparison with it, and Pitt proclaming that "it surpassed all the eloquence of ancient and modern times'.

For a further five months, Burke was to marshal the charges against Hastings, but by the spring Fox was embroiled in an altogether more delicate affair. For all his championship of the Whigs, the Prince of Wales was becoming a heavy liability, and not just for the weight of his debts. The government press had been carrying hints of a secret marriage for more than a year, and on 20 April, during a debate on the parlous state of the prince's finances, John Rolle, a Tory member for Devonshire, urged that the gossip 'immediately affected the constitution, both in Church and State'.

There was no escaping the implication. If the rumours were true, then the marriage was void, while if there should be a Catholic connection then the prince had effectively excluded himself from the succession under the Act of Settlement. In attempting to lay the gossip, Sheridan made it worse by declaring that the prince was happy to have 'every part of his conduct laid open', and two days later Fox was compelled into an outright denial to the House. The story was 'a calumny, destitute of all foundation . . . monstrous . . . a report of a fact which has not the smallest degree of foundation, a report of fact actually impossible to happen'. Rolle was not satisfied. Had Fox authority for such an assertion? Fox answered that he had, and the House went on to vote the prince £160,000. One member, however, still had his reservations: Pitt remarking *soto voce* to a neighbour on the Treasury bench: 'Villain, be sure thou prove my love a whore.'

It was to be another twenty-four hours before Fox learned the truth. At Brooks's the following evening a member took him aside to report: 'Mr Fox, I hear that you have denied in the House the Prince's marriage to Mrs Fitzherbert. You have been misinformed; I was at the marriage.'

Sixteen months before the prince had lied to Fox, and now Fox had lied to the House. His embarrassment was acute, and compounded by the difficulty that if he should withdraw his statement it could lead not only to a parliamentary crisis, but also to a change in the succession to the throne. So much for friendship. As his father had never tired of saying: 'Never trust as I did.'

But if Fox was embarrassed, the prince was desperate. Mrs Fitzherbert had been deeply offended by Fox's statement, and tackled about the matter the following morning the prince had attempted to bluff his way out of the difficulty: 'Only conceive, Maria, what Fox did yesterday; he went down to the House, and denied you and I were man and wife.' Apparently she had been less than satisfied, and now Fox himself knew the truth. Unless something was done, and urgently, there was no chance that Parliament would stand by their offer to help to pay off his debts, and a strong possibility that he would be debarred from the throne.

His only hope lay in persuading a member, any member, to speak for him in the House, as much to satisfy Mrs Fitzherbert's honour as to secure his own finances. Charles Grey, at 23-years-old already a prominent Whig, was the prince's first choice, to be sharply rebuffed by the rejoinder that Grey could say nothing without calling into question Fox's veracity. It brought the meeting to an abrupt end, but not before the prince had remarked: 'Well, if nobody else will, Sheridan must.'

And Sheridan did, in a speech to the Commons that tested even his sophistical skills. His only advantage was that the ministry was as anxious as the Opposition to avoid a crisis, Pitt having spent the previous weekend in delicate negotiations to safeguard the prince's financial settlement, and in a short speech Sheridan achieved the near impossible, persuading the House to pursue the matter no further, while assuaging Mrs Fitzherbert's pride. The prince was delighted, ordering building to recommence on the Dome of his Brighton pavillion, though in obtaining an increased allowance he had lost his Dear Friend.

When the House rose that summer, the prince set off in pursuit of Fox in the hope of making reparations, to be widely shunned by the Whig establishment. By September, Fox was the guest of Thomas Coke at Holkham for the partridge shooting. The prince wrote proposing a visit, to be reminded: 'Holkham is open to *strangers* on Tuesdays.' The snub was of regal proportions, but the prince was undeterred. He arrived at the house to find that Fox had left on hearing that Mrs Armistead had been taken ill at St Anne's Hill, but still undiscouraged he twice proposed a toast over dinner that evening 'To the health of the best man in England – Mr Fox.'

Almost a year was to pass before there was to be a reconciliation, a year in which Warren Hastings was finally brought to trial, and during which there was growing evidence of George III's apparent insanity. Impelled by his sense of outrage, Burke had pursued his case against Hastings through the Commons for almost two years, and by February 1788, Hastings stood arraigned on twenty-one charges. The trial was set for Westminster Hall, and for weeks before it had been cast as the event of the London season. If the leading trial managers were not sufficient to command attention – Burke with his erudition, Sheridan his wit, and Fox his imagery – then there was always the accused. A diminutive figure in his plain crimson coloured suit, this was the man who had once ruled India and who now stood charged with 'high crimes and misdemeanours'. Sir Gilbert Elliot wondered whether Hastings would survive the week, though there was little sympathy for him as the press of spectators (Mrs Fitzherbert in the royal box, the queen and princesses in the Duke of Newcastle's gallery) watched the Lords Spiritual and Temporal process into the hall and take their places for the trial.

The first day was occupied with legal formalities, but on 14 February Burke opened the case. It was to be among the finest orations of his career, lasting for four days, and concluding:

I impeach, therefore, Warren Hastings in the name of our Holy Religion, which he has degraded. I impeach him in the name of the English Constitution, which he has violated and broken. I impeach him in the name of the Indian millions, whom he has sacrificed to Injustice . . . . And I conjure this High and Sacred Court to let not these pleadings be heard in vain.

Men wept, women fainted, and Fanny Burney (no Whig lover) confessed to feeling quite overpowered. And this was only the beginning. Three days later, the Quality were up at six in the morning to be at Westminster by nine and 'there wait shivering without fires' until eleven when Fox moved the Benares charge. He was not in best form, having drunk too much the night before, but while Miss Burney found it a speech of 'uninterrupted passion and vehemence', there was no gainsaying that Fox remained consistent in his prosecution of injustice. Burke might rail that he viewed the case as much from the political as from the moral standpoint, but this did nothing to diminish his rage against inhumanity, wherever perpetrated – in India or America, the Indies or Africa.

As the seventeen managers continued to press their charges against Hastings at the opening of a trial that was to last for seven years, and to end with Hasting's acquital, the business of the Commons continued, and on 8 May, in the absence of William Wilberforce, Pitt proposed a debate on the abolition of slavery for the next session of Parliament. Fox was hot in support – *the trade ought not to be regulated, but destroyed*' – though critical of Pitt for not committing himself on the question, and for the delay in addressing an issue that revolted against every principle of justice.

Impulsive as always, Fox demanded immediate action, careless of the long history of the trade – the first African slaves having been sold in the Lisbon markets in 1444. Little more than half a century later, with the opening up of the New World, the Portuguese and then the Spaniards began to make regular shipments of slaves across the Atlantic, but another 200 years were to pass before England took a major hand in the trade. By the 1760s, however, Chatham was boasting that Britain had established a near monopoly of slaving, and Liverpool had overtaken Bristol as the largest slaving port in the world.

While the boast revealed something of the under-belly of Chatham's populism, it told little of the horror of the trade he espoused, and it was not until 1786 that the Committee for the Abolition of the Slave Trade was established, with Granville Sharp as its chairman and Wilberforce its most articulate voice. Pitt was to spend the next twenty years pledging himself to Wilberforce's cause, though doing little to further it, and it was finally left to Fox to introduce the bill that succeeded in abolishing the 'flesh trade'.

During the summer of 1788, however, Pitt had other things on his mind. On 11 June the king was taken ill with a series of abdominal 'spasms'. Although George reassured him the following evening 'I certainly mend, but have been pretty well purged this day', the question remained: what if the king should be seriously incapacitated and the Prince of Wales come in? Within a week it appeared that George was on his way to recovery, and in July the royal family set off on a tour of the West Country. Temporarily it seemed as if the alarm was unfounded, and while Pitt holidayed at his newly acquired country house, Fox set off on a European tour with Mrs Armistead.

Committed to doing no more than enjoying themselves, the couple travelled at a leisurely pace through France and Switzerland, to spend two days at Lausanne with Edward Gibbon. For more than two decades the two men's friendship had over-ridden their political differences, and on Fox's departure Gibbon was to write of him: 'Perhaps no human being was more perfectly exempt from the taint of malevolence, vanity, or falsehood.' By mid September, Fox and Mrs Armistead had crossed into Italy blissfully unaware that a new crisis was in the making. Together they studied the works of the great Italian artists and toured recently excavated Roman remains, and while Fox once read a newspaper, it was only to follow the racing results. The world of London may have seemed far distant, but there was to be no escaping it.

On 17 October the king had another 'spasmodic byleous attack', and over the next fortnight there was little improvement in his condition. Even before his West Country holiday there had been hints of a recurrance of mental instability – not least, an increase in the incoherence of his conversation – and now the symptoms reappeared. In an attempt to allay public concern, George held a levee at Kew on 24 October 'to stop further lies and fall of stocks', but the following day, on an outing in Windsor Park, he startled his coachman by shaking hands with an oak tree, mistaking it for the King of Prussia. There could be no mistake, George III was mad.

At first, the word was put about that the king was suffering from gout, but while he displayed his backside to his attendants in an attempt to disprove the story, there was no disguising the truth for long. By the close of the month the Opposition were already aware that something was seriously amiss, and over dinner on 3 November George broke down completely. The Prince of Wales, just back from Brighthelmstone, told later of how he had to restrain his father's violence, while the queen had a fit of 'violent hysterics'. Within hours the news was out, and in London the Whigs were galvanized into unaccustomed activity. If the king was indeed insane, what of the succession?

The generally held view was that the prince would be appointed Regent, with full royal powers, and then dismiss Pitt and call in the Whigs. Pitt himself was pessimistic ('there was more ground for fear than for hope'), but while Burke hustled down from Yorkshire, and Sheridan opened negotiations with Thurlow (careless of the latter's role in defeating the coalition's India Bill), there was neither sign nor news of Fox. In the first week of November, the Duke of Portland posted relays of messengers to scour northern Italy for the Whig's lost leader, and eventually they tracked him down in Bologna.

During his tour, Fox had heard indirectly that his favourite nephew, Lord Holland, had been taken ill, and his first thought on seeing the messenger was that 'Dear Young 'Un' was dead. On hearing the truth, he was so relieved that he collapsed and 'cried violently for some time' before considering the full import of the news. Virtually overnight the whole complexion of politics had changed, and without allowing him a moments rest, the messenger was posted north again to arrange relays of horses for Fox and Mrs Armistead's return journey across Europe. Leaving Bologna on 15 November they were in Lyons three days later, to hear that George III was dead.

The report was ill-found, though the king's condition was continuing to deteriorate, but it acted as a further spur to Fox. Exhausted by the strain, Mrs Armistead remained in Lyons while Fox pressed northwards considering all the while the likely composition of the new Whig ministry: Portland would be there, as would Burke and Sheridan and Grey, all talented men, and trustworthy too. In Paris the news was that the king still lived, and it would be a Regency instead, though that would make little difference to Fox's ministerial plans.

All that was needed was to get to England, though by the time he reached Calais, Fox himself was ill. Possibly it was the pell-mell nature of the journey, possibly an ill-prepared meal taken en route that was the cause of the trouble, but by the time he reached London on 24 November his condition gave growing cause for concern, Wraxall writing that Fox's body was emaciated, his countenance sickly, his eyes swollen, and 'his stockings hung upon his legs'. This was hardly the man to take command of a party fired by the prospect of government – unaware that on the day of Fox's return Pitt had received the first piece of encouraging news since the crisis began.

Seven doctors were already in attendance on George when Doctor Anthony Addington was called in, the first specialist in mental disorders to examine the king. His diagnosis was encouraging, a complete recovery could be expected, though the treatment should continue unchanged. Initially, Pitt was cautious. Addington's was only one opinion in eight, it would be premature to be too optimistic. Better to let the Whigs live with their illusions for a little longer, and for the prince to continue entertaining his expectations at Brooks's, where members had adopted the habit of referring to a court card as The Lunatic. Only time would resolve the issue, and Pitt played for time, but with growing confidence that given the king's recovery he would, after all, win out.

On 4 December, and heavily dosed with laudanum, Fox was in his place in the Commons to hear a report on the king's illness from the Privy Council, who had examined the royal doctors. The prognosis was hopeful, yet inconclusive, and six days later Pitt moved for a committee of the House to examine precedents relating a Regency. By now the minister's tactics were plain – to delay, and delay, and delay again – and Fox was quick to mock the proposal. The House knew well enough that no such precedents existed, while:

> There is here among us an heir apparent, of full age and capacity to take upon him the royal authority. In my opinion the Prince of Wales possesses as clear a right to assume the reins of Government, and to exercise the sovereign power during His Majesty's incapacity, as he would have in case of a natural demise.

The remark was a gift to Pitt. With the aside that now he would 'unwhig the gentlemen for ever', he rose to advance the rights of Parliament against those of the Crown, for 'The assertion of such a right, either in the Prince of Wales or any other individual, is little less than treason to the constitution.' Fox, for so long the critic of prerogative, was hoist by his own petard and while, two days later, he was to accept that the prince's right to the Regency ultimately turned on the verdict of the Commons and the Lords, the damage was beyond repair. As *The Times* reported, Fox's statement had shown up the Whigs for what they were, men born to mislead.

Although aware of his growing unpopularity out-of-doors, Fox none the less remained confident, writing to Liz Armistead on 15 December: 'We shall have some hard fights in the House of Commons this week and next, in some of which I feel that we shall be beat; but whether we are or not, I think it certain that in about a fortnight we shall come in . . . . The King himself (notwithstanding the reports which you may possibly hear) is certainly worse, and perfectly mad. I believe that the chance of his recovery is very small indeed.'

In this he was the victim of his own wishful thinking, for while Pitt deployed his majorities to block effective progress on the Regency issue, the king was showing gradual yet marked signs of improvement, in spite of the savage treatment meted out to him. Behind locked doors in his room at Kew, and often tied down on his bed, George was subjected to a regime of purging and leeching, leeching and purging to the point where his equerry once heard him praying piteously 'that either God be pleased to restore him to his senses, or permit that he might die immediately'. By January, however, sanity was returning, if still punctuated by spells of irrationality, and the Whigs were in growing disarray.

A sick man himself, a debate in mid December had to be postponed because he was too weak to reach the House, Fox was ordered to Bath by his doctors in February, leaving his party in the Commons virtually leaderless. Not that it made a great deal of difference. While an emasculated Regency Bill was passed by the House on 12 February, discussions on the bill in the Lords were postponed until the following week when it was announced that George III was now convalescent. The crisis was over, and on 23 February the king was to write: 'It is with infinite satisfaction that I renew my correspondence with Mr Pitt.'

It is unlikely that Fox missed the irony. Once again, it seemed that the positions were reversed, the Duchess of Devonshire reporting that in recent months Pitt had become 'almost the republican', while as for Fox, his public reputation was again in ruins and his party close to collapse – and all this when England had so recently been celebrating the Glorious Revolution of 1688. A century before, the Whigs had known what they were about, but now they had resorted to 'that habitual spirit of despondency and fear that characterises the party', though there were indications, however slight, that the old humour was not entirely lost.

A scatter of Revolution Societies throughout England had celebrated the centenary of William III's landing at Torbay with 'uncommon festivities', and the powerful London Society had not only decided to organize the friends of liberty on a more effective basis, but also to codify its principles turning on a belief in the sovereignty of the people, the liberty of conscience, the right to trial by jury, and the freedom of the press. When set against Pitt and his carefully marshalled power it was only a small beginning, but for Fox the society's newly drafted constitution expressed much of his own political creed.

For two decades Fox had been a radical in the making, two decades during which he had outlived his extravagant past and learned by his mistakes where his future lay. And there had been mistakes enough. The Shelburne ministry, the North coalition, the Regency crisis, all were open to interpretation, defying absolute conclusions – right or wrong. Yet if each was an error on Fox's part, they did nothing to disguise the growing coherence of his political views. The American war ('All the late American acts are tending to increase the power of the Crown, and to demolish the rights of the people'); the India Bill ('If he should fall in this, he should fall in a great and glorious cause, struggling . . . for the people of Great Britain and India, for many, many millions of souls'); and the contest between Crown and Commons ('Here Ministers played the double part, enslaving the Commons into obedience to the Crown'), had taught Fox the nature of power – and if, on 5 November 1788, he had raised a glass to the Glorious Revolution of 1688, he can have had little idea of the part he was to play in the revolution still to come.

8

'The Majesty of the People'

The morning of Tuesday, 5 May 1789 was sunlit and warm, though the 1200 deputies gathering at the Salle des Menus Plaisirs du Roi at Versailles found the place cold and noisome, as if long unused. They had been summoned for eight o'clock, but it was past midday before Louis XVI appeared to open the first meeting of the Estates General to be held since 1614 with a warning that an exaggerated desire for change seemed to be abroad which, unless handled with wisdom and moderation, 'might completely pervert public opinion'. The applause was dutiful, though not prolonged, and after further speeches the Estates adjourned until the following day.

Unbeknowingly, the French Revolution had begun, though news of the assembly caused little stir when it reached London three days later. Perhaps Louis was finally coming to accept that there was something to Voltaire's advocacy of a mixed constitution on the English model, that 'masterpiece of legislation' according to Montesquieu. If so, only time would tell; meanwhile Fox had other business to hand. Late on the morning of the 8th, after meeting a deputation of Dissenting ministers, he rode to the House to support a motion for the abolition of the Test and Corporation Acts. Twenty years previously he had been strongly opposed to lifting the harsh proscriptions placed on Dissenters, but, as with so much else, that too had changed, though not simply on grounds of expediency.

Always mindful of the vote of the Lords Spiritual, Pitt again opposed the motion, maintaining that an Established

Church was a political necessity. Fox disagreed. Some distinction had to be drawn between religious beliefs and civil government, no government having the right to inquire into a man's private opinions on the grounds that at some point in the future he might act on them. Indeed, for government to say 'As you think, so you must act' was as mischievous as it was tyrannical.

The following morning the press were complimentary to Fox, although the motion had been voted out. The bogey of Dissent, of the possibility that given their civil rights Dissenters might challenge the authority of the Established Church, was too much for the conscience of members, and they were quick to follow North and Pitt into the opposition lobby, while Burke stayed away from the House. His absence was significant. In the previous couple of years there had been growing differences between Fox and his long-time mentor as to the management of Whig affairs, though on 12 May Burke was quick enough to join Fox and Pitt in support of Wilberforce's proposal that a committee of the Commons examine his report on the slave trade.

Twelve months before, the House had received more than a hundred petitions demanding the abolition of the trade, while from France the Marquis de Lafayette had written to the Whigs offering his full support in effecting 'the destruction of a traffick so disgracing to Mankind'. Possibly it was this that Fox had in mind when damning 'a trade in flesh that was so scandalous that it was to the last degree infamous', or possibly it was news of the more recent events at Versailles: 'If there was any great and enlightened nation now existing in Europe, it was France, which was as likely as any nation on the face of the globe, to act on the present subject with warmth and enthusiasm.'

Only a week had passed since the Estates General had assembled, yet it seemed that Fox was already moderating his traditional hostility, not so much to France as to her government. The Bourbons still ruled, but driven by financial necessity their absolutism had been breached. All that remained to be seen was what would emerge, and dismissing the jeremiad that the most dangerous moment for an authoritarian government is the moment at which it begins to reform, Fox rested his hopes for the future on the verities of the *philosophes,* and the moderation of men such as Lafayette and Condorcet. In an age of reason, reason must out.

And the news from Paris was certainly encouraging. By mid June, tired of the obstructive tactics of the nobility and the clergy who formed the first two Estates, the 600 deputies of the Third Estate, representing the Commons, declared that 'the General Will of the people, expressed in a National Assembly, can and must draw up a Constitution'. With its echo of Rousseau, the upper houses might have been cautious of the general will, but by 19 June a majority of the clergy, together with eighty nobles, had joined the new Assembly.

The conservatives at Court were not inactive, however. On 20 June, Versailles was placarded with notices announcing a *séance royale* for the 22nd, and the Chamber of the Third Estate was closed on the pretext of preparing for the royal session. The deputies were undeterred. They moved to the royal tennis court and, with only one dissenting vote, took a solemn oath that the Assembly would go on meeting 'wherever circumstances may dictate, until the Constitution of the Realm is set up and consolidated on firm foundations'.

The king had two alternatives: either to make significant concessions to the Assembly, or to side with the reactionary party in Court. He compromised, fatally. At the *seance royale* on the 22nd, he produced his own reform programme (parliamentary control of taxation, reform of the law, freedom of the press, internal free trade), but closed the session with the veiled threat that he might well dissolve the assembly altogether. The response was immediate, the Comte de Mirabeau asserting: 'We will not move from our places here except at the point of a bayonet.' The impasse was complete. Either the king or the Assembly must stand down – and on 27 June Louis accepted the Assembly's terms.

That night Paris was *en fête*, while Versailles issued marching orders to six regiments to concentrate around the capital. Reaction was on the move. Four days later a further ten regiments were ordered to deploy around Paris (a move denounced by Mirabeau as counter-revolutionary), and by 11 July Louis had exiled virtually all his liberal ministers. The following day Paris heard of their dismissal, and, allied to the troop concentration around the city, this reinforced growing suspicions of a Court conspiracy against the National Assembly and the hopes it represented.

That afternoon there was a clash between German cavalry and a crowd on the Place Louis XV, and by the morning of the 14th rumours of an imminent attack on Paris were widespread. Barricades began to appear on the streets; a search for weapons was organized; word went abroad that the arms and ammunition stored at the Arsenal had been transferred to the Bastille; a march to the fortress began; a volley of grape shot swept the Faubourg Saint-Antoine; a hundred of the crowd fell, and the assault on the fortress began. By late afternoon the Bastille had fallen and its seven prisoners released.

Paris was tense that night. The fall of the Bastille might be regarded as near miraculous, but how would the king react? At Versailles, Louis went to bed after hearing all that had happened, but could think of nothing more to write in his diary than: 'Rien'. The crisis had robbed him of a day's sport, he had taken neither a stag nor a boar. At his *levee* the following morning, Louis was inclined to dismiss the events of the previous day. 'Is this a rebellion?' he asked the Duc de la Rochefoucauld-Liancourt. 'No sire', replied the duke 'this is a revolution', and while the Comte d'Artois advised him to flee to the protection of the troops that remained loyal, the queen began burning her papers, packing her jewels.

Indecisive as ever, Louis remained to compromise with the National Assembly. On the 15th he ordered the withdrawal of all troops from Paris, and the following day rode into the city to announce the recall of his liberal ministers. With a tricolour cockade pinned to his hat, Louis mounted the great staircase of the *Hôtel de Ville* to cries of 'Vive le Roi' from an ecstatic crowd, and for the Comte d'Estaing to whisper 'Sire, with that cockade and the Third Estate you will conquer Europe.'

186

The following day, the British Ambassador, the Duke of Dorset, was reporting in his dispatch to Pitt:

> Thus, my Lord, the greatest revolution we know anything of has been effected with the loss of very few lives; from this moment we may consider France as a free country, the King as a very limited Monarch, and the Nobility as reduced to a level with the rest of the country.

The summary was representative of a broad spectrum of liberal opinion. From Paris, Thomas Jefferson, now US Minister to France, was writing to his long-time friend Tom Paine in London: 'a tranquillity is now established here and tolerably well throughout the kingdom, and I think there is now no possibility of anything hindering their final establishment of a good constitution'. Fox agreed, entirely: 'How much the greatest event it is that ever happened in the world, & how much the best', while even Pitt considered that 'the present convulsions of France must sooner or later terminate in general harmony and good order'. Only one man of any political standing disagreed – Edmund Burke.

At 60 years of age, Burke was rapidly loosing his political faith. It was not so much he that was leaving the party, more that the party was leaving him. Within months of the opening of the Hastings's trial, Sheridan had remarked that he wished 'Hastings would run away, and Burke after him', and now here was Fox drumming up the events in France. Sheridan was bad enough, the pedant in Burke finding his theatricality insufferable, but it was Fox that concerned him most.

For a quarter of a century the inspired, yet increasingly irrascible Irishman had cast himself in the role of guardian of the Whig conscience, formulating a philosophy designed 'To bring the dispositions that are lovely in private life into the service and conduct of the commonwealth; so to be patriots, as not to forget we are gentlemen'. An elitist formula, of power legitimized by paternalism, it was admirably suited to the tastes of the Whig grandees of Rockingham's generation, but since Rockingham's death it seemed that Fox and his acolytes had been sapping at the foundations not so much of

Burke's, but of their own patrimony. No question, they still paid lip service to the old order, still drank to the Glorious Revolution, and yet. . . .

When the House broke for the summer, Fox retired to the delights of St Anne's Hill, while at his country seat at Beaconsfield, Burke brooded darkly on the future. The news from France was mixed. The countryside remained unsettled, but Paris appeared calm, while at Versailles the Assembly had already begun to draft a constitution that recognized nothing as valid, only reason's right. The notion sounded well enough in theory, but in practice what were the principles that were so quickly being transmuted into the doctrine of the Rights of Man?

An echo of the American Declaration, their appeal was seductive ('Men are born free and always continue free, and equal in respect of their rights. . . .The end of all political associations is the preservation of the natural and imprescriptible rights of man'), but for Burke they struck at the very heart of good government, of constitution building in the abstract. For to Burke the past was sacrosanct. It was only there, in the weave and warp of history, that true reason could be found, it only being necessary to adapt at the margins (as with his own plan for economical reform) to safeguard the core. Yet now these new metaphysicians, besotted by their *philosophe,* were standing reason on its head in the hope of building a future by abandoning the past.

The notion was absurd, denying reason itself, and by October it seemed that events in France were already bearing out Burke's worst fears. Although there had been a good harvest, there were growing food shortages in Paris, commentators reporting that there was 'serious suffering from want of bread'. And while the capital grew restless for supplies, it seemed that the Court at Versailles was once again conspiring against the revolution. The Flanders regiment had been ordered into the town, allegedly to reinforce the local guard, but on 1 October at a dinner held for the garrison the national cockade was trampled under foot as the regimental band played *'O Richard, O mon Roi, l'univers t'abandonne'* and ladies of the Court distributed the white cockade of the Bourbons.

Five days later, as the National Assembly met to learn that Louis XVI was still refusing to promulgate sections of the proposed constitution, the women of Paris began a march to Versailles to represent their own grievances to the king. The next twenty-four hours were confused – elements of the crowd broke into the palace; Marie Antoinette, half dressed, fled to her husband's room in fear of her life; the king appeared on a balcony above the courtyard to cheers of 'Vive le Roi' – but by the morning of the 6th order had been restored, thanks, in part, to Louis's undertaking that he, the queen and their children would return to Paris with their 'good and faithful subjects'.

Burke was sceptical. The rights of man or, in this case, of woman, may have been unleashed on the march to Versailles – but what of the rights of kings? By mid October he was writing to a correspondent in Paris:

> You may have made a revolution, but not a reformation. You may have subverted monarchy, but not recovered freedom. . . . You are now to live in a new order of things, under a plan of government of which no man can speak from experience. . . . You have theories enough concerning the rights of man; it may not be amiss to add a small degree of attention to their nature and disposition. . . . Great powers reside in those who make great changes. Their own moderation is their only check; and if this virtue is not paramount in their minds, their acts will taste more of their power than of their wisdom.

Haunted by his imaginings, Burke was virtually alone with his fears. The world would heed him soon enough, but in the meantime Wordsworth dreamt his dreams on Westminster Bridge, Fox proposed a toast 'To the Majesty of the People', and on 4 November Dr Richard Price, a Unitarian divine, spoke at a dinner of the Revolution Society in the city, and contemplated: 'I have lived to see the rights of man better understood than ever; and nations panting for liberty which seemed to have lost the idea of it.' The

Society immediately adopted an address of congratulation to the National Assembly, the first of a flood of compliments addressed to the French by English reformers.

Inspired by events in France, the radical movement, largely quiescent for more than half a decade, was stirring again. Hesitantly at first, but with burgeoning confidence, clubs and societies formed or re-formed. While varying widely in their social composition, they shared common cause in their admiration for the French experiment, and their demand for reform closer to home, the young Francis Place writing: 'The Revolution. . .induced men to look beyond mere party struggles. It taught them to despise the jugglery of party.'

When the House returned in January 1790, Fox must have wondered at Place's comment. The débâcle of the 1784 election, followed by five years of fruitless opposition, had seriously tested the political stamina of the Whigs. Once they had mocked Pitt as the Angry boy, but now he appeared invulnerable, while the growing hostility between Fox's two lieutenants, Sheridan and Burke, did not augur well. During the Regency crisis, each had suspected the other's intentions, and now they had divided radically in their interpretation of the recent developments in France. Both powerful figures, and egocentric, their enmity was contagious and threatened the unity of the party itself. For Fox, it was to prove a bruising test of leadership, demanding the subordination of his own, strongly held views in the wider interest of maintaining a credible Opposition.

The first trial came on 6 February with a debate on the army estimates in which Pitt had called for a small increase in the armed forces, to be opposed by Fox who, in his turn, was opposed by Burke. In a tirade that presaged much that was to come, not least, the growing frenzy of his views, Burke raged against the French Revolution. As a political entity it seemed that France was 'expunged out of the system of Europe', while as for the recent declarations of the National Assembly they were little better than 'a sort of institute and digest of anarchy, called the rights of man'. Fox was placatory, he had 'learnt more from his right honourable friend than from all the men with whom he had ever conversed', but Sheridan was not to be put down. Rejecting Burke, Sheridan wondered whether he had now become 'an advocate of despotism', for Burke to reply that from this time on they were 'separated in politics'.

Pitt was delighted, it seemed the Whigs were dividing before his eyes, and that evening a hurried conference was held at Burlington House. Only ten days before, Fox had convened a similar meeting which had ended with Burke fleeing the room, shouting that he would never be reconciled 'to a Man [Sheridan] who maintain'd opinions equally diabolical, ferocious & cruel'. For five hours on the night of the 6th, Burke and Sheridan debated their positions, Fox holding the ring between them, but the outcome was a cholerous as before. At three in the morning, the talks ended in deadlock, with Burke complaining that Sheridan had ambitions on the leadership of the party itself.

As jealous of his standing among the Whigs as Sheridan was conscious of his vanity, Burke was beyond reconciliation. Events in France had crystallized the fundamental differences that existed at the heart of the Whig philosophy. Sooner or later the party would have to decide where its future lay, and while the final rupture might be delayed the outcome became inevitable when Burke flounced out of the meeting at Burlington House in the early hours of 7 February. Compromise was no longer a viable option; it was as much the personalities as the principles involved that were soon to rip the party apart.

Through March and April, the Whig leadership sparred for position – Fox renewing the motion for the repeal of the Test and Corporation Acts, and Burke opposing; Burke opposing a motion for the reform of Parliament maintaining that no sane man would repair his house during the hurricane season, and Fox recommending it with the riposte 'What season was more proper to set about a repair in, than when a hurricane was near?' Ill-fitted by temperament to play the mediator, Fox's temper was sorely tested by Burke's retreat from his former principles. Sure enough, he still continued his pursuit of Hastings, but what of the time when he held that 'although Government certainly is an institution of Divine authority,

191

yet its forms and the persons who administer it, all originate from the people', or, again, when he had quoted Tully to assert '*La populace ce n'est jamais par envie d'attaquer qu'elle se soulève, mais par impatience de souffrir*'.

Then Burke had waxed strongly enough on 'The Causes of the present Discontents', but while the discontents remained Burke himself had changed. No question, this new Burke was eloquent in defence of his new position; and no question, either, that a man had a right to amend his views, yet to Fox it may well have seemed that his former mentor was now unconscionably anxious to exorcise his past – though still laying claim to the Whig inheritance. Ultimately, the situation was untenable, but while impatient for the final breach to occur, Pitt was not without his troubles.

In 1789, the Spanish had seized English merchantmen in protest against the establishment of an English settlement at Nootka Sound, on the west coast of what is now Vancouver Island. For almost a year the dispute was waged through diplomatic channels, but in April 1790, Pitt went to the Commons to raise £1 million credit to fit the navy for war. Fox supported the move wholeheartedly, and after three further months of sabre rattling Spain backed down, conceding the English right to Nootka Sound. Pitt's power play had proved successful, though the experience was to have significant repercussions. Meanwhile, at home the general elections reinforced the ministerial majority.

For a fourth time Fox stood for Westminster, having hoped, if briefly, that the seat would be uncontested. Although he had recently had a good run on the horses, winning 6000 guineas on his filly Seagull at Ascot, the price of his candidature was high, and rising. If there was one seat in the kingdom which Pitt coveted, it was Westminster, and once again Lord Hood stood against Fox, each man agreeing that he would run no other candidates. It was an unsavoury arrangement, and ideally suited to the reforming zeal of Horne Tooke. Fifteen years had passed since the former Vicar of Brentford had launched his diatribe against the Speaker of the House. In the years between he had established himself as a leading figure of the reform movement, and now he offered himself as an independent candidate, inveighing against an aristocratic conspiracy that shared out political spoils 'like thieves divide their booty'.

The polls remained open for three weeks, the Treasury investing heavily in Hood's candidature, and Fox's principle supporters raising £12,000 to defray the expense of 'courting and cajolling, entertaining, and pressing the constituents to vote'. At the close, Fox topped the poll, defeating Hood and Horne Tooke by comfortable margins, and then withdrew to St Anne's Hill for the summer.

It was five years since Liz Armistead had first engaged his affection, five years in which the frustrations of politics had been eased as much by the affection as the sympathetic intelligence of 'Dear Liz'. Both had lived life to the full when young but now, with Fox in his forty-first year, they enjoyed the pleasure of each other's company as much as they had ever enjoyed that of society, one visitor that August writing 'A few days ago I made a visit at St Anne's Hill, and found our blue and buff chief surrounded by the arts, lolling in the shade. Mrs Armistead was with him; a harper was playing soft music; books of botany lying about. . .and thus you see, like Solomon, he is to seek wisdom in the search of herbs and flowers.'

Burke was soon to put an end to Fox's idyll. A half day's ride north of St Anne's he was already completing the final stages of his *Reflections on the Revolution in France*. The first shock of the revolution may have appeared to have abated, a crowd of 300,000 having attended a *Fete de la Federation* in Paris on 14 July 1790, to hear Louis pledge himself to the new constitution, but Burke was now obsessed by his fears. The age of chivalry was passing, to be replaced by 'all the nakedness and solitude of metaphysical abstraction'.

The *Reflections* had one, over-riding goal – to alert Europe to the dangers of revolution and, thus, mobilize the forces of counter-revolution. They made little pretence either at objectivity or formal structure ('I beg leave to throw out my thoughts, and express my feelings just as they arise in my mind'), relying on prescription to extirpate innovation.

The idea of the fabrication of a new government is enough
to fill us with horror and disgust . . . . All the reformations
we have hitherto made have preceded upon the principle of
reference to antiquity . . . . By this means our liberty becomes
a noble freedom. It carries a noble and imposing aspect. It has
a pedigree and illustrating ancestors . . . . We procure reverence to our civil institutions . . . on account of their age, and
on account of those from whom they are descended.

Allowing for modest adaptation, the future for Burke was
to be a repeat performance of the past; against which he
ranged innovation and its spawn, anarchy:

Amidst assassination, massacre, and confiscation, perpetrated or contemplated, they [the National Assembly] are
forming plans for the good of future society . . . . They have a
power given to them, like that of the evil principle, to subvert
and destroy, but none to construct . . . . We are taught to
look with horror on those children of their country who are
prompt rashly to hack that aged parent to pieces, and put
him into the kettle of the magicians, in the hope that by their
poisonous weeds and wild incantations, they may regenerate
the paternal constitution.

Reflections was published on 1 November 1790, and Fox
was quick to recognize its implications. Burke had declared
war not so much on Fox's own position of studied neutrality,
more on the party for which Burke himself had worked for
so long and so hard. Quite deliberately, he was forcing a
showdown within the party, and was reported to be 'in very
good spirits' whenever the book was mentioned, apparently
careless of its consequences.

Within days, Sheridan had promised a reply to Burke, and
while Fox struggled to hold his forces together, the government press mercilessly harried his position ('The *Party* know
not what to do with Edmund – he is as dangerous as a
mine'), and Pitt delighted at the growing disarray among
the Whigs. It was only a matter of time before the party
broke, though his expectations of a final breach were to be
disappointed in the early months of 1791. Due to Fox's firm,

yet conciliatory leadership, the Opposition remained intact and in March it seemed, for an instant, as if Pitt might be in trouble of his own making.

Encouraged by the success of his power play against Spain, Pitt now decided to test the metal of the Russians who had been at war with Turkey for almost three years. Pleading the interest of the Porte, an ultimatum was dispatched to Catherine of Russia demanding the immediate cessation of hostilities, and the restoration of all occupied territories to Turkey, not least the Black Sea fortress of Oczakow which had been taken early in the campaign. On 28 March 1791, Pitt went to Parliament for funds to augment the navy 'to add weight to our representations'. Fox was scathing in reply, first raking Pitt's case for its inconsistencies, then warning of the hazard of going to war for the sake of a single town. The House was impressed, and while the government's majority was safe grave doubts had been sown about the wisdom of Pitt's policy, more especially in the Cabinet, which was seriously split. Britain was in no mood for war.

Two weeks later, a series of resolutions tabled by Charles Grey calling for Britain to preserve the peace were defeated by a much reduced government majority, and Fox was writing to Mrs Armistead that the ministry 'made a terrible figure indeed in the debate'. After six years in opposition, it seemed that the Whigs had at last found a chink in Pitt's hitherto impregnable armour, and on 15 April the Oczakow issue was debated for a third time. Pitt's defence of his policy was as perfunctory as it was evasive, for he had already determined to retreat from his previous position, and for once Fox had a captive, even sympathetic audience when he rose to speak.

Little more than an hour later, whatever advantages he commanded had been lost; destroyed by a short, yet deadly outburst of temper. For almost a year Fox had held his personal feelings in check in the interests of party unity, subordinating his opinions to those of Burke and Sheridan. Always a passionate man, the provocations to speak out had been enormous; none the less, he had played the diplomatic part, placating Burke's pride, reining in Sheridan's extravagances, coaxing the party from day to day with the assurance that they were still capable of beating Pitt if only they stood together. And now, with Oczakow, it seemed that their time had come – until Fox himself made a fatal slip.

After castigating Pitt for his handling of foreign affairs, he turned to reviewing affairs in Europe, more especially, conditions in France:

> With regard to the change of system that had taken place in that country, he knew different opinions were entertained upon the point by different men; he for one admired the new constitution, considered altogether, as the most stupendous and glorious edifice of liberty which had been erected on the foundations of human integrity in any time or country.

As soon as Fox returned to his seat, Burke was on his feet 'in much visible emotion' attempting to catch the Speaker's eye, but was forced to give way to the division that had been called. The outcome of the debate was virtually irrelevant. Fox's brief outburst, and all it implied, had saved Pitt's face. The minister's precipitate retreat over Oczakow was forgotten, over-shadowed by the now imminent breach between Burke and the Whigs. As if orchestrated, the government press concentrated on rumours that Burke was intent on a confrontation with Fox, and on 20 April Fox went so far as to accuse him of being a government agent. The following day, Burke touched briefly on their differences in a debate in the House, and after reflecting that 'however dear he considered his friendship, there was something still dearer in his mind – the love of his country', he promised to enlarge on his theme during the forthcoming debate on the Quebec Bill.

Two weeks were to pass before Burke was to have the opportunity of fulfilling his promise; two weeks in which London was alive with rumours (that Burke was in discussion with Pitt; that Pitt was conniving to set Burke at Fox's throat; that the Whig grandees were desperate to ensure Fox's silence when the Quebec Bill came before the House); and two weeks during which bitterness appeared to corrode Burke's entire being. The elder statesman of Whiggery was determined on a root and branch purge of the party's radical sentiments to 'counteract the Impression which must be produced by Fox's last panegryric on the French Revolution'. The step might be a dangerous one, for all the while Pitt watched and waited, but it was necessary for the well-being of Whiggism itself – and on 6 May Burke rose in his place in the Commons as soon as the Quebec Bill was tabled.

In a garble of logic, he referred first to Canada and then to France, next to America, then to France again: 'The National Assembly had boasted that they would establish a fabric of government which time itself could not destroy . . . . The Assembly now continued nearly two years in possession of the absolute authority they had usurped . . . . They had a King such as they wished, who was no King; over whom the Marquis de la Fayette, chief gaoler of Paris, mounted guard . . . .'

Burke was called to order, Fox rose: 'It seemed that this was a day of privilege, when any gentleman might stand up, select any mark, and abuse any government he chose.' Tempers were fraying, but Pitt remained cool. The confrontation was brewing up nicely, though he could not support a motion that 'dissertations on the French constitution' were out of order – that would blunt the thrust of Burke's attack. As for Fox, it appeared that he was as anxious as Burke himself to bring matters to a head, claiming to be at a loss to understand how anyone who had once defended the 'Rights of Man' in America could now condemn them as 'chimerical and visionary'. Why, it was Burke who had taught him that 'no revolt of a nation was caused without provocation', and no denial by his master would persuade him to repudiate the lesson.

Burke's reply began coolly enough, but his temper was always fissile:

He felt desirous of pointing out the danger of perpetually extolling that preposterous edifice [the French constitution] on all occasions . . . all that was then doing in France could never serve the cause of liberty, but would inevitably tend to promote that of tyranny, oppression, injustice, and anarchy . . . . What principally weighed with him was the danger

197

Plate 2 Fox and Burke – the great falling-out between friends over the French Revolution. Pitt is seated to Burke's left, delighting in the Whigs' troubles; Sheridan is on his feet on Fox's right, calling for 'Order, order . . . .' (Unknown artist, 1791)

that threatened our own government . . . . Were there not clubs in every quarter, who met and voted resolutions of an alarming tendency? . . . A time of scarcity and tumult might come, when the greatest danger was to be dreaded from a class of people, whom he might now term low intriguers and contemptible clubbists.

A gaunt yet commanding figure, Burke then turned on Fox to savage the man who he claimed had 'ripped up the whole course and tenour of his private life'. Grey protested. Burke continued: he had frequently differed from Fox in the past, but this had never interfered with their friendship. On this occasion, however, the case was different. 'It was certainly indiscreet at his time of life to provoke enemies . . . yet if his firm and steady adherence to the British constitution placed him in such a dilemma, he would risk all, and as his public duty and public prudence taught him, with his last breath, exclaim *"Fly from the French Constitution"*.'

Quietly Fox exclaimed that there was no loss of friendship and then to the astonishment of all save, possibly, Pitt, Burke burst out that he knew the price of his conduct: 'He had done his duty at the price of his friend, their friendship was at an end.' Arguably, it was among the greatest shocks of Fox's life. Friendship had been the staple of his political career, yet here was Burke dismissing it as little more than a caprice. Fox wept, and struggling for coherence recalled that since his school days he had been honoured by Burke's friendship, a friendship that had lasted for twenty–five years, through twenty of which they had acted together 'and lived on terms of most familiar intimacy'. Surely so much could not be staked on a single difference? Surely there was more to friendship than that? Lolling back on the Treasury benches, Pitt stole a smile from his limited reserve of good nature. The issue had gone too far for reconciliation. There could be no turning back. The rift between Burke and Fox was simply the prelude to the break up of the Whig party itself.

* * *

If Pitt was elated and Burke temporarily isolated (the only support he received during the debate had come from the government front bench), then Fox was close to despair. Whatever his critics might say, he had sacrificed much in the Whig interest, but the loss of Burke was almost too much to bear: 'You will easily imagine how much I felt the separation from persons with whom I had so long been in the habit of agreeing; it seemed someway as if I had the world to begin anew, and, if I could have done it with honour, what I should best have liked would have been to retire from politics.'

Temporarily, all the old fire had gone. The government's majority was virtually unassailable, the more so since 'the great falling out'. In the following week the press made much of 'Fox versus Burke', one evening paper noting that while both remained Whigs, Burke took the aristocratic part and Fox the republican. The generalization was as glib as it was dangerous, but if Fox hated the extremes equally, he was all too soon to be crushed between them for political opinion in Britain was polarizing rapidly, precipitated by developments in France. In June, Louis XVI's flight to Varenne, leading to the first calls for the establishment of a republic, bolstered the confidence of reaction in Britain. Where, only recently, reform had commanded widespread sympathy, it was now becoming suspect for, once started, where would it end? Perhaps Burke was right to maintain that the best constitutions were 'founded on the wisdom of antiquity, and sanctioned by the experience of time', for as the French were discovering, the problem was to determine exactly where the Rights of Man lay.

And as with the French revolutionaries, so with radicals in Britain. They had no doubts about the need, rather about the nature of reform; existing and emergent political clubs each drafting their own programme of demands. The Society for Constitutional Information, to which Pitt had belonged, and which had been virtually moribund for half a decade, again set about lobbying for the diffusion of political knowledge. The largely working-class London Corresponding Society, founded by the shoemaker Thomas Hardy, and soon to beget imitators throughout Britain, adopted the formula advocated by the Duke of Richmond in 1783 that 'the right of voting universally to every man . . . is the only reform that can be effectual and permanent'. The altogether more aristocratic Association of the Friends of the People, founded by Grey, pressed for a limited extension of the franchise that was finally to find expression in the Reform Bill of 1832, while the long-standing Revolution Societies toasted the Rights of Man and Tom Paine.

The son of an East Anglian staymaker, Paine had emigrated to the colonies in 1774, to play a seminal role in the American war before returning to Europe fired by the radicalism of the Declaration of Independence which he may well have helped to draft. In March 1791, he published the *Rights of Man*, as much a radical testament as a critique of Burke's *Reflections* at which it was directed. The work exploded in the public's consciousness, the Society for Constitutional Information alone ordering 25,000 copies, for Pitt to confess to Lady Hester Stanhope: 'Paine is right, but what am I to do? If I were to encourage Tom Paine's opinions I should have a bloody revolution.'

Rights was to become the touchstone of radical opinion, and the focus of reactionary execration. Pitt may have accepted that Paine was right, after all little more than a decade had passed since he himself had asserted that 'The House of Commons has but a subordinate existence, it is the organ of the people's voice', but his radical enthusiasms were a thing of the past and soon to be publicly expunged by the adoption of coercive legislation to which Burke was to lend his wholehearted support.

On 14 July 1791, a group of Birmingham reformers, mostly from the middle class, and many of them Dissenters, held a dinner to celebrate the fall of the Bastille. It was the trigger for three days of rioting. Under the rallying call of 'Church and King' the mob ran amok through the city, burning down non-conformist chapels, looting the homes of Dissenters, and destroying the laboratory and library of Dr Joseph Priestley, one of the foremost scientists of the day. If not amused, George III was invigorated, writing two days later 'I cannot but feel better pleased that Priestley is the sufferer for the doctrines he and his party have instilled; and that the people see them in their true light.'

Whether the Birmingham riot was actively promoted or not, king and country mobs were soon to become common-place, reaction conspiring to conflate French with English affairs to make a bogey of dissent, whatever its nationality or political aims. And all the while, Burke continued to sap away at the foundations of Whig unity. Since his break with Fox in May, the party had indulged in an orgy of soul-searching, but still remained intact, thanks largely to Fox's determination to continue playing the mediator and hold the middle ground. To Burke in his self-imposed exile the situation was intolerable. He had made his sacrifice, to be met with rejection, and on 1 August he published his *Appeal from the New to the Old Whigs*.

The distinction was as clearly drawn – on the one hand, of a constitution settled by compact that 'no power existing of force can alter'; on the other, of a constitution careless of contractual rights and holding 'that the people are essentially their own rule, and their will the measure of their conduct' – as was the demand it made upon the Whigs to state their position. The challenge had been thrown out, if indirectly, with *Reflections*, had been reiterated on 6 May, and now here it was for a third time – and for a third time Fox refused to be drawn.

Half a lifetime at Westminster, and the lessons of his former mentor, had tempered his impulsiveness. He might weep at his separation from Burke, but the tearaway that had been Fox had gone, replaced by an altogether shrewder politician who recognized the dangers of being drawn further into dispute with a man whose whole, cankered purpose was to divide the party that he had once adorned, and in September Fox set off on his annual round of the great Whig country houses. The party and its managers needed to be steadied, reassured, and at Wentworth and Chatsworth and Holkham Fox talked-up moderation, and if he entered Doncaster to a peal of bells, then York went one better by giving him the freedom of the city 'in token of his brilliant and unrivalled abilities in support of the British Constitution, upon the principles of the Glorious Revolution, of the just rights of every degree of citizen, and the peace, liberty and happiness of mankind'.

Once again, Burke was frustrated, writing that Fox's reception in the north was 'a slap to me'; once again Pitt's hopes of an early dissolution of the Whigs were disappointed; and once again Fox was in his place to lead the Opposition when the Commons reassembled in January 1792. The King's Speech was a mirror image of his own and his Prime Minister's private opinions – both men had growing doubts about developments in France, yet George maintained that the tranquillity of European affairs allowed for a reduction in the armed forces; both men recalled Birmingham, yet George asserted that 'the continued and progressive improvement' in domestic affairs was based on an attachment to a constitution that united 'the inestimable blessings of liberty and order'.

Fox was quick to expose the deceit. After a brief review of foreign affairs, he turned on the claim that liberty and order were well found when king and country mobs could sack the homes of Dissenters meeting to demand a voice in the management of their own affairs:

> It was impossible not to know, and not to lament, that towards the close of the eighteenth century, men, instead of following the progress of knowledge and liberality, had revived the spirit and practice of the darkest and most barbarous ages . . . . Instead of passing over such acts in silence, ought not His Majesty's sentiments to have gone forth applying to them every epithet expressive of abomination? . . . When men were found so deluded as to suppose that their general object was not disagreeable to government . . . it might do much more mischief than Ministers were aware of.

The House was silent, the charge was plain: that tacitly the king and his ministers approved the conduct of the mob in Birmingham on Bastille night 1791, with all that implied for the future. Propelled by developments in France and the consequent revival of the reform movement in Britain, the pattern of action and reaction was taking shape; the king,

Pitt and their majority defending the constitutional status quo by whatever means they thought appropriate against the radicals' generally modest demands for reforming the franchise.

As if anticipating much of what was to come, more especially the fine tuning of the judiciary, Fox had introduced a Libel Bill in the previous parliamentary session. It was consistent with all that he had represented since the death of Lord Holland – his championship of the colonists, and his prosecution of Warren Hastings; his support for the abolition of slavery, and his opposition to the Test and Corporation Acts; and, most notably, his defence of the people against prerogative – and it remains one of the two major pieces of legislation for which Fox was directly responsible.

Some years before, Lord Mansfield had ruled that the question of whether a publication was libellous was a pure question of law, to be decided by the judges, the jury only having to decide whether or not the defendant had published it. The ruling, a reversion to the practices of the Star Chamber according to one leading jurist, challenged the whole concept of trial by jury, and with Pitt's support, Fox's bill to correct the abuse was passed as a Declaratory Act in 1792 – within weeks of the ministry issuing a Royal Proclamation against 'divers wicked seditious writings'.

In late February, Tom Paine published the second part of his *Rights of Man*, subsequently to become one of the best-sellers of all time. To Burke, once again among the targets of Paine's polemic, it was too much. The man should be put away, and already careless of the 'progressive improvement' in domestic affairs, Pitt agreed. The radical movement, for all the constraint of its demands, was growing apace. Within months of its foundation, the London Corresponding Society had attracted more than 12,000 members at a subscription of a penny a week, while Grey's Association of the Friends of the People was busy canvassing the support of the Quality at a subscription of 5 guineas a year.

Reaction followed events at home and abroad with a horrid fascination. As the old marching song had it, it seemed that the world was being turned upside down, and while

Burke infected Pitt with new and dark forebodings, Grey introduced a bill for parliamentary reform against Fox's better advice. In view of the government's commanding majority, he felt that such a measure was likely to do more harm than good, but Grey was undeterred. The franchise was rotten through and through, latest evidence showing that seventy-one peers and ninety-one commoners returned more than 300 members to the Commons, and on 30 April Grey gave notice that he intended to introduce a Reform Bill in the coming session of parliament – reminding Pitt and Fox that they had both declared themselves 'unequivocably on the subject'.

Pitt rose to the taunt; there was a suspicion abroad that the motion for reform 'was nothing more than the preliminary to the overthrow of our whole system of present government', and Fox was lukewarm. Only the month before he had written to a long-standing friend: 'You seem to dread the prevalence of Paine's opinions, while I am much more afraid of the total annihilation of all principles of liberty & resistance . . . . We both hate the two extremes equally, but we differ in our opinions with respect to the quarter from which the danger is most pressing.' Almost twenty years had passed since he had first challenged executive power, but now it was not so much the mood of the Commons that discouraged him from taking a strong line on reform, more the recognition that by declaring wholeheartedly for Grey and his friends he would compromise his hard won role as mediator among the Whigs.

His discretion was to do him little good, Burke interrupting his speech to rail against any notion of reform; and the king later remarking that as Fox had spoken in support of the motion, it made little difference if he was a friend of the people or not for 'if men are to be found willing to overturn the Constitution of this Country, it is most providential that they so easily cast off the mask'.

George. Pitt. Burke. All were now infected by the virus of fear, but uncertain where the greatest danger lay – from out-of-doors, with Paine and his popular writings, or from within the Commons itself, with Grey and his more radical friends. Since the King's Speech in January it seemed that there had been a remarkable shift as much in the state of the nation as in the government's views, and on 25 May came the Royal Proclamation against seditious practices aimed, on the one hand, at stamping out pamphleteers like Paine, and on the other hand, at exploiting the widening breach between the opposing wings of the Whig party.

Opposing the measure in the Commons, Fox had no doubt about the proclamation's purpose:

> The plain intention of this proclamation was to strive to make a division between that great body of united patriots, know by the name of the Whig interest . . . . It was not a republican opinion that we had to dread in this country; there was no tincture of republicanism in the country. If there was a prevailing tendency to riot, it was on the other side. It was the high church spirit, and the indisposition to all reform, which marked more than anything else, the temper of the times.

Events were to bear him out. During the summer, 'king and country' mobs rampaged throughout the country, taking Paine as their prime target. In Lincoln he was hung in effigy 'amidst a vast multitude of spectators', in Leeds his image was whipped through the streets, while one small village reported that the executioner's hands 'ran with blood' from pounding a caricature of Paine to pieces. But if Pitt and his agents drummed up reaction out-of-doors, they played an altogether more subtle game at Westminster. The Royal Proclamation had been successful in building on Burke's foundations to create further dissension in the Whig ranks, the right of the party voting with the government. It was clear that the old alliance of interests was becoming increasingly unstable.

What better time for Pitt to reinforce his own ministry by holding out the temptations of office to the more conservative elements in the party, thus condemning the radicals to virtually permanent opposition? Certainly, the mood among the Whig grandees was sympathetic to such a junction – a sentiment carefully nurtured by Burke. At a meeting in

Burlington House in early June, Burke held that by his support for the revolution in France, for reform, for the abolition of the Test and Corporation Acts, and for much else besides, Fox had forfeited his right to lead the Whigs in the Commons, and that in the present, troubled times 'A union of all the abilities, and all the weight of this country was necessary.'

Whether Burke was playing Pitt's game or not, the party's titular head, Portland, and the talented but devious Loughborough liked the sound of his words. Grey and his friends were becoming an embarrassment. The old guard had had enough of reform. Well aware of the divide, Pitt exploited it skilfully to create further dissent among the Whig hierarchy, but if Portland was keen for a coalition, he was equally anxious to maintain his party intact. Always indecisive, he now found himself trapped between two, seemingly irreconcilable demands, and turned to Fox for advice.

Initially the response was encouraging. Fox appeared to welcome a coalition ('It was so damned right . . . that I cannot help thinking it must be'), but with the caveat that the new ministry was headed up by a neutral man, and that both offices and patronage were equally shared. Portland was as quick to grasp that such terms would be intolerable to Pitt, as Fox was as quick to reappraise his position. Albeit implicitly, what was being asked of him was to desert such friends as Fitzpatrick and Grey, men who shared his comradeship at Brooks's and whose company he relished at St Anne's Hill. It was too high a price to pay for an arrangement with Pitt. No question, if the divide were to come he would have to make the choice, meanwhile he set about convincing Portland that Pitt had only entered into the negotiations in order to break the Whigs. By the close of June, Fox's strategy was successful. The talks were broken off.

Having exposed the rift among the Whigs, however, Pitt was not discouraged. The party was close to disintegration, and events in France during the summer of 1792 did nothing to allay the suspicions of its grandees that the friends of the people were agents of subversion closer to home. In April, Austria had declared war on France, and on 1 August the Duke of Brunswick, commanding the Austrian forces already deep inside French territory, issued a manifesto threatening to 'deliver up Paris to military execution and complete destruction' if any violence was offered to Louis XVI or his queen. Recognizing its danger, Louis repudiated the manifesto, but the damage was done, one deputy proclaiming: 'The moment the danger exists, every Citizen is a soldier'. The theory of revolutionary nationalism, of the defence of revolution by a nation in arms was born. Three days later, all but one of the Paris sections petitioned for the deposition of the king, and within the fortnight Louis was deposed and imprisoned with his family in the Temple.

Between racing at Newmarket and relaxing at St Anne's Hill, Fox followed developments closely. The Brunswick manifesto horrified him, and he was alarmed at the arrest of the king ('It seems as if the Jacobins had determined to do something as revolting to the feelings of mankind as the Duke of Brunswick's proclamation.'), but he applauded the later defeat of Brunswick by French arms at Valmy: 'No! No public event excepting Saratoga and Yorktown, ever happened that gave me so much delight.'

Portland, however, placed a very different interpretation on events. It seemed that Burke's worst fears were being realized, that the revolution was running out of control, and Pitt was alert to play on the already frayed nerves of the Whig grandees. Since the failure of the previous negotiations, he had discreetly stage-managed the growing confusion in the party, flattering their innate vanity (in July, Portland was offered the Order of the Garter), and cosseting their taste for power.

By August, coalition talks had been reopened – but again, Fox was the sticking point, for again he insisted that Pitt quit the Treasury if terms were to be agreed. It was an impossible demand which the king would never accept, but while the negotiations had broken down by the end of the month, Pitt had again tested the nerve of the Whigs. The only question that remained to be answered was how long Portland could withstand such pressure, how long he and his more conservative colleagues could resist the temptations of office in defence of a radical position for which they no longer had any heart?

They might be an unconscionable time about it, but eventually the Whigs must break, and as the year advanced Fox's position became progressively more difficult. In France, conditions appeared to be degenerating rapidly, 1200 prisoners in seven Paris gaols being slaughtered by the mob in September, while in London Grey and his friends intensified their campaign for parliamentary reform, to the growing consternation of Portland and the grandees. And all the while Pitt awaited his opportunity. Eighteen months had passed since Burke had first breached the Whig position, six since he himself had exploited the breach; all that was now needed was patience aided, as required, by political stratagem.

On 1 December Pitt issued a proclamation calling up the militia on the ground of 'acts of riot and insurrection'. Fox was incensed: 'None of our friends have sanctioned this most detestable measure, and I hope none will.' He was too optimistic. Burke was already at Portland's ear, and if he did not have material enough for mischief making on the 1st, he had more than enough on the 5th. On the previous evening, at the recently formed Whig Club, Fox had toasted the House of Brunswick rather than the king, explaining that he would never forget the principles which had placed the Hanoverians on the throne:

> For the same reason, I am attached to the *Constitution, according to the principles asserted at the Revolution* . . . .
> It follows, therefore, that I am, and I declare myself to be an advocate *for 'The Rights of the People'*, upon whose rights alone can, in my opinion, be founded any real, sound, and legitimate government, since the very end and object of all just government is the SECURITY, FREEDOM, AND HAPPINESS OF THE PEOPLE.

Burke was delighted, Portland was furious, and Pitt was quick to exploit this new advantage. He offered Portland a preview of the King's Speech for the opening of parliament, and on 12 December the Whigs peers agreed to accept the address without opposition. As the meeting broke up early on the morning of the 13th, Fox arrived to inform those who remained that he strongly disapproved of their decision, declaring with an oath 'that there was no address at this moment Pitt could frame, he would not propose an amendment too, and divide the House upon'.

Twenty-four years a politician, Fox must have known where his ultimatum would lead. The Whigs were dividing against themselves; soon the choice of friendships would have to be made. Burke had worked his phantasms well, for he no longer lived alone with them. Carefully fostered by the right, from 10,000 pulpits and as many country seats, they were coming to haunt England as well, and if Fox himself deplored the growing violence in France, he was equally troubled by the growing reaction at home. All he had long represented now seemed at risk, not least the lesson that he had learned from Burke twenty, no, nearer to thirty years before:

> If ever the time should come when this House shall be found prompt to execute, and slow to inquire; ready to punish the excesses of the people, and slow to listen to their grievances . . . ready to invest magistrates with large powers, and slow to inquire into the exercise of them; ready to entertain notions of the military power as incorporated in the constitution – when you learn this in the air of St James's, then the business is done, then the House of Commons will change that character which it receives from the people only.

That was Burke as he should be remembered, and it was time that his words were remembered again. On the afternoon of 13 December Fox rose in his place in the Commons to table an amendment to the King's Speech. The time for compromise had passed, as much for the sake of his own integrity as that of the party which he had served for so long. In contrast to the bland assurances of less than twelve months before, the ministry was now claiming that Britain was in an insurrectionary mood, that there was a spirit of tumult and disorder abroad which could only be contained by force:

An insurrection! Where is it? Where has it reared its head? Good God, an insurrection in Britain! No wonder the militia were called out . . . . But where is it? Two gentlemen have delivered sentiments in commendation and illustration of the speech; and yet, though this insurrection has existed for fourteen days, they have given us no light whatever, no clue, no information where to find it . . . . I will take it upon me to say, sir, that it is not the notoriety of the insurrections which prevents these gentlemen from communicating to us the particulars, but their non-existence.

Behind him, the Opposition shifted uneasily. Fox was going too far, but for Burke he could go as far as he liked if it would finally expose those 'unclean spirits' of dissent and reform, those dark and metaphysical vapourings that threatened the soul of the party itself. For too long Fox had dissembled, allowing the Whigs to escape the decision that had to be made, but now he dissembled no longer:

But what are the doctrines they [the government] desire to set up? That Englishmen are not to dare to have any genuine feelings of their own; that they must not rejoice but by rule; that they must not think but by order; that no man shall dare to exercise his faculties . . . but according to the instructions he shall receive . . . . So then, by this new scheme of tyranny, we are not to judge of the conduct of men by their overt acts, but to arrogate to ourselves at once the province and the power of the Deity; we are to arraign a man for his secret thoughts, and to punish him because we choose to believe him guilty! What innocence can be safe against such power?

An echo of his speech to the Whig Club a fortnight before, it delighted Grey and Pitt in equal parts; the former because there could be no further question about where Fox's sympathies lay, the latter, because he could see, at last, an end to his long struggle to break the Whigs. After this, there could be no retractions, for what was he saying now:

Our constitution was not made, thank God, in a day. It is the result of gradual and progressive wisdom but . . . now it seems the constitution is complete. Now we are to stand still.

211

Plate 3 Pitt (left, backed by Dundas) feigns shock at Burke's (right) allegation that daggers are being issued to English jacobins. Fox (centre) looks on horrified, as Sheridan whispers over his shoulder. (Gillray, 1792)

We are to deride the practice and wisdom of our forefathers; we are to elevate ourselves with the constitution in our hands, and to hold it forth to a wondering world as a model of human perfection. Away with all further improvement, for it is impossible! Away with all further ammelioration for the state of man in society, for it is needless.

And for those who questioned this doctrine, what of them? Only the previous day one of Portland's closest allies had confided that England was quieter than usual, and the Scottish insurrection had consisted of planting a Liberty Tree in Perth, yet the proclamation of 1 December demanded near absolute power to stamp out this figment of Dissent:

What have you done? Taken upon you by your own authority to suppress them – to erect every man not merely into an inquisitor, but into a judge, a spy, an informer – to set father against father, brother against brother . . . and in this way you expect to maintain the peace and tranquillity of this country! You have gone upon the principles of slavery in your proceedings; you neglect in your conduct the foundation of all legitimate government, the rights of the people; and, setting up this bugbear, you spread a panic for the very purpose of sanctifying this infringement, while the infringement engenders the evil which you dread.

The thing was done. At three in the morning the House divided, only fifty members voting with Fox (among them Sheridan and Grey, Lord George Cavendish and Lord John Russell, the advocate Thomas Erskine, the brewer Samuel Whitbread, and the putative Junius, Philip Francis), to give Pitt a 240 vote majority. As Fox's old friend Gibbon remarked: 'He uttered everything his worst enemy could wish. Every man in the street asked, Is he mad?' Many Whigs believed so, but Burke had another explanation. At a meeting of the Whig grandees at Burlington House later in the week he suggested that Fox had been seduced by ambition and come to believe 'that a government like ours is not a proper one for great talents to display themselves in'.

When the meeting closed, Portland remained 'benumbed

and paralysed' for two hours, shocked by the advice of his friends that there should be no further delay in breaking with Fox. A week later, with Portland still undecided, Sir Gilbert Elliot took matters into his own hands. On 28 December he informed the Commons that he had the Duke's permission to announce Portland's disassociation from Fox. The blow was as bitter as his separation from Burke, and he was to write to Liz Armistead that evening: 'I cannot help loving the D. of P, and if with him the Duke of Devonshire & Lord Fitzwilliam are to go, I never can have any comfort in politics again.'

The note made no mention of Burke's performance in the Commons that same afternoon. In a histrionic gesture, he had pulled a dagger from his coat, thrown it on the floor of the House, all the while raging: 'This is what you are to gain by an alliance with France. Wherever their principles are introduced, their practices must follow.' The irony cannot have escaped Fox, that in defence of his own, now fevered principles, Burke had helped cut down the party whose love he had once claimed.

9

'God Almighty Made That Man'

Save for the eyes, there is little to distinguish Karl Anton Hickel's portrait of Fox from a gallery of similar works of the late eighteenth century. The rest may be a cliché, but the eyes are different, dark images of hurt and bewilderment. Thirty years had passed since Reynolds had painted the young Etonian, self-possessed and arrogant, but all that had changed. The surety has gone, and against an idyllic backcloth of a small country house set amid hills and trees, the portly, middle-aged Fox gazes into the middle distance, as if wondering at all he has lost – the hopes he had held, and the friends with whom he had shared them.

On 24 January 1793, Fox celebrated his forty-fourth birthday, and the defection from the Whigs had already begun. Slowly at first, but in increasing numbers they hurried to make their peace with Pitt. The hurt was deep, that they could abandon all they had represented for so long, and yet perhaps the cause was in himself. Possibly Burke had been right, and what passed for principles were in fact only vanities and that he, too, was covetous of power. Possibly there were further compromises that he could have made in the interests of party, though to do so would have been to mock the principles that he had represented since the death of his father almost half a lifetime ago, and in his room in South Street, Mayfair, he re-read the proofs of his *Letter to the Electors of Westminster* which was to be published before the week's end.

For the first time in his political career, Fox was committing himself to print, and the forty-three page pamphlet, which was to run to sixteen reprints before the year was out, was as much a plea for calm against the growing clamour for war with France, as a defence of Parliament against the encroachment of executive power under the pretext of maintaining law and order nearer home. It was to make little difference. The previous Tuesday, Louis XVI had gone to the guillotine in the Place de la Revolution, precursor to the Reign of Terror, and on 1 February, the National Convention declared war on Britain.

Less than a year before, Pitt had been hoping for fifteen years of peace to consolidate the achievements of a programme which, in the previous decade, had transformed the national finances. Where, however, he had proved masterly as Chancellor, he was to prove a pale shadow of his father as a war minister – save in combating dissent at home. The opening campaign of the ill-assorted First Coalition (Prussia, Austria, Spain, Holland, Sardinia and Britain) was damned by indecision, and ended disastrously. Under the command of the Duke of York, an ill-equipped British expeditionary force landed in Holland in late February, and by mid-summer was in full retreat, the young commanding officer of the 33rd Regiment, Lieutenant Colonel Arthur Wellesley, saying later that it was in Flanders that he learned how not to fight a battle.

What Burke's Crusade of Kings lacked abroad, however, was more than compensated for by the growing ferocity of repression in Britain itself. Even before the outbreak of the war, John Reeves had founded the Association for the Protection of Property against Republicans and Levellers to co-ordinate the attack on the reform movement, while the law in the shape of the magistracy was diligent in prosecuting Dissent whatever its form, and wherever it was found. At Plymouth the Reverend William Winterbotham was sentenced to four years imprisonment for preaching that the authority of kings was bounded by laws; in London, several illiterate bill-stickers were imprisoned for six months apiece for posting notices that the London Corresponding Society stood for the purity of the constitution; in Newark a printer was imprisoned for four years for reprinting an address of the Constitutional Society; and in Marylebone, an attorney was sent to the pillory for being overheard to say: 'I am for equality . . . . Why, no King!'

The Sheffield Constitutional Society might insist on a declaration from all new recruits that: 'I solemnly declare myself an enemy of all conspiracies, tumults, and riotous proceedings . . . my only wish and design is for a speedy reformation, and an equal representation in the House of Commons', but it made little difference. The Friends of the People and the London Corresponding Society might protest that their only objective was parliamentary reform, but they protested in vain.

In Britain, as in France, a reign of terror had begun. What had once been an unreasoning fear of reform now found substance in the progress of events in France, and while the revolution degenerated into anarchy, counter-revolution in Britain marshalled all the forces of repression to check what one Whig defector wildly described as the murderous, atheistic, profligate agents of dissent. He was not alone in his views. The Whigs were caught up in the mounting hysteria, and if Fox's position in the debate of December 1792 was not sufficient excuse for their defection, then the war with France was.

Prinny had already abandoned Fox and sought a meeting with Pitt to ensure him of his 'loyal attachment to our present happy Constitution'. He was soon to be followed by twenty-one Whig MPs, while on 20 February a further large group of Portland's supporters quit the Whig Club in protest at what they regarded as Fox's now irredeemably radical views. Carlisle and Fitzwilliam, friends since his school-days; Devonshire and Lord Spencer, so often his companions at Chatsworth House; the mercurial Windham and the trusted Tom Grenville, all had gone – and with them more than sixty others. The king was delighted, not least that his wayward son was back in the royal fold; Pitt was relieved, he had seen off the Whigs at last; and Fox was left with the cold consolation that 'while

the French are doing all in their power to make the name
of liberty odious to the world, the despots [at home]
are conducting themselves so as to show that tyranny is
worse'.

Only a handful in the Commons agreed, though they
were a distinguished and loyal band (among them Sheridan,
Grey, Erskine, Francis, Adam and Whitbread), Thurlow
writing: 'There are but forty of them but every man would
be hanged for Fox.' If certain of the Whigs had had
their way, they could well have been, Lady Malmesbury
remarking that 'As for Fox and Grey, I wish they would
utter treason at once, and be beheaded or hanged', but
as it was the Foxties regrouped to mount a defence
of English liberties against the now massed ranks of a
ministry bent on stamping out any trace of dissent, however mild.

Through March and into April, Fox and Erskine, Fox
and Whitbread, Fox and Adam opposed the Traitorous
Correspondence Bill ('a Bill much better calculated to
entrapping individuals, than for guarding them against
the perils of high treason' according to Fox), and on
7 May Grey again tabled a motion for parliamentary
reform. The whole system, he maintained, was as archaic
as it was corrupt, Cornwall having more MPs than the
combined total of Yorkshire, Middlesex and Rutland,
while the majority of the House was elected by less
than 15,000 people, or a two hundredth part of the
male, adult population. Surely the time had come to
correct such abuses and 'redress the evil' of the
franchise.

Pitt disagreed. Ten years had passed since he had
reminded the freeholders of Cambridge that 'The House
of Commons has but a subordinate existence, it is the
organ of the people's voice', and as many since he
had tabled his own proposals for reform, but now was
not the time for such measures. Tomorrow, possibly,
but not today when even moderation was excited by
the 'violent spirits' of what had passed in France; by
'the wild and illusive' theories of men who talked up

the Rights of Man only to establish the worst sort of despotism.

> In what is called the government of the multitude, they are not the many who govern the few, but the few who govern the many. It is a species of tyranny, which adds insult to the wretchedness of its subjects, by styling its own arbitrary decrees the voice of the people . . . . Such is the nature of those principles connected with the right of individual suffrage.

An echo of Burke, Pitt's defence of the status quo was artfully turned, deliberately confusing the modest demands for parliamentary reform with the spectre of revolution, but even without raising such a bogey he was confident of his majority when he returned to his seat. For almost two days the debate continued, and Fox apologised for the lateness of the hour when he rose to support Grey early in the morning of 9 May, and to mock Pitt for faithlessness to his former principles: 'If the opinions which the right honourable gentleman formerly professed . . . were so very erroneous, and pregnant with such alarming consequences as he now depicted, it was but natural to suppose that he would have . . . expressed humiliation instead of triumph in recapitulating the enormous mischiefs to which his former errors might have exposed the country.'

Time and again Fox taunted the minister with his past, to deride Pitt's defence of established practice:

> If for the essence of our constitution we were to repair to a cottage on Salisbury plain or, for the sake of antiquity more reverend, let us take Stonehenge for Old Sarum; then might we undertake pilgrimages to that sacred shrine, and tell each admiring stranger 'Look not for the causes of our envied condition in the system of our government and laws; here resides the hallowed deposit of all the happiness we enjoy

. . . to expose Pitt's fears of the majority:

True, the majority might sometimes oppress the minority, and the minority might be justified in resisting such oppression, even by force, but as a general rule, though not without exception, the majority in the community must decide for the whole, because in human affairs there was no umpire but human reason . . . . What was the criterion of truth but the general sense of mankind.

. . . to lay the grounds for Fox's claim to the Whig's inheritance:

He was ready to say with Locke, that government originated not only for, but from the people, and the people were the legitimate sovereignty in every community. If such writings as are now branded as subversive of all government had not been read and studied, would the parliament of 1640 have done those great and glorious things, but for which we might be now receiving the mandates of a despot like . . . any other slaves.

Only one thing further needed to be said, that the objection to the timing of the measure was a fallacy: 'This manner of postponing . . . what could not be denied to be fit, was more properly the object of ridicule than argument, the time must come when the House would be unable to disguise, even from themselves, the necessity of inquiring into the state of representation.'

At four in the morning the House divided, and Thurlow's forecast proved correct – forty members voting for Grey's motion, and 282 voting against. It was a foretaste of much that was to come, of voting in small minorities. Little more than a month later Fox's motion for the re-establishment of peace with France collected only forty-seven votes. Writing to his nephew, Lord Holland, Fox compared himself with Sisyphus: 'nothing remains but to get together the remains of our party, and begin . . . to roll up the stone again, which long before it reaches the summit, may probably roll down again'.

But while the majority of Whigs divorced themselves

from Fox the politician, many still admired Fox the man, a committee of the Whig Club 'as respectable as fortune, rank, and character could make it' meeting at the Crown and Anchor Tavern in June 1793 to raise a subscription to relieve him of debt and provide him with an income for the future. Within six months, £61,000 had been raised to settle with his creditors and provide him with an annuity of £2000 a year for life. Nervous of Fox's response, one subscriber wondered to a friend; 'How do you think Fox will take it?', to be told 'Why, quarterly' – which he did, with a charming letter of thanks to all concerned.

The gesture was a handsome one, and more than enough to provide Fox with a comfortable living since he had finally quit gambling, and the subscription list a roll-call of old friends and colleagues (Spencer and Fitzwilliam and Devonshire), though there was one notable absentee – Edmund Burke. In the two years since their separation, Burke's growing horror of political developments had been matched only by his growing animosity to Fox, as if the measures and the man had become fused in his mind. Where, once, there had only been friendship, there was now only enmity envenomed by fear, and while the Whig Club canvassed subscriptions, Burke drafted his *Fifty Four Articles of Impeachment against the Rt Hon C.J. Fox.*

Published in September 1793, the indictment captures much of the tortured nature of Burke's character, at one and the same time craven and arrogant, fawning yet supercilious. For thirty years a party to, but never a fully accepted member of the Whig establishment, Burke may well have secretly envied Fox who represented all that Burke himself would like to have been, and considered that he, too, had been betrayed by what he regarded as Fox's betrayal of the Whigs.

In my journey . . . through life, I met Mr Fox in my road; and I travelled with him very cheerfully as long as he appeared to me to pursue the same direction with those in whose company I set out. In the latter stage of our progress, a new scheme of liberty and equality was produced in the world, which either dazzled his imagination, or was suited to some new walks of ambition, which were then opened to his view . . . .

The evidence mocked the notion. If Fox had ambitions he would have done better to join the hue and cry against reform and settle for a place in Pitt's ministry, but through fifty-four articles and ninety-four pages Burke developed his charge: the horrors of the revolution which Fox espoused were too well known to bear repetition, not least 'the pillage and destruction of the more eminent orders and classes of the community'; the absurdity of Fox's proposal for re-establishing peace, not least on the grounds of non-interference in the domestic affairs of a sovereign state; the dangers of subversion closer to home, not least, of the 'Cabals and Conspiracies of the French Faction in England' to which Fox was a party.

It had all been said before, but now, in a *mélange* of half truths, Fox was cast in the role of the man who, virtually single-handed, was threatening 'the whole Constitution, virtual and actual, together with the safety and independence of this nation, and of the peace and settlement of every state now in the Christian world'. The notion was absurd, the product of a distempered mind, though Fox may well have been entertained to learn that this was where his ambition had been leading since his road had parted from Burke's. True enough, he had ambition, though it bore no resemblance to Burke's imaginings. Abroad he called for peace, which was not to condone the excesses of a revolution that now ruled by terror, while at home he called for reform, which was not to sanction the more extreme demands of the republicans. Better, perhaps, if Burke had looked to the ambitions of the executive with its growing taste for coercion.

Three weeks before the *Articles of Impeachment* appeared, the first treason trial opened in Edinburgh. Late in 1792 a young Scottish advocate, Thomas Muir, had helped to form the Friends of the Constitution and of the People in Glasgow, a society to which no one was admitted without first declaring their allegiance to king, Lords and Commons. In August 1793, Muir was arraigned on charges of sedition, for a trial that was to parody justice – Lord Braxfield, the Lord Justice Clerk, whispering to one juror as he passed behind the bench 'Come awa', Maaster Horner, come awa', and help us to hang ane o' thae damned scoondrels.'

It was the beginning of a charade which was to end with one judge, Swinton, regretting that as torture had been abolished there was no punishment adequate for Muir's offence, and another instructing the jury that the defendant had disguised his ambition for rebellion by talking-up reform, before reminding them that 'A government . . . should be just like a corporation; and in this country it is made up of the landed interest, which alone has a right to be represented.' The outcome was preordained, Muir being sentenced to fourteen years transportation for doing little more than echoing Pitt's sentiments of a decade before.

Within the month, the Reverend T. F. Palmer, a Unitarian minister and fellow of Queens College Cambridge, was sentenced to seven years transportation for recommending Paine to members of the Dundee Friends of Liberty – the 'mildest' of punishments according to the bench. Pitt agreed. He had no doubts about the legality of the Scottish trials, holding that the judges would have been culpable if they had not used their discretionary powers 'for the present punishment of such daring delinquents and the suppression of doctrines so dangerous to the country'. What Fox had long feared was coming to pass; reaction was now animating the whole apparatus of the state.

Even at St Anne's Hill there was no escaping the nightmare, Fox writing towards the year's end:

> There is such a barefaced contempt of principle and justice in every step we take, that it is quite disgusting to think that it can be endured. *France is worse* is the only answer, and perhaps that is true, for the horrors there grow every day worse . . . . At home, we imitate the French as well as we can, and in the trials of Muir and Palmer in particular, I do not think that we fall very far short of the original . . . . You will easily believe that I shall not acquiesce to this tyranny without effort, but I am far from sanguine for success. We live

in times of violence and extremes, and all those who are for creating or even retaining checks upon power are considered as enemies to order.

The King's Speech at the opening of the new session of Parliament in January 1794, was much the same mixture as before, exuding confidence in the progress of British arms abroad, and 'unspeakable satisfaction' at the tranquil condition of domestic affairs, and Fox handled it with much the same, closely reasoned contempt. The origin of the war was now a secondary matter, the object was to conclude it. All were generally agreed upon that, the problem was the terms. The government protested that the war was a defensive one, to protect its allies, but the suspicion was that their real objective was 'the subversion of the ruling power in France'. If these were the only terms acceptable to the ministry and its allies, then their hopes were doomed. He abhorred the conduct of Frenchman to Frenchman as much as any man, of the crimes at which humanity shuddered, but one thing was now abundantly clear:

Whatever have been the contest of parties in France, and whatever the consequences to which they have led, the war has produced in that country not only union, but what is still worse for the allies, a degree of energy which it is impossible to withstand . . . . And if it were not too presumptuous for a man to reckon on his own life, I might say, that I expect to live to see Great Britain treat with that very Jacobin government with which you now refuse to treat – and God grant that it may not be under circumstances less favourable for making peace than the present.

Fox's amendment, that subject to the defence and safety of Britain peace negotiations be opened with France went down by 218 votes. Pitt's juggernaut was on the move, crushing opposition in the House as ruthlessly as dissent out-of-doors. In the next three months, Fox was to speak sixteen times – opposing the quartering of Hessian troops in Britain; supporting a call for an inquiry into the trials of

Muir and Palmer; opposing a proposal to raise volunteer militia without Parliament's consent; supporting a motion for a separate peace with France – and sixteen times he spoke to no effect, Pitt deploying his majority to the point where, by late April, the Foxites could divide only thirty-four votes.

And worse was to come. On 12 May the first report of the Committee of Secrecy was presented to the House. Established to examine papers seized on government orders from the London Corresponding Society and the Society for Constitutional Information, the Committee's findings were as biased as its composition was prejudiced, consisting, as it did, only of Pitt and his nominees (Dundas, the Home Secretary, Burke and Windham). Only four months had passed since George III had reflected on the 'steady loyalty and firm attachment to the established constitution . . . prevalent among all ranks of my people', yet it now appeared that the entire country was at risk from subversion, an underground plot having been discovered to hold a convention to demand parliamentary reform.

The ministry feigned horror, and its placemen responded. How long had it been since Burke had first warned of the dangers of levelling spirits – three, no four years? Now it seemed that his worst fears were being confirmed. Universal suffrage. Annual parliaments. They smacked of treason, and worse. Four days after the report was submitted, Pitt was to exploit the induced panic among his own back benchers to move for the suspension of habeas corpus and bring in a bill for the arrest of all persons suspected of conspiring against the government. Although sick, Fox spoke briefly against both measures, but at the close the government commanded a 162 vote majority. The Committee of Secrecy had done its work well. Terror had put reason to flight.

Twenty-four hours later the bill was given its third reading, and as Windham sat down after delivering a tirade against that 'most lamentable of evils', universal suffrage, Fox rose to speak. Still a sick man, his face grey and his clothes hanging baggy around him, he protested both the grounds for, and the intent of the bill. It was one more step in Pitt's ladder 'towards the complete extinction of liberty'. The Aliens Bill was an anodyne, the Treasonable Practices Bill gentle medicine, and after the suspension of habeas corpus, what next?

> Would he [Pitt] still further go on in the exact and horrid imitation of the men who now held France in anarchy, and establish a revolutionary tribunal or what, perhaps, he would call an anti-revolutionary tribunal? Where would he stop? What limits did he propose to make? . . . Good God, what was to be done after this? Under the colour of pretended alarms, were they to go on to an unlimited infringement and demolition of all the strongest and most beautiful parts of the constitution?

For almost an hour Fox denounced the measure, pointing and counter-pointing his charge of the ministry's bad faith with the example of France ('Thus they follow the example of men they pretend to abhor'), to wonder that Pitt's battery of punitive measures were directed against 'some low persons, without property or consideration . . . who were found to entertain opinions about parliamentary reform'. The whole made a nonsense of reason, for in pursuit of liberty Pitt was imperilling liberty itself.

Close to exhaustion, Fox returned to his seat, though he already knew that it had all been to no avail. Six weeks before, the Portland Whigs had told him, with the 'strongest expressions of personal friendship', that the time had come for the dissolution of the party, and when the House divided at three on Sunday morning the Foxites mustered only thirty-three votes. The Habeas Corpus Act, long-time a staple of English law, was suspended, and the ministry was free to make 'terror the order of the day'. Which they did, with the active support of Portland, Fitzwilliam and Windham who joined the ministry in July.

Britain was fast becoming an armed camp, the newly recruited militia tapping into Pitt's network of informers and agent provocateurs, and the Anti-Jacobin Society, subsidized from the government's Secret Fund, whipping up reaction on the streets. Inflamed as much by Francophobia as by a concern for the constitution, the country was becoming increasingly hostile to any mention of reform, and only days before the final dissolution of the Whigs a mob raging 'TREASON, TREASON' sacked the home of Thomas Hardy, Secretary of the London Corresponding Society, an event which led directly to the death of his pregnant wife. As for Hardy and the other senior officers of the LCS, they were already under arrest and held in the Tower. As Fox was to remark, the intensity of Pitt's campaign against dissent at home more than compensated for the failures of his operations overseas.

With his party irrevocably divided, and with his career apparently in ruins, there were moments that summer of 1794 when Fox seriously considered quitting the contest of Westminster for the peace of St Anne's Hill, as revealed in his letters to his young nephew, Lord Holland. Their tone is in turn bitter ('I have nothing to say for my old friends . . . but I cannot forget how long I lived in friendship with them.'); despondent ('I am now quite sick of politics, and attend only because I think it is my duty to do so.'); philosophical ('Though weak, we are right, and that must be our comfort.'); and escapist ('Idleness, fine weather, Ariosto, a little Spanish, and the constant company of a person I love . . . more and more every day, make me as happy as I am capable of being.').

Quarter of a century had passed since Fox had first entered the Commons, and it was with more than his accustomed fondness for verse that he was now given to quoting Cowper:

> Oh! for a lodge in some vast wilderness,
> Some boundless contiguity of shade,
> Where rumour of oppression and deceit,
> Of successful or unsuccessful war,
> Might never reach me more! My ear is pained,
> My soul is sick with every day's report
> Of wrong and outrage with which earth is filled.

The prospect was beguiling, and momentarily Fox found it irresistible. There had been a time when it was impossible to respond not to what others expected of him, more to what he expected of himself; when he had fled from the contradictions that he found within himself in a fury of high living. By 1794, those days had long gone, and in laying the ghost of his own inheritance Fox was discovering a tranquillity that he had never known before.

For all the political disasters, and their hurt, that summer was an idyll for Fox – a round of boating and gardening ('the place looking beautiful beyond description, and the nightingales singing'); of writing and reading ('the greatest resource of all, literature, I am fonder of every day'); of the occasional small house party ('I am sorry to tell you that the Duke of Bedford has overtaken me at tennis, and beat me, even'); and always of Dear Liz. For ten years she had been building an alternative life for Fox, and as the world of politics collapsed around him he was coming to depend upon her more and more:

> She is a comfort to me in every misfortune, and makes me enjoy doubly every pleasant circumstance of life; there is to me a charm and delight in her society, which time does not in the least wear off, and for real goodness of heart if she ever had an equal, she never had a superior . . . . The Lady of the Hill is one continual source of happiness to me.

But even at St Anne's Hill there was no escaping the press of events. The Foxites demanded their leader, and he may well have remembered his own sharp criticism of Rockingham's threatened withdrawal from politics in the dark days of 1776. What was it he had written then, that 'a secession at present would be considered as running away from the conquerors'. The same applied again. Pitt was firmly in the saddle, and it was no longer the colonists' liberties that were at stake, but those of free-born Englishmen.

The state trial of Thomas Hardy, Horne Tooke, John Thelwall and six other officers of the London Corresponding Society opened at the Old Bailey on 25 October. With memories still fresh of Muir's trial, the rump of the Whigs were keenly aware of their possible fate if the English bench should imitate Scottish justice, Charles Grey writing: 'I believe that I shall attend [the trial] in order to learn how to conduct myself when my turn comes.'

The charge against the defendants was high treason and 'compassing the death of the King' for which, if found guilty, there could only be one verdict – death. For eight days, the prosecution advanced its case, based, in large part, on the Committee of Secrecy's report to the Commons – and for eight days the defence, under Erskine, exposed the charge, and its substantiation, for what it was: a fabrication. The government's spies broke under cross-examination, paid informers retracted their evidence, and Pitt and the Duke of Richmond were both subpoened to establish that they, too, had once been advocates of electoral reform which was no more than the defendants were demanding. In fact, no evidence whatsoever existed of a conspiracy to subvert the constitution. At the close there was uproar, Erskine having to appeal to the crowd for order, and three hours later the jury returned with a verdict of not guilty – an indictment as much of Pitt's suspension of habeas corpus as the evidence on which the measure had been based.

* * *

Superficially, Pitt's position appeared impregnable when Parliament returned four days after Christmas 1794. Assured of the king's support and guaranteed a three figure majority in the Commons, he may well have laughed at the retort of one Foxite when taunted that the entire Opposition had ridden to the House in a single coach: 'This is a calumny. We should have filled *two*.' Yet the appearance was deceptive. Ten years had passed since Pitt had first kissed the king's hand, but now a sick man, and increasingly fond of his madeira and port, there were growing signs of distress at home (wheat prices were to double in the first six months of 1795), while the First Coalition was already breaking up under mounting pressure from French arms, a decimated British army being left to defend the Netherlands for which Britain had originally gone to war.

As early as November 1794, Lord Auckland had been urging Pitt to negotiate for peace, and in late January one of his few close friends, Wilberforce, joined in the call to end the war on much the same grounds as those previously advocated by Fox – non-interference in the internal affairs of France. Fox himself was delighted, perhaps the government's majority was not as sound as it seemed, though his delight was short-lived, for while Pitt's biographers record that he had one of his rare sleepless nights he was to win the division by a comfortable 179 votes.

Discouraged, but undeterred, Fox was to renew the attack in March, moving for a Committee of the House on the State of the Nation. Even the government press was compelled to report that the speech was a brilliant performance, reinforcing, as it did, the Common's growing doubts about the continuation of the war, about the stability of the continental alliance, about the increasing strain being placed on the nation's finances, and about the re-emergence of tensions in Ireland. For four hours Fox pursued the logic of his case, to conclude by demanding that Pitt be called to account for bringing Britain 'to the verge of ruin by the obstinacy and madness of his conduct'. Pitt's reply was to whip-in his back benchers to secure his majority.

All the reasoning might be with Fox, but the vote remained with the ministry. Seemingly members were careless of the fact that, one by one, Britain was being abandoned by her continental allies, each in their turn suing for peace with France, and that Ireland was growing restless again. Inspired by the French example, Catholics and Presbyterians excluded from the Irish Parliament took common cause in calling for reform, Grattan declaring: 'The Irish Protestant can never be free until the Irish Catholic has ceased to be a slave.' In 1793, Pitt had pressurized the Dublin Parliament to pass an Irish Relief Bill, giving Catholics the same voting rights as Protestants and allowing them to hold certain minor civil service posts, but his coalition with Portland had created new problems.

Among the terms of the deal had been an agreement that Fitzwilliam should replace the Earl of Westmorland as Lord

Shrine at St Anns Hill.

Plate 4 Fox at prayer before the altar of revolution at his country home, St Anne's Hill. (Gillray, 1798)

Lieutenant of Ireland. In January 1794, Fox's one-time friend took up his post, to be recalled within three months for giving the impression that he favoured Grattan's plan for Catholic emancipation. George III was incensed, writing that Fitzwilliam had condemned 'the labour of ages' for the defence of Irish religion and property, and Pitt hastily backed away from any further thought of reform – leaving Catholics and Presbyterians to turn their attention to more radical means of achieving their demands. As Fox was to say: 'I no longer apprehend any danger to Ireland from disputes between Catholics and Protestants; what I apprehend is the alienation of the whole Irish people from the English government.'

A call in the Commons for an inquiry into Fitzwilliam's dismissal was heavily out-voted, and at the close of the session the Foxites were no better off than when they began, a beleaguered minority to be dismissed, almost contemptuously, by Pitt. His foreign policy might be in disarray, his domestic policy open to question, but they posed no threat to his power, while as for Fox a recent Gillray cartoon had captured his situation exactly – on his knees before a revolutionary altar at St Anne's Hill.

With his saturnine features and a figure of which the young Palmerston was to say 'I have never seen a man so fat in all my life', Fox was a natural subject for caricaturists, their attacks on him becoming increasingly poisonous during the 1790s, culminating in a cartoon of his severed head wearing the French *bonnet rouge* mounted on a pike above the heads of his political compatriots. The protraction as much as the venom of such assaults can only have reinforced Fox's growing desire to retreat from politics – and on 28 September 1795 he finally married The Lady of the Hill at the hamlet of Wyton in Huntingdonshire.

Why they should have waited ten years to marry, and why they should have been so secretive about the marriage subsequently still remains a mystery. One suggested explanation is that Mrs Armistead had been married previously, and it was only on her first husband's death that she was free to remarry, while Fox himself provided only a part explanation

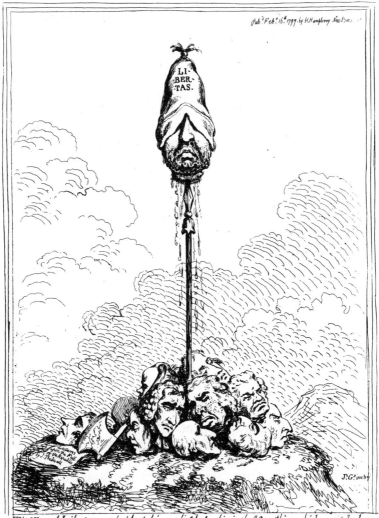

Plate 5 Fox's dismembered head, wearing the *bonnet rouge*, above a pile of heads of his radical friends. (Gillray, 1797)

in a letter of 25 September: 'In case of anything happening to me, I am sure you having been my legal wife will make your situation less uncomfortable.' Seven years were to pass before the marriage was made public, for Mrs Armistead (as she continued to be known) to write somewhat ruefully that 'a Secret which need never have been one is now divulged'. Fox's behaviour contrasts, forcibly, with his otherwise open character, and it may be that he feared for his private happiness once it became public knowledge; that he did not wish to risk the love he had found with Dear Liz by exposing it to the brutal and brutalizing effect of politics.

Whatever the reason, Fox was back to the cockpit of Westminster within a fortnight of the marriage, holding that secession was 'the measure that a shabby fellow would take in our circumstances'. Only days before Lord Auckland, a colleague of Pitt, had published his *Remarks on the Apparent Circumstances of the War* in which he called for a negotiated end to hostilities, to the fury of Burke who wrote that a regicide peace would lead to Britain's 'utter and irretrievable ruin', while on 19 October the Whig Club, now a stronghold of the Foxites, met to discuss Opposition tactics for the forthcoming parliamentary session at which Fox urged that an association be formed in an attempt to check the government's coercive ambitions.

Ten days later, the king's coach was mobbed on its way to the opening of the Commons, a stone shattering one of its windows. George III remained calm, remarking simply 'My Lord, I have been shot at', but Pitt was quick to exploit the situation. Although unsubstantiated by any concrete evidence (as indicated by the trial of Hardy, Thelwall and Horne Tooke), he, too, was now obsessed by the fear that revolution was imminent, and on 10 November he moved to extend government power by introducing what have since become known as the Two Acts – the first to make spoken and written words, even if not followed by an overt act, a treasonable offence; the second to ban all public meetings not approved by magistrates.

Fox's reply was immediate – 'These are means so dreadful . . . that it may be a matter of question whether any good they produce can possibly compensate for the evils with which they are necessarily attended' – and by mid November mass protests against the measures were being organized. On the 12th, the London Corresponding Society mounted a demonstration at Copenhagen Fields, attended by 200,000 'men, women and children'; on the 16th, Fox himself presided over a meeting in Westminster Yard; while by the 23rd ninety-four petitions carrying more than 130,000 signatures had reached Westminster from as far afield as Portsmouth and Edinburgh.

Meanwhile, the Foxites fought the acts stage by stage through Parliament, though, for all the public's support, Fox himself was not sanguine, writing on 17 November:

> The House of Commons is very bad indeed, and really seems to like these violent measures, which I consider as a symptom that the country, or at least the higher classes, are of the same opinion. However it is clear that *here* [in his Westminster constituency] we have the popularity, and I suspect that we shall have it universally among the lower classes. I cannot tell you how much I dislike this state of things; but I cannot submit quite passively to Mr Hume's Euthanasia which is coming on very fast.

The reference was to Hume's discussion of the dangers of arbitrary government, an echo of Fox's long-time fear of executive power. Where during the American war it had been George and North, it was now George and Pitt, and rather than losing his head in six months if he should resign, as Pitt was reported to have remarked, there were signs that he had lost it already. In the month to 10 December, Fox spoke ten times against the Sedition and Treason Bills, reviling the motives for their introduction, and stressing their dangers to English liberties:

> He [Pitt] admitted that by the passing of the bill, the people would have lost a great deal. A great deal! Aye, all that is worth preserving. For you will have lost the spirit, the fire, the freedom, the boldness, the energy of the British character,

and with them its best virtue. I say, it is not the written law of the constitution of England, it is not the law that is found in books, that has constituted the true principle of freedom in any country, at any time. No, it is the energy and boldness of a man's mind . . . . This is the principle which gives life to liberty; without it the human character is a stranger to freedom.

At the third reading the Opposition divided forty-five votes, and the Treason and Sedition Bills became law. Again Pitt had invoked freedom only to shackle it, though before public dissent was effectively silenced the London Corresponding Society passed a motion that:

The thanks of this meeting be given to the Rt Hon. Charles James Fox, M.P, for his firm, determined, and unequivocal opposition to these Bills both in and out of Parliament. And more especially, for his manly and constitutional declaration 'That neither the Commons, nor the Lords, nor the King . . . can be considered as having the power to enslave the people; but that they may separately, or unitedly do such acts as would justify the resistance of the people'.

The spirit of the words had been sanctified by a Civil War and a Glorious Revolution, but Pitt was careless of them, and as the old year turned into the new what resistance remained had been driven underground by his draconian legislation. No extremist, Fox deplored all that he heard and saw. While he had as little time for universal suffrage as for Jacobin tyranny, he had even less for a regime that hunted down the rights of free speech and free assembly with a ferocity that put talk of English liberties to shame. Yet it seemed that nothing could now check the advance of 'a system of cruelty and oppression worse that any devised by the See of Rome, or the Spanish Inquisition'.

An exaggeration perhaps, but in the fell days of 1796 it may have appeared to Fox that Pitt had unleashed all the dark forces of chauvinism and bigotry, the only question being, for what purpose – certainly not to bolster his own authority, that was unquestioned, as was that of his master, George III. But if not for personal aggrandizement, then for what? Half a lifetime had passed since Wilkes and the Whigs had suspected the king's ambitions on power; twenty years since a nameless Bostonian had feared that 'the BRITISH CONSTITUTION seems fast tottering into fatal and inevitable ruin', yet in pleading defence of the constitution, George and his ministers now appeared hell-bent on undoing it. Undoubtedly, there were dangers from France, though they paled into insignificance when set against the dangers from within Britain itself.

But what was to be done? Thirteen years out of office, and the leader of little more than a rump of the once great Whig connection, Fox was fast despairing of the prospects for the future. Down the years few men had fought harder for their beliefs, but while the grounds of his policies had been consistent enough, the critics were still quick to damn him not so much for abandoning his father's patrimony ('It is a matter of infinite regret . . . too see a man who, from his birth and talents, might fairly have aspired to proud pre-eminence') as the principles that they entailed, to fulminate that 'By every art, intrigue, and contrivance, Fox studies to banish from the minds of men all public motives and public principles.'

Motives. Principles. Fox's critics made a butt of the words, but they still cut deep, to reinforce his growing desire to retire from active politics to the calm of St Anne's Hill. Indeed, the temptation became the greater as the prospects for the Opposition continued to deteriorate, the Foxites mustering only twenty-three votes in a division in February, while in May Fox's own motion on the conduct of the war went down by 174 votes – though not before he had delivered a stinging attack on Burke:

> In a masterly performance he charmed all the world with the brilliancy of his genius, fascinated the country with the powers of his eloquence and, in as far as that cause tended to produce the effect, plunged the country into all the calamities of war . . . . Never, certainly, was a nation more dazzled than the people of this country were by the brilliancy of this

performance! Much of the lustre of his opponents, as well as of his friends, was drawn from the influence of this dazzling orb; but it was the brilliance of a fatal comet, which bore terror and desolation in its train.

The ministry was as dismissive of the censure as the king was delighted at its rejection, for he was fast coming to regard Fox as 'an open enemy of his country'. In fact, George's only regret was that the electors of Westminster did not share his opinion. Confident of 'the most convincing proof of the attachment to our happy Constitution', he called a general election in late May, at which Sir Alan Gardner, the government candidate, and Fox were comfortably re-turned as the members for Westminster. As in the past, Fox was chaired through the constituency by his triumphant supporters – though neither the Prince of Wales nor the Whig grandees any longer cheered his passage.

The election confirmed Pitt's majority, and when the Commons reassembled in October the Foxites remained a small and embattled group, though momentarily encouraged by the opening of the King's Speech. During the summer the continental war had progressed from bad to worse. Holland and Prussia had already made their peace with France, and in a brief but brilliant campaign, the young French commander, Bonaparte, had annexed Austria's north Italian possessions, while in October Spain declared war on Britain. Pitt's coalition was in ruins, and with fears of a French invasion George announced the opening of negotiations to end 'the calamities of war'.

After three years of campaigning, and having been forced to abandon all pretence of intervening in the internal affairs of France, Pitt had finally been driven to follow Fox's advice – with few bargaining counters with which to trade. Fox was scathing ('I cannot forget how often I have advised this measure, nor how often, without success, I have pressed it upon ministers'), and throughout the autumn and into the winter he harassed Pitt and his ministry as much for their incompetence in conducting the war as the pretext they made of it to enforce their iron rule at home:

Show me a Parliament since the year 1688 . . . that has diminished the best and dearest rights of the people, so shamelessly, so wickedly, as the last Parliament have done! Show me a Parliament since that period that has so uniformly sacrificed the liberty of the subject to increase the influence of government, as the last Parliament have done! . . . Should this Parliament be like the last one (God in his mercy avert it) this country will soon be in a condition in which it will be of little importance whether it have a Parliament or not.

He was soon to be disappointed. By December, the peace talks had collapsed, the French employing their strategic advantages to demand unacceptable concessions, and the Commons had succumbed, once again, to Mr Hume's euthanasia. Five days after Christmas 1796, Pitt moved an address of thanks to the king for informing the House of the breakdown of negotiations. In reply, Fox reminded the House of the time when, as a young member, the first minister had complimented the Rockinghams on destroying a ministry that had prosecuted the American war, and invoked them to introduce radical reform 'otherwise Ministers may, on future occasions, arise, who will again plunge the country into more bloody and expensive wars'. The years between had flouted the intention, for Pitt to become the agent of his own prophecy, his predictions having been 'fatally accomplished'. At the division, the Foxites won thirty-seven votes.

Apparently nothing that was said or done could halt the inexorable progress of the ministry, and reaction. Parliament was little more than a tool of the executive, and coercion had silenced the voice of dissent out-of-doors. Burke, penning his final, maddened Philippic against any settlement with France, in which he stigmatized Pitt as weak and charged the liverymen of London with high treason, may have applauded the situation, but not Fox. The darkness was very close at hand, and on 27 May 1797, he announced his secession from the Commons.

Grey had again tabled a Reform Bill, having re-drafted his proposals of four years before, and again Pitt had rejected it outright, asserting that the Opposition employed talk of reform not so much to disguise their own ambition, or even that of their party, but to cloak their intention of extinguishing 'every branch of the constitution'. It was late in the evening when Fox rose to reply, knowing from the outset that his task was hopeless. The government benches were crowded, Pitt's majority was safely in place, yet for a last time the attempt had to be made. The ministry pleaded that these were troubled times, but trouble of whose making – the ministry or the public that the ministry claimed to represent?

In two hours, Fox reviewed much of what he had learned in his twenty-eight years as a Commons' man – the lessons of American independence, of the ingrained presumptions of the Crown, of the dangers of executive power – all the while punctuating his defence of Grey's modest proposals with memories of Pitt's former views. Not so distantly he, too, had damned the defects of representation to talk-up reform, yet now . . . .

A roly-poly figure, Fox fleered the minister and his government, and on the benches opposite there was silence, for there was no one to answer the charge:

> What reliance can the people have for any vestige of the constitution that is yet left to us? Or rather, what privilege, what right, what security had not already been violated?
> . . . And seeing that in no one instance have they [the government's supporters] hesitated to go the full length of every outrage that was conceived by the Minister – that they have been touched by no scruples – deterred by no sense of duty – corrected by no experience of calamity – checked by no admonition or remonstrance . . . that they have never imposed a single restraint upon abuse, may not gentlemen feel that the reform which they previously thought unnecessary is now indispensable?

Surely, no one who would deny the rights of man to be governed well, yet the ministry continued to deny that right, preferring a system which Pitt had once condemned as a 'national disease' to reform. And if reform was not undertaken, if 'a system so defective and vicious in all its parts' was not corrected, what then? Britain's fate would be inevitable. She would be 'driven to a convulsion that would overthrow everything'.

Fox paused, there was no sound or movement, then in a quiet voice he announced his own and his followers withdrawal from Parliament:

> I hear it said 'You do nothing but mischief when you are here; and yet we should be sorry to see you away.' I do not know how we shall be able to satisfy the gentlemen who feel towards us in this way. If we cannot do our duty without mischief, nor please them with doing nothing, I know but of one way by which we can give them content, and that is, by putting an end to our existence . . . . I certainly do think that I may devote more of my time to my private pursuits, and the retirement which I love, than I have hitherto done; I certainly think I need not devote much of it to fruitless exertions, and to idle talk, in this House.

Resignation? Certainly. Bitterness? Perhaps. Cowardice? Never. In the years since he had broken with North the one-time rake and hell-raiser had dared all for his principles, sacrificing friendship for enmity, reputation for rejection, the prospect of office for long years of opposition. In his time, Charles James Fox had been many things, but a coward, never. Once the rebel had found his cause he was not to be distracted from it – for all the blandishments of power and place. Small wonder that Horne Took, no lover of Fox, was once heard to exclaim: 'God Almighty made that man to show his omnipotence' – a tribute as much to the rebel as to all that he represented.

10

'A Lodge in Some Vast Wilderness'

Edmund Burke died at his home on 9 July 1797, seven weeks after the Foxite secession. During Burke's last illness, Fox visited Beaconsfield, to be refused an interview, while in answer to a message inquiring after his health Burke wrote the chilling reply that 'it has cost Mr Burke the most heartfelt pain to obey the stern voice of duty in rending a long friendship asunder, but that he deemed this sacrifice necessary'. Even when dying there was to be no reconciliation – yet only days before his death Burke was heard to say of Fox that 'He was made to be loved.'

Whether sincere, or simply mawkish sentiment, the fact remains that for six years Burke had pursued an unremitting vendetta against the man who had been first his disciple and then his friend; a vendetta which, once opened, had breached the party to which Burke claimed allegiance, and in which his public rancour was only matched by his private spite. The rising young Tory politician, George Canning, might say of his death 'Here is but one event, but that is an event for the world – Burke is dead', yet Burke's genius had been seriously flawed by the dark imaginings that haunted his later years, even Pitt coming to suspect his counsel.

On hearing of Burke's death, Fox wept. All the old enmity was forgotten, and it was only Burke's instruction that he be buried at Beaconsfield that prevented Fox from pursuing his proposal that he be interred in Westminster Abbey. Unlike

George III, Pitt and Burke himself, Fox was never a good hater, his rivals as well as his friends testifying to the truth of Lord Grenville's remark that he was a man 'whose friendship it was a pleasure to cultivate'. In politics he could be as wounding as the situation demanded, but in private life . . . .

. . . In private life, Fox bore no grudges and never wanted for friends. At Eton, at Brooks's, at Newmarket, he had always commanded a following, but the years at St Anne's Hill had transformed his notions of friendship as much as they transformed Fox himself. The old hell-raiser had long gone, his last recorded bet at Brooks's being dated 24 March 1794, and John Bernard Trotter, Fox's secretary in the last years of his life, was to provide a brief sketch of the simplicity of his lifestyle following the retreat from Westminster:

> In summer, he rose between six and seven, in winter before eight . . . . After breakfast, which took place between eight and nine in the summer, and a little after nine in the winter, he usually read some Italian author with Mrs Fox, and then spent the time preceding dinner at his literary studies, in which the Greek poets bore a principal part. A frugal but plentiful dinner took place at three, or half past two in the summer, and at four in the winter; and a few glasses of wine were followed by coffee. The evening was dedicated to walking and conversation to tea time, when reading aloud, in history, commenced, and continued till near ten. A light supper of fruit, pastry, or something very trifling finished the day, and at half past ten the family were gone to rest.

Almost thirty years had passed since Newcombe, the Master of Hertford, had remarked with astonishment on Fox's appetite for learning, and in 1797, the pedant again replaced the politician. In more than a hundred letters to his nephew, Lord Holland, he provided an insight into his reading matter (Homer, Virgil and Ariosto are read annually, and Shakespeare, Euripides and Dryden almost as often) commenting pungently on each – 'You see, I have never done with Homer . . . Dryden wants a certain degree of easy playfulness that belongs to Ariosto . . . Medea is the best of all the Greek tragedies, though the choruses are not so poetical as in some others . . . Burns writes the best pastorals in any modern language.'

Fox's scholarship was as eclectic (one day elaborating his defence of the song of the nightingale as 'a merry note', the next arguing the exact dates of the Trojan war) as his enthusiasms were unbounded, Mrs Armistead once having to confiscate a newly arrived copy of Fanny Burney's latest book, *Camilla,* which he began to read aloud at dinner.

For all of his literary interests, however, and for all of Wordsworth's and Coleridge's youthful admiration of his stand during the opening phase of the French Revolution, Fox developed few contacts with the school of brilliant young poets and writers that emerged towards the turn of the century. Where, once, he had been a member of Johnson's Club, and had numbered Boswell and Gibbon among his friends, he had out-lived both the club and most of its members, and while he maintained a passing acquaintance with George Crabbe, and dined occasionally with Wordsworth (who presented him with a copy of his *Lyrical Ballads*), Fox's only close literary associate was the scholar Gilbert Wakefield.

In 1796, Wakefield dedicated his edition of Lucretius to Fox, and on hearing that the book was not selling well, Fox suggested wryly that the dedication might account for its poor reception. It was the beginning of a friendship that was to last for five years, the two men corresponding regularly on literary matters, and occasionally on more down-to-earth topics – Wakefield once reproaching Fox for the pleasure he obtained from partridge shooting which 'misbecomes a man of letters'. A Unitarian and a radical, Wakefield was tried for sedition in 1799, following the publication of a pamphlet criticizing the government and its policies, and was sentenced to two years in Dorchester jail, during which time his correspondence with Fox continued, to end, unaccountably, on his release.

Not that Fox's pleasures were limited to literature and the classics. There was plenty to entertain him besides, the recollections of visitors to St Anne's Hill being punctuated with vignettes of Fox in a beige apron playing the role of a gardener, of Fox with his notebook listing every flower and plant on the small estate, of Fox lying silent in the grass for hours on end trying to teach the birds to think he was dead, Fox the tennis player a trifle fatigued after a single's match, and, always, of Fox the adoring husband of the Lady of the Hill: 'for real goodness of heart, if she ever had an equal, she never had a superior'.

Small wonder he was jealous of time spent away from St Anne's, and steadfastly resisted his friends' pleas to return to the Commons, writing to Lord Lauderdale in November 1797:

> I indeed, even supposing Royal prejudices out of the way and all other objections of the kind, feel such an extreme aversion to the situation of the First Minister that I am sure I should act very ill a part that I so much dislike.

The bitterness was deep-seated. Seemingly Pitt's repressive policies were rapidly bringing on 'Mr Hume's euthanasia', while as for Fox, he was subject to the nagging suspicion that his name could well become a liability to his own party. Sheridan and Grey sought to dissuade him but in the three years to 1800 Fox only made a handful of appearances in the Commons – to oppose Pitt's plans to treble assessed taxes, to praise Pitt's speech in support of Wilberforce during a debate on the slave trade, and to table a motion condemning the use of torture to extort confessions in Ireland:

> When an Irishman is tortured, an Englishman is tortured; for the same men who, in violation of the laws of their country, and every dictate of humanity, dare to put Irishmen to torture, when they think it expedient, will not hesitate to put Englishmen to torture also.

Fox's critics have been quick enough to identify the apparent shifts in his policies, careless of the consistency of his concern for human rights. When judged by twentieth-century standards he may fall well short of the ideal, when measured by those of the eighteenth century he was a humanist in advance of his times. On India and Ireland, on religious toleration and the slave trade, on American independence and the French Revolution, on the rights of man against those of prerogative he staked his reputation against those of reaction, to be ostracized in private life, and vilified in public – the freeholders of Kent burning a live fox to show their contempt for a man who had once been their neighbour; Pitt actively considering his incarceration in the Tower.

On 24 January 1798, Fox's forty-ninth birthday, a public dinner was held at the Crown and Anchor Tavern, with the Duke of Norfolk in the chair. In proposing the toast to Fox, Norfolk drew a comparison with Washington ('Not twenty years ago, the illustrious George Washington had no more than two thousand men to rally round him when his country was attacked. This day, two thousand men are assembled in this place; I leave you to make the application'), and in responding to a toast to himself he invited the company 'to drink our Sovereign's health – the Majesty of the People'.

With the country in paranoic mood, these were dangerous sentiments even for a grandee, and Pitt was quick to exploit them. Asserting that Norfolk's remarks 'will hardly prove to be much short of treason', the Duke was stripped of the command of his militia regiment and dismissed as Lord Lieutenant of the West Riding. Fox was enraged as much as Norfolk was insulted: 'The toast relating to the sovereignty of the people will be universally and I believe truly considered as the cause of your removal, and thus you will be looked up to as the marked champion of that Sovereignty under which King William and the Brunswick kings have held their thrones.'

Personal expressions of disapproval were not enough, however. The humiliation of Norfolk demanded something more, and at a meeting of the Whig Club at the Freemason's Tavern in May, Fox repeated word for word the now notorious toast to the people's sovereignty. It was a calculated, yet dangerous gesture. Within the month, the trial opened at Maidstone of five United Irishman on charges of conspiring to enlist French aid for their cause, while Ireland itself was in open rebellion –

southern Catholics and northern Protestants, each aggrieved though for different reasons, campaigning separately against a British force commanded by General Lake. Under near-draconian law, England remained quiescent, but for Fox to proclaim the Majesty of the People was to taunt Pitt's authority, and he was quick to react. Although hesitant to mount a prosecution in case it should fail, he seriously considered ordering Fox to attend the House to be reprimanded by the Speaker after which, should he repeat the offending toast, he would be committed to the Tower for the remainder of the parliamentary session.

In a letter to Wilberforce, Pitt weighed the options carefully, to conclude that even a spell in the Tower would not serve for 'at the end of three weeks he [Fox] might be led home in procession, and have the glory of breaking windows'. Eventually a combination of caution and mean-mindedness prevailed – Pitt advising the king to strike Fox's name from the Privy Council list, which he did with considerable enthusiasm. The Intrepid Fox, as a commemorative medal of the period described him, could no longer be addressed as Right Honourable. However petty, it must have seemed that there was little further point in exposing himself in pursuit of the causes he had so long championed. A time would come when the free-born Englishman's rights would once again assert themselves; in the meantime, better St Anne's Hill, and at breakfast on his fiftieth birthday Fox presented Dear Liz with a commemorative verse:

> Of years I have now half a century passed
> And none of the fifty so blessed as the last.
> How it happens that my troubles thus daily should cease,
> And my happiness thus with my years should increase,
> This defiance of Nature's more general laws,
> You alone can explain, who alone are the cause.

After more than thirty years, it seemed that Fox had had his fill of politics, though his new-found leisure was soon to

Plate 6 Fox (left) and the Duke of Norfolk consulting one another after being struck off the Privy Council for toasting 'Our Sovereign Lord, the People'. (Gillray, 1798)

be overtaken by the press of events at home and abroad, and if he had addressed himself as keenly to the former as he did to the latter the course of Irish history might well have been different.

In 1782, the ill-fated Rockingham ministry had sought to settle the Irish question by extending legislative independence to the Irish Parliament, and allowing it to manage its own internal affairs. Within a quarter of a century, however, the country was at flashpoint again. What, in practise, did independence signify, if executive power was vested in a viceroy appointed by London? As Fox's long-time friend, Henry Grattan was to say: 'Let the kingly power that forms one estate in our constitution, continue for ever; but let it be, as by the principles and laws of these countries it should be, one estate only – and not a power constituting one estate, corrupting another, and influencing a third.'

The words might well have been Fox's, but he ignored them. The spring of 1798 at St Anne's was too precious to lose, and while he pottered about his garden and listened for the nightingale, conditions in Ireland continued to deteriorate. Now it was not so much a matter of constitutional niceties, more of religious bigotry. For half a decade, Pitt had been struggling to keep the various and embittered factions (Catholic, Anglican, Presbyterian) from each other's throats, but conditions were beyond his control, and by May the whole country was embroiled in what amounted to a religious civil war.

With peace restored by the autumn, and with Ireland little better than an armed camp, Pitt determined to formulate a plan to resolve the Irish question for once and for always. A number of solutions offered themselves, but only one appeared feasible – to extinguish Irish independence by dissolving the Irish Parliament, a notably corrupt institution, and uniting the two countries under the legislature of Westminster. Superficially the scheme was an attractive one, for while it would allow for token Catholic representation at Westminster, it would ensure that such representation was in a permanent minority, though Pitt was well aware of the implied committment if such a deal were to be struck – emancipation for Irish catholics.

Fox was diametrically opposed to the plan. Somewhat naively, he trusted Grattan's assurances that it was the English Cabinet rather than Irish Protestants who were opposed to making any concessions to Catholic interests, and even before the insurrection he had made his own position plain:

> I know of no way of governing mankind but by conciliating them; and according to the forcible way which the Irish have of expressing their meaning, I know of no mode of governing the people, but by letting them have their own way. And what shall we lose by it? If Ireland is to be governed by conceding to all her ways and wishes, will she be less useful to Britain? What is she now? Little more than a diversion for the enemy?

The echo was of all that Fox had learned in arguing the case of the American Colonists, but the idea of self-government for Ireland was too much for Pitt, recognizing, as he did, the true nature of the religious rivalry that divided the country, and constrained, as he was, by the weight of Protestant opinion at Court and in his own Cabinet. Privately, he might accept the case for emancipation, meanwhile he progressed his plans for the Union, while Fox idled away his time keeping good Whig company and writing doggerel on the death of a friend's two dogs.

In January 1799, details of the proposed Union were published in Dublin, to be sympathetically received by the Catholic community. The Protestant reaction was very different, and in the spring the Irish Lower House threw out the deal. If MPs were to vote for their own extinction, then it would be at a price. Alarmed, Pitt resorted to bribery and corruption on a scale unprecedented even in Irish politics, eventually paying more than £1.2 million in compensation to the owners of 'close boroughs' and creating twenty new Irish peerages in order to buy a working majority for his plan which was finally approved in March 1800.

Two months later, Fox made his objections to the Union

clear, first at a meeting of the Whig Club, then in a letter to his nephew, Dear Young 'Un:

> If it were only for the state of representation in their House of Commons, I should object to it (Union), but when you add the state of the country, it is the most monstrous proposition ever made . . . . I never had the least liking to the measure, though I confess I have attended less to the arguments *pro* and *con* than perhaps I otherwise should have done . . . . You know, I dare say, that my general principle in politics is very much against the *one* and *indivisible*, and if I were to allow myself a leaning to any extreme it would be to that of Federalism.

By then, however, it was too late. Fox had neglected the arguments *pro* and *con* for too long. While Sheridan and Grey had done their best to oppose the bill's passage through the Commons, their leaders continuing absence from the House had robbed the Opposition of its cutting edge. Against the deep-rooted prejudices of Members it is unlikely that Fox's appearance would have changed the outcome; none the less, his failure to articulate a constructive alternative to Pitt's proposals was to have long-standing and tragic consequences. On 1 August 1800, the Act of Union became law – while Fox pleasured himself at St Anne's Hill.

The reasons for Fox's neglect of the Irish question remain inexplicable. His long-standing friendship with Grattan, his affection for the Irish themselves, his championship of the Irish settlement of 1782 ('He had rather see Ireland totally separated from the Crown of England than kept in obedience only by force') all indicated where his sympathies lay – yet for more than two years he virtually foreswore the issue, preferring to concentrate his attention on continental affairs, while considering writing a history of James II.

After the fiasco of the First Coalition, a second had been formed led by Austria and Russia and funded, once again, largely by the English Exchequer. Initially, the allies were successful, and on Christmas Day 1799, Napoleon wrote personally to George III to explore the possibility of a negotiated peace. The king was contemptuous, as was

Pitt, who drafted a reply which was as inept as it was offensive, suggesting, among other things, that the Consul General would do well to consider restoring the Bourbons to their throne. When he heard the news, Fox was astounded. After seven years of war, England was hungry for peace and with the allies temporarily in the ascendant there could be no better time to secure a settlement, instead of which Pitt and his master had spurned the offer outright. 'Surely' Fox wrote 'they must be mad.'

The ministry's answer was debated in the House on 3 February 1800, and all Fox's friends urged him to be present. Since 1794 he had been pressing for a peaceable solution to the conflict, and now the opportunity had offered itself, to be rejected, out of hand, by Pitt. Unwillingly, Fox agreed to attend, but on arriving in London he learned that the debate had been postponed for a day due to Pitt's illness, at which Lord Holland saw 'tears steal down his cheeks, so vexed was he at being detained from his garden, his books, and his cheerful life in the country'.

The old Fox was long gone, and with him some of the old confidence, for as he walked to the House on the afternoon of the 3rd he confessed nervousness to his nephew, and hoped that it would not spoil his speech. He need have had no cause for concern, he never spoke better in his life. Since early morning the House had been crowded, but it was 4.30 before Fox rose in his place. In moving thanks to the king, Dundas had earlier reiterated the view that Britain should pause and wait on events before negotiating with Napoleon. Fox was to put the notion to devastating use. After a scathing, three-hour review of the ministry's policy, delivered without a single note, he directed his final challenge to Pitt himself:

> In former wars a man might at least, have some feeling, some interest, that served to balance in his mind the impressions which a scene of carnage and of death must inflict . . . . But if a man were present now at a field of slaughter, and were to inquire for what they were fighting – 'Fighting!' would be the answer; 'they are not fighting, they are *pausing*.' 'Why is that man expiring? Why is that other writhing with agony? What

means this implacable fury?' The answer must be 'You are quite wrong, sir; you deceive yourself. They are not fighting. Do not disturb them; they are merely *pausing*. This man is not expiring with agony – that man is not dead – he is only *pausing* . . . . All you see, sir, is nothing like fighting – there is no harm, cruelty or bloodshed in it whatever; there is nothing more than a political *pause*. It is merely an experiment to see whether Bonaparte will not behave himself better than heretofore; and in the meantime we have agreed to *pause*, in pure friendship.

No one rose to reply. Yet again, the House was under the spell of the magician, and while the government whipped in its majority, the moral victory remained with Fox who retired, once more, to St Anne's Hill. He had made his point, and determined not to reappear at Westminster during the remainder of the session. As for Pitt, he was soon to regret his perfunctory dismissal of Napoleon's peace overture. By midsummer, the Second Coalition was close to ruins, Napoleon's decisive victory over the Austrians at Marengo being closely followed by Moreau's defeat of a second Austrian army at Ulm. On his return to Paris, Napoleon opened a diplomatic offensive which, within months, had virtually isolated Britain.

In one of his rare public appearances, at a meeting to commemorate the anniversary of his election for Westminster, Fox bitterly denounced Pitt's strategy. After reasserting his opinion that 'the only legitimate Sovereign is the People', he poured scorn on the claim that Britain had any right to interfere in the internal affairs of France, maintaining that the sole aim of ministerial policy was to PROMOTE THE CAUSE OF DESPOTISM. The audience was ecstatic, Fox was their Man of the People again.

*   *   *

The New Year opened badly for the Whigs. Pitt and his ministry appeared firmly entrenched, and Fox resisted all blandishments to come up to Town. Since 1797 he had

253

been contemplating a history of the early life of James II and increasingly begrudged the distractions of politics. By his own admission he was a slow writer, though he found the subject compelling enough for as his nephew, Lord Holland, noted, he regarded the Glorious Revolution of 1688 as 'the most signal triumph of that cause to which his public life had been devoted' – a cause that demanded renewed attention at the opening of the nineteenth century.

The apparent calm of January 1801 was illusory, however, for even as Fox 'juggled' with his words a new crisis was blowing up. At first the rumour that the king and Pitt had had a falling out was little more than a whisper, but by the close of the month it was the loudest whisper of all. The Act of Union had come into effect on New Year's Day, and Pitt set about attempting to redeem his unwritten pledge of emancipation to Irish Catholics. It was an honourable undertaking that was to break him. Although commanding a Cabinet majority, five of its members were against him, not least the Lord Chancellor, Loughborough, who in thirty years in politics, had made a profession of betrayal. In a private memorandum to George III, Loughborough pointed out that Catholic emancipation conflicted directly with the Coronation oath that undertook, at all times, to maintain the Protestant religion.

The king reacted in characteristic fashion, raging at a levee on 28 January:'I shall reckon any man my personal enemy who proposes any such measure. The most Jacobinical thing I have ever heard of.' The news of the split could no longer be disguised, and while a more chastened George pitifully begged Pitt to drop his proposals ('I shall still hope that his sense of duty will prevent his retiring from his present situation to the end of my life'), Pitt remained adamant. The impasse was complete, and on 5 February Pitt resigned, for George III to have a further breakdown, which he was to blame upon Pitt, and for Fox to ponder the future.

Henry Addington, the son of the king's former physician, had been named Prime Minister by George before his collapse, to the surprise of all, save George himself. The man was a political nonentity and the appointment caused as much mirth as astonishment, for George Canning to write:

> Pitt is to Addington
> As London is to Paddington.

While the astonishment continued, however, the laughter was much shorter lived. Yet again, the king had set his own stamp on government. True, measures had been the cause of Pitt's fall, but as George had indicated it was men not measures that he regarded as the touchstone of sovereignty, Fox remarking: 'The King's power is, as we know, great; and when exerted in conjunction with his ally, the Church . . . will not be easily foiled; and you may be sure that the Ministry is quite one to his heart's content.'

Almost three decades had passed since he had warned of the ambitions of the Crown, but little seemed to have changed. George was, indeed, content with his new ministry, and as such Fox saw little profit in abandoning either his country seat or his historical research, though by the spring of 1801 a new distraction had begun to emerge. In February, Austria had concluded a separate peace with France at Luneville, and little more than six weeks later Napoleon persuaded Tsar Paul to abandon the Second Coalition in favour of a League of Armed Neutrality against Britain. With the exception of Portugal, Britain once more stood alone against France – and Addington opened negotiations for peace.

The news was received with delight, especially at St Anne's Hill. After eight years of war, it seemed that Fox's views were finally to be redeemed, but as had happened too often before he was to sacrifice much of his new standing by the extravagance of his reception of the news. The Preliminaries of Peace were signed on 2 October, with Britain making major concessions to France, and eight days later at the Shakespeare Tavern, Fox was extolling the event in terms that were to embarrass even his closest friends:

The peace was glorious to France, glorious to the First Consul. Ought it not to be so? Ought not glory to be the reward of such a glorious struggle. France had set an example to all the nations of the earth, and, above all, to Great Britain.

The peace might be welcome, but this was going too far. Both Grey and Sheridan warned Fox to curb his enthusiasm and, penitent, he begged them to speak before him in the debates that were to come that 'he might not get into a scrape'. The damage was already done, however, and if the public were shocked at his outburst, then Coleridge was to articulate their views in two savage letters addressed to Fox in the *Morning Post*:

Did you utter one word of alarm at the attrocious ambition of the First Consul? One sentiment of pity or indignation at the iron despotism under which this upstart Corsican has reduced forty millions of your fellow-creatures? Not a syllable! Not a breathing! You *exulted,* Sir that the war had ended as it ought to end, gloriously for France, ignominiously for Great Britain! For the spirit of a man and a patriot you abandoned yourself to the low and womanish temper, which finds in a triumphant 'Did I not tell you so, now?', a pleasure that overpowered, and sunk into oblivion, all the dangers and all the disgrace of a whole nation, and that nation your country.

And this from a man who, like Wordsworth, had been one of Fox's keenest admirers; who had once written to Southey: 'except Fox, I, you, or anybody might learn to speak better than any man in the House'; and who, through the long years of war, had consistently espoused Fox's pacific cause. It was little use Fox protesting his contrition. Once more he had proved to be his own worst enemy, for in one short outburst he had ceded virtually all that he had won in eight years of opposing the war with France. Small wonder that Grey scolded him, and Charles Yorke wondered whether he was a villain, or mad.

The Treaty of Amiens was signed on 27 March 1802 and what should have been a celebration for Fox ended as a triumph for Pitt, the Commons voting him thanks by name and holding a dinner to mark the end of hostilities. Fox cannot have failed to appreciate the irony, and his success at heading the poll at the Westminster election in July can have done little to assuage his bitterness. For eight years he had campaigned against war, warning of the folly of Britain trying to impose her will on the government of France, yet at the close it was Pitt who was eulogized as 'The Pilot that weathered the Storm.'

The hurt was deep, though there was to be some compensation from the reception he received in France. At the war's end, English society renewed its pilgrimage to Paris, and in early August Mr and Mrs Fox (Mrs Armistead was to sign herself with her married name for the first time on 1 August) and John Bernard Trotter, Fox's secretary, crossed from Dover to Calais and proceeded in leisurely fashion via Ghent, Antwerp, Brussels and Lille to the French capital. Ostensibly the purpose of the trip was to further research into the history of James II, and while Fox spent his mornings among the archives of the Ministry of Foreign Affairs the rest of his days were spent in a round of entertainments and civic functions.

If London suspected him, then Paris regarded him as a hero. He dined with Talleyrand and Lafayette, relished the company of Madame Recamier's salon, was invited to become a member of the Institut National des Sciences et des Arts, and on a visit to the theatre shortly after his arrival was embarrassed to find that 'every eye was fixed on him and every tongue resounded Fox! Fox'. The First Consul was among the audience, and while Trotter was to note that the reception he received was overshadowed by that accorded to Fox, Napoleon was quick to invite the visitor to a levee at the Palais de Tuileries. Casting himself for the moment as the man of peace, it suited the First Consul to be seen associating with Fox, though even before the meeting Fox may have begun to have doubts about his host.

On a visit to the Louvre, now crowded with art treasures accumulated by Napoleon during his Italian campaigns, there was a shout that the First Consul was passing below. Fox crossed to the windows, but on seeing the splendour of the Napoleon's entourage he 'lifted up his hands with disgust and impatience', then turned quickly away to resume his tour of the gallery. This was not the modesty of a man who now professed peace and republicanism, rather a display of imperial conceit.

And the levée itself was not a resounding success. Napoleon was effusive: 'Ah, Mr Fox, I have heard with pleasure of your arrival. I have desired much to see you.' Fox remained silent. 'I have long admired in you the orator and friend of his country who, in constantly raising his voice for peace, consulted the country's best interests – those of Europe – and of the human race.' Still Fox did not speak, and still the First Consul continued to protest his regard, for the meeting to end with Fox having said little in reply.

The two men were to meet again, but again the meeting ended coolly. While Fox welcomed a scheme to build a Channel tunnel, he emphatically denied the suggestion that Pitt and Windham had planned an attempt on Napoleon's life: 'Premier Consul, otez vous cela de votre tête.' As Lady Bessborough reported later: 'Buonaparte after a moment walked away in silence, and so they parted', leaving Fox to wonder whether, behind the bonhomie, he had detected something altogether more sinister – the true nature of Napoleon's ambition.

If so, it must have fuelled the fears that his trust both in France and her First Consul had been misplaced. Less than a year had passed since he had confessed to friends that 'the triumph of the French government over the English does in fact afford me a degree of pleasure which is very difficult to disguise', and to admit otherwise would be to admit that he had been wrong not so much in his evaluation of Napoleon, more of the character of the revolution that had transformed France.

It was the beginning of November before the Foxs quit Paris, and on the 17th they finally reached 'dear, dear home' – for Fox to find himself regarded as an agent of the republic. His meetings with Napoleon had aroused widespread suspicion, and while he now took to maintaining that if liberty was *asleep* in France, then it was *dead* in England, he still struggled to safeguard what was left of the peace. To abandon that would be to abandon all that he had represented for almost a decade, yet all the evidence indicated the extent of the First Consul's burgeoning ambition.

Napoleon proclaimed himself President of the Cisalpine Republic – and Fox protested he meant 'nothing insulting' to England. Napoleon demanded the payment of German indemnities – and Fox maintained that 'he was quite right in that affair'. Napoleon reinforced his garrisons in the Low Countries and ordered a major expansion of the French fleet – and still Fox continued to talk-up peace. As if unwilling to recognize what he already feared, Fox sought to deny the inevitability of war, writing to Lord Holland in mid December that he would go, once again, to Westminster: 'but it will be for a very short time; only while there is hope of contributing to prevent war'.

By the New Year, however, even Fox's faith was waning. For half a year he had resisted his suspicions of Napoleon, for half a year he had clung to his pacific beliefs, but by the spring of 1803 it was no longer possible to deny the First Consul's intentions. The man was exploiting the peace to pursue his expansionist ends, and on 9 March Fox supported Addington's proposals to reinforce the navy and embody the militia. If war was to come, it would be a different war from that fought by Pitt. Then the issue had been the right of France to settle her own affairs; now it was the extent of Napoleon's aspirations. In twelve months he had breached the Treaty of Amiens on a dozen occasions, while a recently published, secret report revealed his designs on the Levant.

The danger to Britain's oriental trade was clear and Addington, who had fought hard to save the peace, finally nerved himself to take a stand over Britain's continuing occupation of Malta. Contrary to the terms of the treaty under which Britain had agreed to cede the island to the Order of St John, she refused to withdraw, and within days of France issuing an ultimatum on the matter the British Ambassador to Paris was recalled. Six days later, on 18 May, Britain and France were once again at war.

* * *

The Commons was crowded on 24 May, and if the main concern was to debate the declaration of war, then the question of the exact state of the parties was of almost equal importance. Addington's ministry had been vulnerable from the outset, and earlier in the year he tentatively explored the possibility of Pitt returning to the Treasury bench, to be perfunctorily rebuffed. As for Fox, who now commanded seventy votes in the House, his first preference was for an arrangement with the Grenvilles, apparently careless of the hard line they had adopted towards any accommodation with France, an issue that had led to their break with Pitt over the peace terms of 1802.

As the *Morning Chronicle* noted, 'it was a case of all against all', though one thing was clear – that Addington would have to go. On the afternoon of the 24th, the Prime Minister appeared in the House in full dress uniform, for Sheridan to quip that here was 'a sheep in wolf's clothing', and Grey to note: 'We are now actually at war, and can only say God send us a safe deliverance! which under such Ministers can hardly be hoped.' The three major contenders for office – Pitt, William Wyndham Grenville and Fox – were to speak in the debate on the declaration of hostilities. Pitt's speech, the first he had made for almost a year, was a triumph. He was strong in support of the war, and even Sheridan felt compelled to write: 'Detesting the Dog as I do, I cannot withdraw this just tribute to the Scoundrel's talents.'

Thomas Grenville was to echo Pitt, but such was the press of speakers that it was 25 May before Fox was called, to deliver what was generally agreed to be the greatest speech of his life. He had a well nigh impossible task, not so much to oppose the declaration of war, more to dispute the grounds on which it had been declared. Pitt's long-time ally, Wilberforce, had already touched on the point ('Malta is indeed a valuable possession, but the most valuable of all the possessions of this country is its good faith'), and Fox was to enlarge on it for almost three hours.

Thirty-three years had passed since he had made his maiden speech, twenty since he had gone into opposition, but none of the old magic, the old charisma had been lost. It was all there – the grasp of detail, the close reasoning, the humorous asides, the acerbic comments – all delivered in a pell-mell of words that could reduce the House to laughter one moment, and a ministry to shame the next. Burke had once asserted that Fox grew by degrees to be the most wonderful debater that the world had ever known, and that May evening of 1803 he so mesmerized the House that Sheridan, called from the chamber by Lady Bessborough, wrote in reply: 'I have done what I would do for no one breathing but you – Left the House while Fox was speaking.' And this from the greatest dramatist of his age.

On rising, Fox was silent for a moment, and the packed benches fell silent too. To new members, it may have seemed improbable that this portly figure, standing four square to the dispatch box, should have become something of a legend in his own lifetime. His whole appearance belied the reputation, and then Fox spoke, quietly at first, but with increasing force. All turned on the distinction between an insult and an injury, and if the former was no ground for hostility, then the latter demanded negotiation first, with war as a last resort. Essentially a pacific approach that has subsequently become the touchstone of diplomacy, Fox's prescription was largely alien to eighteenth-century practice, yet this was to be the measure of his support, or otherwise for the war.

Napoleon had outraged the people of Switzerland ('an act of violent injustice'), had attempted to subvert the small republic of St Domingo ('a material blot in the character of Bonaparte'), had behaved with infamy towards the Dutch ('an act no less despicable for its meanness, than hateful for its atrocity'), but on each occasion, and with reason, Addington had refrained from hostilities. Now, however, it seemed that the case was different. Although under treaty obligation to evacuate Malta, Britain was now being asked to enter into war in defiance of her own undertakings – but was 'plain, bare, naked Malta' really worth a war?

'After the Ministers had submitted to every encroachment of French ambition, after they had left Switzerland and Holland to their fate . . . he could not think that the war they were now undertaking for Malta, plain Malta, either wise or justifiable.' Instead, Fox pressed the government to accept the Tsar's offer to mediate not only to secure an immediate peace, but also to ensure 'the solid and permanent pacification of Europe'. As much an optimist as a man of peace, Fox's hopes were still-born, heedless as they were both of Napoleon's ambitions and the mood of the House. At the division, the government secured a 331 vote majority, though Wilberforce was among the sixty-seven dissenters.

Three days later, and with Pitt's support, Fox moved a resolution inviting the Tsar to negotiate the differences between Britain and France, but while the ministry accepted the proposition, the prospect for peace had already passed. On the same day, Napoleon had ordered the arrest of all British citizens either living or travelling in France, and began immediate preparations for the invasion of England. For all of his parliamentary support, Addington was not the man for such an emergency, even his best efforts, such as the erection of forts in the Thames, being lampooned:

> If *blocks* can from danger deliver,
> Two places are safe from the French:
> The one is the mouth of the river,
> The other the Treasury Bench.

Addington meant well, but that was not enough, though it was to be almost a year before he finally tendered his resignation. Meanwhile, Britain once again nerved herself for war. There were regular alarms of French landings, and while Pitt, as Lord Warden of the Cinque Ports, drilled the local militia, Fox enrolled in the Chertsey volunteers, between considering an approach to the Home Secretary to see whether he could serve in any capacity in his Westminster constituency and tending his garden at St Anne's Hill. He had fought for the peace as he would now fight the war, but in the absence of any proper equipment ('we have Volunteers in plenty . . . but not a single weapon, pike or gun among them') his time was as well spent in less martial pursuits, and in early June he was writing to Dear Young 'Un who was travelling in Spain:

The nightingales have almost done; but the singing of the other birds, the verdure, the flowers, the lights and shade of this April-like weather make the scene from the window such that I do not envy the orange trees etc. of your southern climates.

Boney might be on the heights above Boulogne assembling his invasion flotilla, but until they attempted a passage it seemed that there was little more that he could do. Only the king had any confidence in Addington, and while his minister continued to dither, Fox cursed his difficulties as a smallholder (his potato crop having failed due to 'some damned worm or other', while rye grass had 'quite got the better' of his clover), and began to consider his strategy for the new term of Parliament. After six years his secession, albeit a partial one, was coming to an end, but what part should the Foxites play in the critical time that lay ahead? Was an Opposition coalition feasible, and if so what of Pitt's and the Grenvilles' mood?

Certainly Pitt's lieutenant, Canning, appeared enthusiastic to achieve a junction between Fox and his chief, but Pitt was quick to make it clear that nothing would induce him to make 'the turning out of the Administration the object of his endeavours'. And the Grenvilles, what of them? An age ago, in the days of Whig unity, Fox had numbered them among his closest friends – Lord Spencer, brother of the beautiful Georgiana; Fitzwilliam and Windham, his school-day contemporaries; and the affable Tom Grenville, whom he had intended to appoint Governor General if his India Bill had become law – but that was before the rupture with Burke and the outbreak of war in 1793. Since then the Grenvilles had been hot for war, as they were once again.

And in this they were not alone. Indeed, what divided the parliamentary factions was not their war aims, in this there was now virtual unanimity, but the personalities involved. All were interested in reaching some sort of accommodation with one or other of the groups, but each was constrained by memories of the past, and all the while, as they manoeuvred for position, Napoleon continued his military build-up across the Straits of Dover. The Royal Navy might be mounting a tight blockade on the French coast, but by October an invasion fleet of some 3000 barges had been assembled, and more than 150,000 French troops were camped around Boulogne.

George III, as bellicose as any of his commanders, was in a frenzy of activity, visiting volunteer camps, reviewing parades of yeomanry, and planning to be 'at the head of his troops' either at Dartford or Chelmsford should 'the usurper' hazard a crossing. By the opening of Parliament in November, however, the king's exertions were beginning to take their toll, Addington having to dissuade him from prefacing his Speech from the Throne with the startling words: 'My Lords and Peacocks of the House of Commons.' Within weeks, George was again to fall victim to a major attack of porphyria, to compound the confusion at Westminster.

Fox, still working on his history of James II ('Yesterday, and not before, died James, Duke of Monmouth'), was increasingly attracted by a junction with the Grenvilles, but was cautioned by Charles Grey, now his closest aide: 'They are certainly able men; their conduct is direct and open . . . but on the other hand, their opposition has appeared to proceed rather from personal disappointment than from public principle; and it is not till they have failed, first, in their endeavours to set up Pitt as the only man who can govern the Country . . . that they have recourse to us.' Always and everywhere there was the shadow of Pitt, yet his position remained enigmatic. He would hold 'no communication, no discourse whatever' with the Addington ministry, but while pursuing a policy a constructive criticism would do nothing to unseat it.

The impasse was to continue through the early months of 1804, but by March Fox had agreed to an informal arrangement with the Grenvilles, while in early April Pitt supported Fox's motion on the state of the national defences, to reduce the government's majority to fifty-two. In despair, Addington made an approach to Pitt to see whether he would be willing to shore up the failing administration. Eldon, the Lord Chancellor, was detailed to handle the negotiations but from the outset a now convalescent George III made his position plain – Pitt was to make no further reference to Catholic emancipation, and Fox was to have no part whatsoever in any plan agreed upon. Now keen to enlist Fox's talents, Pitt rejected the terms outright, and four days later launched a broadside against the ministry, reducing its majority to thirty-seven votes. On 29 April 1804, Addington resigned.

For the next eighteen days Britain was without a ministry, but on 18 May, the date on which Napoleon crowned himself emperor in Paris, Pitt returned to office. On Addington's departure he had written a conciliatory letter to the king saying that if he should be invited to form a government, it should form 'as large a proportion of the weights and talents and connections . . . without reference to former differences and divisions', and, to this end, he intended to consult both Fox and the Grenvilles. George, however, was not to be conciliated. He reprobated Pitt's hostility to Addington, and was horrified at the suggestion 'that Mr Pitt should one moment harbour the thought of bringing such a man [Fox] before his royal notice'. Pitt was adamant, and continued to press the case, but at a meeting on 7 May, George reasserted his opposition to Fox. The Grenvilles, yes; Fox's friends, possibly; but Fox himself, never.

With Fox's approval, Pitt yielded, the former writing to Tom Grenville: 'that he was sure that the King would exclude him, but this ought not on any account to prevent the Grenvilles coming in'. The Grenvilles, however, had other ideas. Without Fox they would remain in Opposition. Two centuries later, their decision continues to provoke controversy. Was their self-denial motivated by pique at not being invited to form their own ministry, a sacrifice to their renewed friendship with Fox, or rancour at Pitt for having supported the Peace of Amiens two years before? The debate continues, but that May of 1804 Pitt's opinion was clear: 'I will teach that proud man [Lord Grenville] that

265

I can do without him, though I think my health such that it may cost me my life.'

Although a sick man, Pitt can have had little idea of how clairvoyant he was to be proved. Always frail, twenty years in office and a growing fondness for drink had taken their toll. As early as 1793, his drinking habits had attracted attention, the *Morning Chronicle* publishing a verse describing his arrival in the Commons with Dundas – 'I cannot see the Speaker, Hal, can you?/ What! Cannot see the Speaker, I see two!' – and as the pressure of business increased, so he drank more, consuming as many as four bottles of wine and port at a single sitting. For a man in good health, it would have proved a dangerous combination; for Pitt it was to prove lethal, his surgeon reporting on a bout of severe illness in June 1803: 'after restless nights he was seized with vomitings almost every morning. The dislike of all kinds of nourishment increased; a spare breakfast was made; & the sight of dinner always brought on Retching'.

Yet this was the man who returned to office in May 1804; the man in whom all Britain save the Opposition now placed its trust to contest the French. For half a century, the name of Pitt had served as a talisman in wartime, but few understood the extent of the problems that the 42-year-old premier faced, both abroad and at home. Even as he was patching together a makeshift ministry, Napoleon was boasting 'Let us be masters of the Channel for six hours and we are masters of the world!', and while the king continued to exhibit his attachment to Addington, Fox considered that Pitt's reappointment was highly advantageous to the new Opposition 'and what is of more consequence in my view, the cause of *Royalism* (in the bad sense of the word) is lowered too'.

The old bogey continued to haunt him, the suspicion as much of royal intentions as of Pitt's dependence on the king. That Pitt had resigned rather than accept George's terms over the issue of Catholic emancipation; that Pitt had voted for the Treaty of Amiens, though the king had little taste for the peace; that Pitt had pressed Fox's own claims to office in the face of George's hostility; and that due to his growing insanity, George himself was no longer capable of managing power, made little difference. All the evidence might belie the illusion, but at 54 years of age, Fox was growing too old to abandon the prejudices of a political lifetime, writing to Lord Lauderdale:

> No strong confederacy (against the Crown) since the Restoration, perhaps not before ever did exist without the accession of obnoxious persons; Shaftesbury, Buckingham etc in Charles II's time; Danby and many others at the time of the Revolution; after the Revolution, many more. . . . In our own times, first the Grenvilles with Rockingham, and afterwards Lord North with us. I know this last instance is always quoted against us because we were ultimately unsuccessful, but, after all that can be said, it will be difficult to show when the power of the Whigs ever made so strong a struggle against the Crown, the Crown being so thoroughly in earnest and exerting all its resources.

The memory, as much of Burke's discontent that 'The power of the crown, almost dead and rotten as prerogative, has grown up anew' as of Dunning's motion that 'the influence of the Crown has increased, is increasing, and ought to be diminished', remained, to colour all else – not least, Fox's relationship with Pitt. For all of his new found independence, it seemed that the man remained a secret agent of George, and there was no forgetting his prosecution of English liberties (of the suspension of habeas corpus, of the Seditious Meetings and Treason Bills) but while, in 1804, the rivals shared a common cause, Fox was unable either to forget or to forgive past differences. He had long doubted Pitt's integrity, and now he was to write 'He is a mean rascal after all', then depart for St Anne's Hill where he was to spend the recess overseeing the construction of a small temple in the grounds of the house.

At Chertsey, the Volunteers still drilled; at nearby Windsor, George still made his dipositions for a French landing; at Walmer, Pitt still considered his plans for the conduct of the war, but by the late summer, Napoleon was on the point of abandoning his invasion plans in favour of a continental campaign. The immediate danger to Britain was passed. But if Britain was safe, Pitt's troubles were only beginning. At the close of the previous parliamentary session he had faced two close-run votes, and for the opening of the new Parliament, Fox was imploring Charles Grey to forego his pleasures in Northumberland: 'Opposition *seems* now more restored. . . . Mind, I say *seems*, for if *you* stay away it will be very far from being so. . . . Do, for God's sake, make up your mind to one unpleasant effort, and come up for the first two months at least of the session.'

Unwillingly, Grey acceded, to find that although the opposition was in full cry, Pitt had succeeded in persuading Addington to join his ministry, bringing with him fifty votes. While Fox expressed his contempt ('Pitt certainly gained more in numbers by his junction with the Doctor that I thought he would'), he was quick to note that by allying himself with a man he had so recently opposed, Pitt had placed his own reputation at risk. For Pitt, however, it was a risk that seemed worth the taking, for all Canning's acerbic remark that Addington was like measles, everyone had him once!

But even as Pitt struggled to reinforce his ministry and patch together a Third Coalition, again involving Russia and Austria, a new crisis was in the making, triggered by charges of alleged misuse of Admiralty funds during Dundas's time as Treasurer of the Navy. Arguably Pitt's closest political ally, and certainly his deepest drinking companion, Dundas had served in government since 1784. With Pitt's return the previous spring, and having only recently taken the title of Lord Melville, Dundas had been appointed First Lord of the Admiralty. Eleven months later, following the publication of the Tenth Report of the Commission of Naval Inquiry, Whitbread moved eleven resolutions of censure against him, claiming misappropriation of public funds. For all his political misgivings, Pitt refused to abandon his long-time friend to the opposition, for Fox to assert: 'I should be ashamed of myself if I belonged to the same class of society as Lord Melville.'

As the debate raged on it seemed that Pitt might yet

command a narrow majority, then Wilberforce rose to speak. His conscience demanded that he vote for the motion. Momentarily there was uproar, for on moral issues Wilberforce was the voice of the Commons, and when the division was called the House divided equally – 216 votes for, 216 against. Lord Fitzharris described what followed:

> The Speaker, Abbott (after looking as white as a sheet, and pausing for ten minutes) gave the casting vote against us. Pitt immediately put on the little cocked hat he was in the habit of wearing, when dressed for the evening, and jammed it deeply over his forehead, and I definitely saw the *tears trickling down his cheeks*.

To Pitt it must have appeared the cruellest cut of all. Since he had first entered the House he had befriended, and been befriended by Wilberforce, yet Wilberforce and his conscience had now delivered Dundas up to the Opposition. To an already desperately sick man, it was a grievous blow, and it was only small compensation when, the following week, Fox flatly refused to agree to an inquiry into Pitt's financial probity, asserting that it would 'make him [Fox] the most miserable of men'. With a terrible inexorability, Pitt's world was collapsing around him, and as spring gave way to summer matters grew even worse.

Intractable as always, George III would have no truck with the emancipation of Irish Catholics. In 1801, and unable to fulfil his implicit pledge on the question, Pitt had resigned, but assured the king on his return that he would not promote the issue again. He proved as good as his word, for when Fox brought a petition for Catholic relief before the Commons in mid May, Pitt spoke strongly against it: 'I ask any gentleman, whether he does not believe, looking to the opinions of the Established Church, of the nobility, of the men of property, of the middling and respectable classes of society – I ask him whether he does not believe . . . that there is the greatest repugnance to this measure.'

Only the king was absent from Pitt's catalogue of esteem – and, implicitly, the king was the target of Fox's attack. It was absurd for Parliament to pretend that the Coronation oath, to which George was pledged, was immutable. Originally drafted by Parliament, and subsequently amended by Parliament, and it would pose no problem for Parliament to amend it again to take note of the Irish case:

> His Majesty's lawful authority is one of the cornerstones of the constitution, but while I shall always exert myself to support that lawful authority, I cannot be silent when I see interested persons endeavouring to extend that influence beyond its due bounds. . . . I could wish to see any sacrifice made for the gratification of the Crown, except the welfare and security of this country. The man who countenances such a sacrifice is not a loyal subject; is not one who loves his King, but one who flatters him in order to betray him.

At the division, the motion was defeated by 214 votes. So much for Pitt's pledge of 1801, though the relief he received by compromising it was short lived. Addington, tetchy that neither of his brothers had been chosen to fill a vacancy at the Admiralty, had only been persuaded to remain in the ministry on the understanding that the appointment was a temporary one, but on 10 July he resigned, taking his faction with him. For a final time, Pitt was isolated, and for a final time he pleaded with the king to allow Grenville and Fox into his ministry.

Possibly in anticipation of Addington's defection, he and the king had discussed the possibility of broadening the ministry on 20 June – but Fox was again the sticking point. Three months later, with Fox growing increasingly confident, Pitt travelled down to Weymouth, where the king was holidaying, to urge the case for a coalition, to be told by George that 'he had taken a positive determination not to admit Mr Fox into his Councils, *even at the hazard of a civil war*'. As Lady Hester Stanhope, Pitt's devoted niece, was to write: 'It was enough to kill a man, it was murder.'

An exaggeration? Certainly, though founded on fact, for Pitt was already a dying man, and however well justified in his own mind, George's consistent refusal to have any dealings with Fox placed both his minister and his ministry in jeopardy. For all but two of twenty-one years, Pitt had sacrificed himself and his health not only to serving his country but also his king, but even at this crisis point George would make no concession to his prejudices, and Pitt returned to London to hear news, first of Napoleon's victory over the Austrians at Ulm, then, forty-eight hours later, of Nelson's death at Trafalgar, and finally, in mid December, of Napoleon's crushing defeat of the Austro-Russian army of Austerlitz. The Third Coalition was in ruins.

Ravaged by gout, and suffering 'excessive weakness and a total debility of digestion', Pitt had been persuaded by friends to travel down to Bath to take the waters, and legend has it that on seeing a map of Europe as he walked from his bedroom, he remarked: 'Roll up that map, it will not be wanted these ten years.' Fox shared his concern, though on different grounds. It had been little short of madness to campaign against 'the first military power in the world' with inferior forces under inferior command – and for this, Pitt had to take a share of the blame.

On New Year's Day 1806, Fox was pressing for a major assault on the enfeebled ministry at the opening of the new parliamentary session, and twenty hours later was writing that even when dying Pitt's final concern would be 'O! let me keep my place.' As with George III, the poison had reached deep into Fox's soul. What had begun two decades before as a conflict of principles, was ending as a conflict of personalities, and it is probable that if Fox had known of Pitt's remark on the day before he left Bath – 'I wish the King may not live to repent, and sooner than he thinks, the rejection of the advice I pressed on him at Weymouth' – he would have been as quick to brand it as suspect, as George had been to condemn it outright.

Lord Wellesley was present when Pitt returned to London on 14 January, and saw that 'the hand of death was fixed upon him'. At first, both friends and foes were unbelieving, but on being convinced Grenville and Fox immediately agreed to suspend all opposition in Parliament. Early in the morning of 23 January 1806, exactly a quarter century after he had first entered the House, William Pitt died with the words: 'Oh, my country! How I leave my country' or, more prosaically: 'I think I could eat one of Bellamy's veal pies.' For more than twenty years, Macaulay's 'tall man in a crowd, who was forced on by those behind him' had led Britain, to see the reputation he had built for himself as a financier and administrator dissipated by the failures of his statesmanship and foreign policy, for as his biographer, Rosebery, noted, if Pitt was made for peace, then Chatham was made for war.

* * *

24 January was Fox's fifty-seventh birthday, but he had little cause for celebration. True, George might well have to call in the Opposition, but his great adversary was dead. Down the years they had developed a near symbiotic relationship, powerful men and superlative orators, each had inspired the best and the worst in the other, but now the debate was ended, for Fox to contemplate to friends: 'Death is a thing without remedy. Besides, it is a very poor way of getting rid of one's enemy. A fair, good debate that turns it out is well, but death – no!' For a moment he was silent, then added that as the news would render future debates flat and uninteresting: 'I think I shall pair with Pitt.'

Fox was to be proved prescient as far as death was concerned, but though unwell himself, he had little time for his own problems that last week of January 1806. For seventy-two hours after Pitt's death, all was speculation, George III sounding out 'any time-server who fancied a place' to avoid calling Fox in, but by the 27th even he had come to realise that there was no escaping what he had so long feared. Grenville was invited to form a government and, from the outset, he made his position clear: 'I can do nothing without consulting

Mr Fox.' With apparent composure, the king replied: 'I suppose so, and meant it to be so.'

On the afternoon that Grenville and Fox set about Cabinet building, a motion was tabled in the Commons for a public funeral for Pitt and the erection of a memorial 'to the memory of that excellent statesman'. The words had applied well to Chatham, but did they apply to his son? A number of members thought otherwise, among them Fox. He had opposed Pitt for twenty-two years, and it would be an act of hypocrisy to praise his statesmanship now. There could be no question about Pitt's talents, his integrity, or his administrative skills, but: 'I cannot consent to confer public honours, on the ground of his being 'an excellent statesman', on the man who, in my opinion, was the sole . . . supporter of a system, which I had early been taught to consider as a bad thing.' Posthumously, Pitt won his final victory over Fox, the House dividing in favour of the motion 258–89.

By early February, the king had approved Grenville's Ministry of All the Talents, with Erskine as Lord Chancellor, Grey as First Lord of the Admiralty, Sheridan as Treasurer of the Navy, Fitzpatrick as Secretary at War, and Fox as Foreign Secretary and Leader of the Commons. The wilderness years were over, and even before the ceremony of kissing the king's hand, Fox was to write 'I am hurried to death and must have forgot twenty things.' There was a prospect of new peace negotiations with France to be explored; the tortured question of Catholic emancipation to be resolved; the long-standing undertaking to tackle the iniquities of the slave trade to be honoured; and all this among the hullabaloo of yet another Westminster election.

Returned unopposed, Fox was to be chaired for a final time through the constituency, and to dine that evening at the Crown and Anchor where, for a final time, he proposed the toast he and his friends had shared so many times before: 'The cause of Liberty all over the world.' Almost thirty years had passed since they had been ridiculed for the hope during the American war; more than ten since they had been reviled for the idea during the early days of the French Revolution, but now it seemed that the Man of the People and his hopes

273

might be redeemed after all. As they passed into the London night, few of the 400 guests appreciated that Fox had less than six months to live.

At 57 years of age, Fox was already sickening with dropsy, and within weeks of taking office had begun to consider resigning, and nominating his nephew, Lord Holland, for the post. Only two things detered him: 'The slave trade and the peace are two such glorious things, I can't give them up, even to you. If I can manage *them*, I will then retire.' He failed to mention his third concern, the Irish question, which, in the light of the pressure of business during what remained of the parliamentary session, he suggested deferring until the following year, though reassuring the Catholic lobby that, should they press the matter, 'I will support it with all my power.'

Meanwhile, he set to the task of peace-making with all his old verve, his aunt, Lady Napier, writing: 'I hear that C. Fox is so thoroughly occupied with the *essential* Business of England, viz, with Bonaparte, that he lets Lord Grenville take a much larger share of the loaves that belongs to him. It is very much like Charles to be above the 2 dary business.' In January, Fox's pre-occupation with peace had appeared unpromising, writing that there appeared to be little chance that '*pacific language*' would receive a sympathetic hearing, but by February all that had changed.

Virtually isolated as a result of Austria's withdrawal from the war, Russia had secretly opened peace negotiations with France early in the New Year – though Fox was only to learn of the news on taking office. While George III proved to be 'as unpleasant as possible', the Cabinet determined to press ahead with a peace overture, a bizarre incident providing the opportunity for a direct approach to the French government. On 20 February Fox was writing to his French counterpart, Talleyrand:

Some days ago, a person I did not know announced to me that he had just disembarked at Gravesend without a pass-port. . . . I conversed with him quite alone in my room, when, after some discourse of little consequence, this scoundrel had the audacity to tell me that, in order to tranquillise all crowned heads, it was necessary to put to death the head of the French nation, and for this purpose a house had been hired at Passy, where, without risk, and with certainty, this desirable project might be executed.

The exposure of the plot on the emperor's life not only produced an effusive reply from Talleyrand (France recognising 'the principle of honour and virtue which have always distinguished Mr Fox'), but also the intimation that Napoleon would welcome an end to the war. Fox reacted swiftly, welcoming the initiative, with the critical provisos that Russia should be included in joint negotiations, and that if there was to be peace there should be no surrender to France. Talleyrand was to concede the first point, but Napoleon had no intention of conceding the second. On the contrary, he now had ambitions on Sicily, hoping to secure it for his brother, Joseph, King of Naples.

The negotiations continued through the spring, but by late April Fox was already despairing of peace, writing to Lord Holland: 'It is not so much the value of the point in dispute, as the manner in which the French fly from their word, that disheartens me. It is not Sicily but the shuffling insincere way in which they act, that shows me they are playing a false game.'

The disillusionment was profound. A man of peace, the possibility of coming to a stable arrangement with France had long been Fox's dream, and one which he believed that he shared with Napoleon, careless of the memory of that day in the Louvre when he had turned from a first floor window on seeing the splendour of the First Consul's entourage. In 1806, he was to learn how wrong he had been, and while the diplomatic charade was to continue until the autumn, the negotiations were doomed from the moment that Fox realised the extent of his illusion, and the reliance that could be placed on Napoleon's word.

Now a desperately sick man, Lord Lauderdale had already noted symptoms of severe dropsy marked by a swelling of the legs and 'the falling off about his neck and chest', Fox was finding it increasingly difficult to walk, and had begun to take the air in a wheelchair pushed by his faithful secretary, Trotter. Whether or not Fox realized that he was dying, however, there remained one more 'glorious thing' to undertake. His hopes of peace might have proved still-born, but on 10 June 1806 he rose for the last time in the Commons to propose the Abolition of the Slave Trade. Pitt had promised much, but had never followed through. Fox was to be as good as his word. The once stocky and animated figure was now drawn, emaciated; the once passionate speaker, whose words had 'darted fire into his audience', was now uncommonly brief. For seventeen years he had supported Wilberforce's call for abolition, and now:

> So fully am I impressed with the vast importance and necessity of obtaining what will be the object of my motion this night, that *if, during the almost forty years that I have had the honour of a seat in Parliament, I had been so fortunate as to accomplish that, and that only, I should think that I had done enough, and could retire from public life with comfort, and the conscious satisfaction, that I had done my duty.*

The House divided 114–15 for the motion. Fox's duty was done. 'The most brilliant and accomplished debater that the world ever saw', the words were Burke's, had made his last speech, and on 17 June Fox went down to the house for the last time. By late in the month, Dear Liz was recording in her diary the steady deterioration of her husband's condition ('Carl not better . . . Carl did not come out of his dressing room, but saw a few people there'), and while there were reprieves ('He has had a charming night, and seems better still'), they proved to be only temporary. There was to be no escaping the Marquis of Buckingham's conclusion: 'I fear that the die is cast respecting Fox, whether his life be protracted for a few months or not.'

As the news spread, friends, colleagues and long-time admirers crowded into his small London home at Stable Yard – among them the Prince of Wales, who requested a daily report on Fox's condition. All the old enmities, the old grievances were forgotten. Fox was dying, and England was as quick to forgive him his mistakes as it was to regret his passing. For all his faults, which he had done so little to disguise, Fox was a man made to be loved, and it was not only the common people who echoed the lines Wordsworth composed on hearing of the gravity of his illness:

> For he must die who is their stay,
> Their glory disappear.

On 7 August Fox's physicians (Dr Moseley and Mr Hawkins) decided that tapping was necessary. When the puncture had been made, Fox asked Lord Holland into the room, and though in intense pain talked cheerfully throughout the operation, later asking to be told plainly when he was in real danger for: 'We neither of us are children, and it would be ridiculous to conceal anything.' Sixteen quarts of fluid were tapped, and for the next four days Fox was prostrate. By mid August, however, there were signs of recovery, and Fox grew restless to return to St Anne's Hill. For twenty years the place had been much more than a home to him, Cowper's 'lodge in some vast wilderness' where he could escape the press of London and find the love of Dear Liz. Now he longed to be there again.

It was only a 20 mile journey, but from concern at the effect on his health arrangements were made to rest overnight at Chiswick House, one of the Duke of Devonshire's many homes. The *Globe* of 28 August described Fox's departure from Stable Yard:

A platform, covered with green baize, was raised from the hall door, gently ascending to the bottom of the carriage, so that he might enter it with more ease than by the gradation of the steps. A crowd of people attended from an early hour at the door. . . . Mr Fox had a brown loose mantle thrown over his shoulders, and wore very wide nankeen pantaloons, and a fur travelling cap. His appearance excited great emotion among the spectators, many of whom shed tears on seeing the change in his countenance, which bore strong marks of the severity of his disease.

Many of Fox's oldest and dearest friends had gathered at Chiswick (Spencer, Fitzwilliam, Townshend), and for a moment it must have seemed as if they had checked the passage of time; that they were still the young blades who had hazarded the days as they had the nights. Momentarily, they remembered, then reality intervened. The late summer weather was fine and clear, and though Trotter wheeled Fox through the gardens and galleries of the great Palladian house, though Holland and his sister, Caroline, read to him his favourite authors ('I liked your reading, young un, but I liked it better before I heard your sister's'), it became clearer by the day that Fox would never see St Anne's Hill again.

A second tapping was decided on, which he talked through 'with all his usual force, accuracy and pleasant natural manners' until fainting from the pain. The following day, Mrs Fox was to write of their slow progress through the grounds: 'He kept my hand in his all the time we were out, made me kiss him several times', and when the Thames came into view, he asked her to recite Denham's lines from *Cooper's Hill*:

> Thames, the most lov'd of all the Ocean's sons
> By his old sire, to his embraces runs;
> Hasting to pay his tribute to the sea,
> Like mortal life to meet eternity.

On Monday, 8 September a 'gush of water' burst from the puncture wound; on Tuesday, he was told of the gravity of his symptoms by Dr Vaughan; and on Wednesday a local clergyman read prayers to the dying man. At the close, Mrs Fox knelt on the bed, and he smiled up at her as she joined together his hands. Long before they had made a pact that, if dying, one would remain with the other, and now Lord Holland was to report: 'Whatever it betokened it was a smile of serenity and goodness such as would have proceeded at that moment only from a disinterested and benevolent heart – from a being loved and beloved by all that approached him.'

Friday night was 'one of horror' according to Trotter, and the following morning Fox lay silent until noon. Then, after bidding Holland farewell, he asked his wife to kiss him, and taking her hand said quietly: 'I die happy, but pity you.' For a moment he drifted, semi-conscious, then finding her still beside him, he fought to say something more, but the effort was too much. All he could manage was: 'It don't signify my dearest dearest Liz.' Charles James Fox died at quarter to six on Saturday, 13 September 1806.

* * *

Fox continues to provoke controversy. Exactly what was he, this descendant of Charles II who was to toast the sovereignty of the people? During his lifetime he was as much admired as reviled, and at his death the nation mourned, even George III confessing: 'I never thought I would regret his death as much as I do.' And today, two centuries later?

No question, Macaulay was right. Fox had a great deal to live down during his early years, the corrupting influence of his father colouring much that he did. Even then, however, there was another Fox – the lover of literature, the dedicated student, the youth who walked with Voltaire in the garden at Ferney. Indeed, Fox the playboy and Fox the politician were of the same mould, each, in this way, rebelling against their past, for if Fox was to hazard his father's fortune at the tables, then he was to chance his political birthright in the Commons.

As with all gamblers, Fox was to make mistakes, grave mistakes, the coalition with North and the Regency crisis to name but two. None the less, the growing consistency of his policies cannot be denied: humane policies, as with his advocacy of religious toleration and anti-slavery; liberal policies, as with his opposition to the prerogative of the Crown, and Pitt's repressive regime; enlightened policies, of which it has been written: 'The independence of Ireland and India are his memorials, and those who now champion the peoples of Africa are only the latest of those who belong to the party of Mr Fox.'

On all the above, Fox was 'to vote in small minorities' which helps give the lie to the charge of his political opportunism. If, indeed, he had been a place seeker, if, indeed, he had been hungry for office, then there were plenty who recognized his talents and would have been happy to employ them. Instead of which Fox advanced policies which were not only to cost him office for almost quarter of a century, but also, and too often, the public favour of which he was said to be so fond.

Of course, it may be that Fox's suspicions of the king and his intentions were too deeply entrenched for him ever to reconcile place with principles, that he was too much of a Whig ever to trade away the power of the grandees, and that he employed the language of liberty simply to cloak the ambitions of the Old Corps. If so, he employed strange means to achieve his ends, choosing to break the party in defence of the Rights of Mankind and the principles of the revolution in France.

Inevitability, Fox's radicalism falls far short of twentieth-century expectations, not least in his preference for extended, rather than universal suffrage. Two centuries on, in fact, the Man of the People may appear as little more than the precursor of a Liberal Party which, having driven through the Reform Bill of 1832, resigned itself to consolidating the power of the emergent middle class and extolling its Victorian values.

To say as much is to judge Fox by our own day, and to diminish what are among his greatest achievements – his role in what A. J. P Taylor has called 'the invention of the modern British constitution' with the establishment of the doctrine that the Crown accepts the authority of the political leader favoured by the majority of the House of Commons; and his defence of English liberties during their hour of greatest need, of which Richard Cobden was to write: 'The annals of Parliament do not record a nobler struggle in a nobler cause.'

Much can be forgiven the playboy if these were to be this achievements; the achievements of the changeling of whom Wm. Hazlitt was to say: 'Fox was in the class of common men, but he was the first in that class.'

Index

281